LORD HIGH EXECUTIONER

The Legendary Mafia Boss ALBERT ANASTASIA

Also by Frank DiMatteo and Michael Benson

Carmine the Snake: Carmine Persico and His Murderous Mafia Family

Also by Frank DiMatteo

The President Street Boys: Growing Up Mafia

Also by Michael Benson

Betrayal in Blood

Killer's Touch

Knife in the Heart

Lethal Embrace
(with Robert Mladinich)

Mommy Deadliest

LORD HIGH EXECUTIONER

The Legendary Mafia Boss ALBERT ANASTASIA

Frank Dimatteo and Michael Benson

CITADEL PRESS
Kensington Publishing Corp.
www.kensingtonbooks

CITADEL PRESS BOOKS are published by

Kensington Publishing Corp.
119 West 40th Street
New York, NY 10018

AUTHORS' NOTE
Although this is a true story, some names and locations have been changed to protect the privacy of the innocent. When possible, the spoken word has been quoted verbatim. However, when that is not possible, conversations have been reconstructed as closely as possible to reality based on the recollections of those who spoke and heard the words. In places there has been a slight editing of spoken words, but only to improve readability. The denotations and connotations of the words remain unaltered. In some cases, witnesses are credited with verbal quotes that in reality only occurred in written form. Some characters may be composites.

ISBN-13: 978-0-8065-4014-6
ISBN-10: 0-8065-4014-1

First hardcover printing: June 2020
First trade paperback printing: May 2021

10 9 8 7 6 5 4 3 2 1

Printed in the United States of America

Electronic edition:

ISBN-13: 978-0-8065-4015-3 (e-book)
ISBN-10: 0-8065-4015-X (e-book)

For Tony Nap

Fix your eyes below, upon the valley,
For now we near the stream of blood, where those
Who injure others violently, boil.
—DANTE's *Inferno*, XII (tr. Allen Mandelbaum)

CONTENTS

INTRODUCTION

Understanding Anastasia

YOU WANT TO UNDERSTAND ALBERT ANASTASIA? You got to know some things right off the bat. He was a psychopathic killer. Not only did he lack a sense of guilt, but also he was a sadist, enjoyed killing, got off on it . . . enjoyed hurting and then killing. He was pure evil, and no one as it turned out was ever really his friend. His kid brother the priest would say that Albert was the poster boy for purity and domesticity—a good family man who liked to stay home and play board games. His wife would defend him, saying he attended church each Sunday. But other than that, it's hard to find anyone who had anything nice to say about him. By all accounts, he was a soulless monster. His presence sent cold chills up and down the spine, the kind of shiver of terror you'd get from being in the presence of the devil himself.

Why was he like that? The facts show a man traumatized and bent early, a man who saw unimaginable mass-scale death and misery as a kid. Hideous images that would always haunt him. Corpses stacked and burning. His mother told him it was the end of the world and he should pray. He saw what men could do when they were terrified and desperate. He was bent from the get-go, and grew into a man unafraid of hell because he'd grown up right in the middle of it.

Another thing you should know is that Anastasia was *versatile*. Many pro killers, then and now, have a specialty: a signature way of bumping a guy off. You got your pocket gun guys, like Jack Ruby, they get in tight and blew out a guy's belly. You got ice pick guys that would put a tiny hole behind the guy's ear, as neat and proper as a tetanus shot.

There were the guys who liked to use their hands on a victim's throat. Some of them got a weird kick out of it, and would let guys live for longer than they needed to just to stretch out the torture.

You had snipers who played the game like they were in a Coney Island arcade shooting ducks for a Kewpie doll. You had rat-tat-tat-tat boys who drove by with a tommy gun and left their victims flat on the sidewalk looking like a discarded suit.

But not Albert. He was what you might call a general practitioner. He enjoyed experimenting with a variety of kill methods. He'd shoot you, strangle you, or stab you with an ice pick. Leave you whole or chop you up. Depended on his mood.

My Uncle Joe said he preferred using his hands. He might've been one of those guys who didn't choke out his victims all at once, let them gasp and sputter a little and then, teeth bared, re-applied the pressure. It was all in the thumbs—and Albert Anastasia had powerful thumbs.

All of his methods involved getting up close and personal. Dishing out death *was* personal, even intimate, and was best administered high and tight. He wanted his victim to smell the garlic on his breath. And even as a kid he was the killer of choice for the bigs, including Al Capone himself.

The third thing you need to know is that, for a large part of his gangster career, Albert Anastasia was a double threat. He was the underboss and then boss of what would one day become known as (spoiler alert) the Gambino crime family. Anastasia was a guy who, with his younger brothers, ruled the Brooklyn waterfront. And, as a second job, he ran Murder Inc. for Lucky Luciano—a gang of professional killers that worked outside the Five Family system—supervising a team of pro's pro gunmen, homicidal maniacs every one, once freelance killers, now under exclusive contract.

Anastasia's crew of killers. These guys, they were everywhere. They could hit you anywhere in the country, and in a lot of places around the world, too. Rule of thumb was: You can't run, they'll catch you, can't hide, they'll find you. Best to not fuck up in the first place.

That was their rep. There was down time, too. Albert's boys wiled away the hours sipping espresso and playing cards in the back of a Brownsville, Brooklyn, candy store, like firemen waiting for the alarm to go off so they could have some excitement.

There would be talk that Albert's personal body count was exaggerated because a lot of guys whacked in his name but not with his expressed approval, which is a load of bullshit. The idea was that if a boss wanted someone whacked, he contacted Albert, Albert sent out a crew of gunmen, and the job was done.

Obviously, Albert himself could have anyone whacked at any time he wanted. (In fact, poor choices in this regard contributed to his downfall.) It was understood that freelance killing was forbidden. You didn't whack anybody without Albert's approval. These things had to go through the proper channels, and in this way the higher-ups were protected.

There is no paper work to refer to, but word was the killers in Albert's employ were given a weekly salary of $200 and then a bonus for a job well done. If they killed for their own personal reasons or took a job on the outside, they themselves could be subject to the final discipline.

Albert's boys didn't just dish out Death. They dealt out Fear by the bucketful, as well. The idea was to let small-time hoods know that crossing the line was a mistake. The more afraid the soldiers of Brooklyn were, the less actual killing would be necessary.

"Make the coroner puke," Anastasia would say.

So Murder Inc.'s trademark was cutting off its victim's dick and shoving it in the corpse's mouth, something that made hits particularly terrifying to survivors. Louis "Pretty" Amberg, whacked in 1935, was a good example. The Jewish killers on the team called it the Schmeckle Special, the *bris* with no *mohel*.

Although Murder Inc. was unparalleled in its body count, it was never a huge organization. As it was done back in Sicily, Lucky Luciano set it up purposefully outside the Five Family structure. In the days before the RICO bullshit, all you needed to skate on a contract kill was plausible deniability. A separate organization doing much of the killing served to insulate the bosses from the blood.

Murder Inc. was not only outside the Five Families, but also outside the Sicilian Mafia, as well. A large chunk of organized crime in Brooklyn back then was Jewish, and those guys were allowed to use Albert's services. Anastasia's second in command, Louis "Lepke" Buchalter, was Jewish—and since many of the boys were originally in Lepke's crew, a large percentage of the killers in the back room were Jewish. Everybody sipped espresso and played cards together. Brooklyn was the *polyglot*.

If a contract came in from a top guy, a boss or an underboss, Albert would just execute it without thinking twice. If a capo or a non-mob businessman wanted a hit done, Albert would run it past Meyer Lansky or Frank Costello, make sure he wasn't stepping on the wrong toes. His organization was supposed to punish insubordinates, not start wars.

Albert would later have his own crime family under his control, a huge organization, but Murder Inc. never involved more than about a dozen men at a time, maybe two dozen all together.

Some of the most famous guys were Martin "Buggsy" Goldstein, Harry "Pittsburgh Phil" Strauss, Louie Capone (no relation), Abraham "Kid Twist" Reles, Allie "Tic Toc" Tannenbaum, Frank "The Dasher" Abandando, Harry "Happy" Maione, Frank Panetta, Anthony "Tony Spring" Romeo, Anthony Maffetore, Seymour "Blue Jaw" Magoon, Angelo Catalano, Mendy Weiss, Charles "Bug" Workman, Jimmy "Dirty Face" Ferraco, Irving Nitzberg, Vito "Chicken Head" Gurino, Jack "Dandy" Parisi, Jacob Drucker, Irving Cohen, Walter Sage, and a few others. But it was a tight group and a tough life. Only a couple of them lived to be old.

And it is important to note that *they* never called it Murder Inc. They didn't call it anything at all. The term Murder Inc. was, like a lot of things in this world, made up by a reporter seeking a hook to lure readers. Albert's crew handled killing in a new cold and businesslike way, so the name fit, and it caught on.

In addition to having friends who were willing to kill for him, Albert was also blessed with loyal followers who were willing to die for him, and who for the most part made him a hard target for those who were jealous of his power.

In this book you're going to hear stories you never heard before. That's because when I was a kid I got to hang out with my uncle Joe Schipani, a.k.a. Joe Shep, who was in a crew with Anastasia and saw some things in person that the rest of the world only got to imagine.

Uncle Joe said that Anastasia wasn't a huge man, but he had a strong upper body, hard arms, a big chest, and a stevedore's hands that could crush a larynx without effort.

Anastasia spoke like a gangster. Uncle Joe told me that when Jimmy Cagney played gangsters in the movies it was like he was doing an Albert Anastasia impression, with more than a little Irish thrown in.

Anastasia spoke in quick bursts, like machine-gun fire, always in a command voice. His skin was olive-complexioned and his hair as black as night. That hair, if left alone, would curl up and form a mop, but Albert used Vitalis with V7, kept it tightly slicked back and usually under a hat, a boater as a youth, and later a fedora.

Back in the day, Uncle Joe, Albert Anastasia, and Frank Costello would go on a wide variety of scores, but their favorites were gambling clubs, the booze flowing. Everybody already had cash out. The men would put handkerchiefs over their faces and stick everyone up. My Uncle Joe would apologize to the men and kiss the ladies' hands. He believed in sentimental value. If the women were married, he allowed them to keep their wedding rings.

Anastasia, on the other hand, would not only want to take wedding rings, he might want to take the finger with it. Not a nice man.

* * *

So in this book, the first ever full-length biography of Albert Anastasia, you're going to learn about some stuff you didn't know before, like what happened to Vincent Mangano. Everybody knows he disappeared off the face of the earth around the same time his brother's body was found in a Brooklyn swamp, but Uncle Joe was there and he told me the chilling details.

You will read about Albert the waterfront czar, king of Red Hook, who with his brother Tough Tony ran the very piers off of which he first touched American soil in 1917. Eventually he ran the labor, and much of the import/export that went on there. He was in charge of the money, and where the money went—in charge of all trade and the lives of those that worked it.

Albert was a record-setter, the first man in the history of American justice to be charged with four separate murders and to go free after each one. And he wasn't done.

You will read about Albert's life from the time he was a small boy, still known as Umberto Anastasio, padding barefoot with his crew from the village of Tropea, Calabria, down 210 stone steps to the beach at Parghelia, all the way to his last day, his sudden demise in a barber chair, and the scent of Wildroot and gunpowder in Grasso's Barber Shop, a legendarily powerful man assassinated with his face wrapped in a hot towel, a wild final scene punctuated by a screaming manicurist and the exploding flashbulbs of tabloid photographers, eager guys wearing their Speed Graphics like masks at a macabre ball. In death, Albert became the most famously photographed stiff in mob history. Plus, all of the daring, treachery, and brutal violence in between, a supporting cast that includes Lucky Luciano, Francesco Castiglia, a.k.a. Frank Costello, Vito Genovese, and U.S. Army generals planning the invasion of Italy during World War II.

This is the first-time-ever complete story of Albert "The Mad Hatter" Anastasia, the Lord High Executioner.

* * *

One quick note before I start the story: Italians back then didn't care about spelling. Especially when it came to surnames. O's and a's are interchangeable. An e can become an a and then go back again. Newspapers tried to keep it straight but every paper had their own spelling for every hood. My dad Rick Dimatteo changed the spelling of his last name on a weekly basis. I asked him why once, and he said, "Throws 'em off." We don't care about spelling that much now either. So I don't want to hear no bullshit about I spelled this guy or that guy's name wrong, because there ain't no wrong. Got it?

OK, our story starts in Italy . . .

ONE
The Land That Dances

UMBERTO ANASTASIO WAS BORN September 26, 1902, in Tropea, a fishing village in Calabria, where men worked hard and remained poor, where each day the men would walk down 210 stone steps to go to work, and at the end of the day with aching knees and ankles, climb back up again to the town on the ridge. Tropea was a shipping town, like Liverpool, England, and New York City, where steam-powered ocean-going cargo vessels docked and stevedores emptied and refilled their hulls.

Umberto's old man was Raffaello Anastasio, and mom was Louisa Nomina de Filippi. His father was neither a fisherman nor a dockworker. He worked the livelong day on the railroad, and was often away from home. It was a time when great technological advances were revolutionizing the rail system in the north of Italy, where electricity allowed quick passage across the Alps to Bernina, Switzerland—but not so much in the south, where smoky coal-burners chugged, heavy with the goods they transported from Tropea to other regions.

Raffaello must've come home sometimes, though, as there were a dozen Anastasio kids, nine sons and three daughters. One son and two daughters died as infants. Raffaello himself died in 1912, cause unknown.

It was a very different world from the one we know today, a world without modern medicine where a simple infection could be deadly, where communication was slow, where trying to get a message from the toe of Italy to someone in the north could take days, and there was always a chance it wouldn't arrive at all.

Some things were the same. As will perhaps always be the case, humans clustered in tribes and were suspicious and hateful of outsiders. The newspapers here in America routinely used phrases like "the evils of Jewish immigration" and "a lynching is expected."

On the day of Umberto's birth, the Mafia had not only taken root in Italy, but in America, as well. It was *the* story in New Orleans, where there were, in the southern half of that delta city, the blood-spattered homes of marked men, subject to savage raids involving axes.

Journalists wrote that the Mafia had arms that could reach around the world. No one could get far enough away to be out of reach of that "cruel society." They speculated that in every city of the United States where Italians gather in any numbers there was an organization that could "avenge a fancied wrong or injury."

Back in Italy, when little Umberto Anastasio was three years old, there was an earthquake that crumbled everything for miles around. The quake itself, epicenter in Monte Leone about eight miles to the east of the Anastasio home, caused a panic, and many were injured as they ran in terror.

In the aftermath, the homeless lived in tents that gave the countryside the appearance of a military camp. The quake caused an old sulfur spring to run dry, so that it emitted nothing but mud and foul-smelling gas. The River Messini swelled, becoming a tumultuous combo of hot and cold water. Sulfur gas rose from the churning waters. Everything stunk to high heaven.

Unlike less lucky areas in Calabria, few people died in Tropea, but there were thousands of wounded. The reason for the lack of fatalities was that there were warning signs that the earth was about to crack open. The underground rumblings were such that most people were outside and out in the open when the quake hit. After the quake, folks walked along the beach where the post-quake waves had deposited thousands of fish to die, including one shark that had been swept ashore just as it bit into the tail of a swordfish.

Tropea didn't lose its sense of community in the crisis. There was no gouging, prices remained the same, and charity was the rule of the day. Those without shelter slept in gardens and under trees. The bishop said mass at a makeshift altar near a disembodied railroad car.

That was the first big quake. It was nothing compared to the one that followed three years later.

The Big One came when Umberto was six years old, three days after Christmas, 1908, the most destructive earthquake in European history. It struck in the middle of the night. Five a.m. Most everyone was in bed, most vulnerable.

History books will tell you that it was a 7.1 on the Richter scale, but truth is, they're guessing. The quake pinned the needles in the primitive measuring equipment of the day. It felt as if the whole toe of the boot of Italy was going to fall into the Mediterranean.

The Bishop of Tropea counted five-hundred churches in his diocese destroyed by the earthquake. Rescue workers at the scenes of the worst damage were traumatized by what they saw. Entire towns and small cities had been flattened. Fourteen-thousand dead in Paimi, twelve-thousand dead in Reggio, two-thousand of them soldiers.

Nothing remained intact. Walls and floors crumbled, sometimes into small chunks. One of the first rescue efforts was by rail, but it came up way short as the quake had wrecked all tracks for many miles around.

The nightmare was vivid in the far-away stares of those who survived it. Rescuers told of living dead moving in lawless groups, packs of monstrous looters. The civilized world ceased to exist and savage instincts were boss. Stripped of humanity itself, they cried out for all of their earthly needs: food, shelter, clothing, and medical attention.

Most horribly, one pack of gray dust-covered figures scavenged like coyotes, dehumanized by desperation, naked some of them—clothes torn off while they extricated themselves from sharp rocks and rubble—skinned, bleeding, scuttling about like spiders in the chalky dust, sticking their boney hands into the pockets of the dead. Looters such as these, when seen by law enforcement, were shot on the spot.

The tidal wave was as harrowing as the earthquake and its aftershocks. It was during this part of the disaster that Umberto Anastasio's home village caught a break. Other villages were wiped from the face of the earth by an ebb and flow both angry and greedy. Even more destructive than the incoming wave was the withdrawal of the water that both preceded and followed it, sucking and then sucking again large chunks of Italy out by the roots like a decaying tooth, a deadly phenomenon caused by a hole forming in the bed of the Mediterranean. Those 210 stone steps that took you from the beach to the village served as a breakwater, as the first and largest wave was estimated at thirty-two feet, and prevented little Umberto from being drowned.

When the sea returned to normal, the visible waters off the Italian shores were speckled with the carcasses of dead animals and various wreckage. Ships at sea were at the mercy of the tidal wave. Some managed to make it to a port with damage, or ruined cargo—many were neither seen nor heard from again.

Threat of disease terrified the living. Death was everywhere, not just decomposing human bodies but animals, too—rotting that brought rats and rats that brought disease. So bodies, human and otherwise, were piled up in the street and torched. When rescuers asked survivors what supplies were needed the most, strong disinfectants to sanitize the maggoty areas topped the list.

It was a world of orphans. Many surviving children had lost their parents. They were numb with grief and stricken with terror. A nice life had transformed into a nightmare in the blink of an eye.

Doctors were few and when one was found alive he was set up in a tent on the outskirts of a destroyed town. If injured were found they'd be carried on stretchers up and over the piles of stone to the doctor who maybe had his black bag with him.

The lucky patients were stretchered to the shore and now and again put on a boat for transport to a real hospital. Those boats had to improvise in the Italian harbors as the tidal wave had washed away the landing quays.

Truth was, there weren't that many survivors. When one was found it was a big deal, and amplified for its note of hope. But for the great majority, there was no hope. For a few moments there it was raining rocks and just about everyone had gotten their skulls crushed.

One doctor in Messina emerged from the thick of the destruction with tales of unbelievable horror. This had been a city of 100,000. There were six-thousand survivors, unhinged by the trauma, limping along on the road to hell. They didn't know that the destruction was localized, and thought that perhaps God had seen fit to tear the whole world down so He could start over.

In the towns like Umberto's where there were survivors but roads were blocked, the living formed tent villages—which was adequate until, on the eleventh day after the quake, the area was hit with a tremendous storm, rain in sheets, hurricane-strength winds. Many who'd survived the earthquake and tidal wave were lost in the Big Blow.

Italy's Queen Elena was in Messina for the quake. She was even slightly injured when she visited a makeshift hospital and a crush of humanity in her direction bruised her royal tits.

In Brooklyn, where many had relatives in Italy, there was a sick concern. In Italian neighborhoods, fraternal organizations and Italian societies established charity funds. Samuel Barber of Neptune Avenue in Coney Island had a ninety-year-old grandmother, a fifty-two-year-old mother, two brothers, and a sister in Messina and feared they were all dead—and feared he'd never know for sure.

Not everyone in Brooklyn was on the same page. One woman had to be hospitalized when she theorized aloud that the quake was a hoax so Italian con artists could fleece honest hard-working people. At that, another woman lost her temper and beat the shit out of her.

Everyone in Umberto's ravaged town wanted to know more about this place in America called Brooklyn. When a rare letter arrived in the mail, people gathered to hear stories of Williamsburg, Red Hook, Bushwick, and Greenpoint.

Another connection between Brooklyn and Italy in 1909 was the Black Hand, which had been powerful in Italy for years but recently spread to New York City. In March 1909, New York Police Lieutenant Joe Petrosini went to Sicily to hunt Black Handers and was there for only a matter of hours when he was blown away with four shots from a revolver.

In Tropea, Umberto's home and surroundings took on the perpetual stink of death. The stone stairs had prevented annihilation, but that didn't mean Tropea hadn't been deeply wounded by the disaster. The region was poor and, despite efforts to raise money in places like Brooklyn in America for aid, there was damage done that would never be repaired.

Umberto's homeland was dealt a blow from which it would never bounce back. The numbers were staggering: maybe 200,000 killed in the quake, aftershocks, and resulting tidal wave. There were reportedly 293 aftershocks!

Umberto saw it and heard it and felt it all, and he emerged from the nightmare a boy without a conscience, a boy who believed life was cheap, that it was okay to climb atop the ghosts of those in his path, cold as ice.

The mass exodus to America started immediately. Cargo ships docked along the Calabrian coast set sail with their hulls jammed with refugees.

The next quake, people believed, would sink Tropea and maybe all of Calabria. The regional tectonic feature known as the Calabrian Arc would give way and like Atlantis itself, there'd be nothing left but underwater ruins.

Secondary to Italy's grief, there were winds of war. In Europe nobody got along with nobody, and there were already chess moves being made. Italy was flirting with France, which brought jealous overtures from Germany and Austro-Hungary. So naturally, many sought to move to other places—places like Brooklyn, New York, where the winds were milder and the land did not dance.

In Tropea, the Anastasio family was torn asunder. Frank went to Australia. The remaining sons worked as soon as they were old enough, on fishing boats, freighters, farms, and on the railroad like the old man.

All back-breaking work.

Two years after his father had died, Umberto, at age twelve, dropped out of school and became a deckhand on a steamship. It was tough work that prepared him well for tougher jobs to follow, and laid the groundwork for a lifelong hatred of physical labor. He became familiar at a tender age with the hideous conditions under which people were expected to work. The seaworthiness of some of his vessels was pretty sketchy, their lifeboats worse.

According to an FBI assessment, Umberto "knocked about some of the toughest ports in the world." And all that that implied. He was a kid unafraid to take a chance, and a gambler. Later there would be a love of the ponies, but at this stage he mostly knelt on guarded street corners and rolled dice.

Of the brothers, Umberto was the leader, three and a half years older than Anthony (a.k.a. Tough Tony), older by six years than Guiseppe (Joseph), about nine years older than Gerardo (a.k.a. Jerry) and he was not naïve about the way of the world.

So Umberto knew by the time he was a teenager that labor was abused, but he did not think about improving those conditions. He thought about more organized and profitable ways to further abuse labor. He couldn't lick management. That was plain to see. Better to *become* management, or management's *muscle*. That was where the power was.

* * *

In Italy there were virtual leaders who presided over ceremonies, and leaders who were actually in charge. The first category was made up of the monarchy. King Humbert dropped dead on July 30, 1900, and King Victor Emmanuel took the throne, but not under the smoothest of circumstances. Victor was thought of as a candy ass by the Italians until they heard him speak, something he could do with electrifying results. Victor's wife was Queen Elena, the gal with the knocked-about knockers, the daughter of Prince Nicholas of Montenegro.

Umberto knew from the time he was a child that King Victor Emmanuel might have been head honcho in many parts of Italy, but there were regions—in particular the mountain district and the poor south—where the murderers and blackmailers of the Mafia were in charge. If you crossed a Mafioso, even an armed guard couldn't keep you from being snatched and disappeared into the night.

Since the dawn of time it has been tradition for law enforcement to turn a blind eye to organized crime, and it was no different in Calabria where, at least since *La Mafia* uprising of 1866, law enforcement often resembled the referee in a modern-day pro wrestling match, always with his back turned at the key moment.

Politicians did more than just look away—they openly *praised* the Mafia. Without organized crime's endorsement, it was difficult getting elected. And police knew a good thing when they saw it.

There were bribes to collect and the Mafia created its own self-policed community. Police could slack off. It was the Mafia that arranged contracts and settled disputes.

A classic crime of the era was a simple fence-free form of robbery, whereby mobsters would steal something and then sell the items back to their owners.

This reminds me of a story I heard once from a movie producer who was in Italy making spaghetti westerns in the 1960s. The real money, he said, came from dubbing them into English and showing them on American TV.

While in Italy for a film's pre-production, he borrowed his

client's Alfa Romeo, paid his visit in Naples, came out of the building and the car was gone, stolen, sending the producer scrambling to the nearest phone to call his client, whom he knew to be well-connected.

The producer explained what had happened and asked, "What do I do?"

The client said, "Stay calm. Don't do anything. The car will be delivered to you in an hour. When it arrives, give the driver $100 for his time."

"But what if the car isn't delivered in an hour?" It seemed implausible. He was in Naples. He'd borrowed the car in Rome. The Alfa could have been stolen by anyone and driven anywhere.

"Don't worry. Sit tight," the client said.

Sure enough, in exactly an hour the car arrived. The producer, now convinced that he was trapped in an episode of the *Twilight Zone*, paid the driver the hundred bucks for his time, got in the car and drove it back to Rome, realizing quickly that there was no point in pondering the matter. Was it a practical joker moving his client's car for a laugh? Was it extortion, an actual theft but also the country's worst-kept secret? It couldn't be a local operation because the car was stolen in Naples and the guy who knew what to do was in Rome. Nope, given a lifetime of contemplation, he was never going to figure out what had just happened.

The movie producer didn't know. But I knew. Didn't matter what city he was in. The car never left the neighborhood. It was a mob thing, mob thinking. This was earning for the most brazen: a fence-free robbery. The thief was cutting out the middleman.

In 1909, the Mafia hit—that is, murder—was already a thing, but back then the Mafia often didn't do its own killing. They contracted out. Sometimes certain Mafiosi formed themselves into a *sette*, a secret society within a secret society, which had its own initiations and rituals, including of course the pledge of *omerta*. And what they did was terrorize the countryside with violence. Some of the most famous of the *sette* were the *Stoppalieri*, the *Fratenanza di Favara*, the *Fratuzzi*, and the *Fratelli Amorosi*. (So those of you who might think that the Syndicate invented Murder Inc., there's nothing new under the sun.)

Although the successful arrest and prosecution of *sette* members was not unknown, it was uncommon, as everyone kept their lips zipped. Witnesses who were foolish enough to cooperate with law enforcement in those instances often had bad things happen to them, and prosecutions imploded under the weight of outside intimidation.

The *settes* didn't care who they whacked. Anyone who wouldn't play ball was iced, and in the year of Umberto's birth, "eminent figure in affairs of state in Sicily" Emanuel Notarbartolo, and zillionaire Francesco Miceli were liquidated because they wouldn't listen.

When a man was designated for death, straws were handed out, and the man who drew the short straw had to carry out the hit, even if the target was his best friend. A man who failed to carry out his grim task would become the next name on the hit list.

Such were the ways of the mystic Italian murder club. When hoods from Europe came to America, they brought their traditions with them, traditions that were bloodthirsty and without conscience.

In 1910, the head of Brooklyn organized crime, Giuseppi Morello, went to jail for six months, leaving a void. Morello's organization was known as the *Camorra,* with crews working both in Brooklyn and Manhattan, especially in Harlem, which was then heavily Italian.

His replacement was Salvatore "Toto" D'Aquila, who operated a crew out of Little Italy under the auspices of Ignazo "Lupo the Wolf" Salette. When Morello was released, he and D'Aquila had a meeting. Instead of divvying up the power, both wanted it all. Morello and his hoods walked out of the meeting and war was declared, which turned out to be a big mistake. Morello's effectiveness had eroded during his time away, and he found himself outgunned.

D'Aquila's killers were everywhere. Morello's men were decimated. Morello was forced into hiding. Eventually, D'Aquila absorbed Morello's *brugad*. The thing about the Camorra was that it was separate although very similar to the Mafia. They were dueling secret societies, both here and back in Italy. While D'Aquila and Morello were battling it out, there was an even bloodier Mafia-Camorra war raging.

The Camorra was run by guys out of Naples and Campagnia, while the Mafia was Sicilian. Both wars reduced the numbers of hoods working in New York, but with thousands of Italian immigrants arriving from Italy every month, there was plenty of talent to replenish the ranks.

Along with hoods killing hoods, the Law was having a brief period of success dealing with organized crime, and entire crews were being wiped out by prosecutions. Why the sudden success? Between the guy who could be bribed and another guy who could be bribed there was a guy who couldn't be bribed.

Organized crime was in a state of chaos with major and minor wars going on, power vacuums opening and filling. There was a lot of action. And this was the state of things when Umberto Anastasio, who would become Albert Anastasia, sailed to America.

TWO

S.S. Sardegna

DURING THE SUMMER OF 1917, almost fifteen-year-old Umberto Anastasio joined the Italian Royal Navy, aboard an ironclad battleship that was aiding the Allied efforts in World War I. The S.S. *Sardegna* was laid down in 1885, launched in 1890, and completed in 1895. The ship was equipped with a main battery of 13½-inch guns and had seen warfare in the Italia-Turkish War of 1911–12. Umberto became an aspiring seaman on the S.S. *Sardegna,* named after the Italian island in the Mediterranean where they cram the little fishes in tin cans. It's a funny name for a ship, which was probably overcrowded.

On September 12, Umberto and the *Sardegna* arrived at the Port of New York, and he was granted shore leave. His feet hit the ground and he disappeared into the urban maze of Red Hook, Brooklyn.

When he failed to return to his ship on September 29, Umberto Anastasio was listed as a deserting seaman and quickly forgotten. Italy, for Umberto, had been a horror story. He considered himself an American from that point on, but his actual citizenship remained in question for almost his entire life.

This is as good of a place as any to point out that Red Hook is where I was born, and where I lived as a kid, and there was no place on Earth, not even in Italy, where the texture of mob life was so ingrained in the structures and the people and the system. Very little English was spoken. You needed some to conduct business.

During the twentieth century, Red Hook was the center of the organized crime universe, dating back to the days of The White Hand and Richard "Peg Leg" Lonergan (the Irish version of The Black Hand), Giuseppe Morello: The Clutch Hand. It would become the stomping grounds of Francesco Ioele (Frankie Yale) and the *Unione Siciliane*. During the Great Depression there was Hooverville: Hoods from the Hobo Jungle, Wise Guys from the Waste Land, the place where Al Capone, Scarface, got his scar, Salvatore "Toto" D'Aquila: The Cheese Importer, first boss of the future Gambino Family, Manfredi "Al" Mineo and the Castellammarese War, Vincenzo Giovanni Mangano; The Executioner, Frank "Wacky" Scalise . . .

And our subject Umberto Anastasia: The Mad Hatter, who was himself followed in Red Hook by Joseph Profaci: The Olive Oil King, and The Gallos: Princes of President Street—which is where I came in. But that was far, far in the future. This was 1917–18.

If teenaged Umberto Anastasio—now a deserter from the Italian Navy and far, far from home—had ambitions to make it in organized crime, and there's every reason to believe he did, he had come to the right place.

Teenaged Umberto was used to death. People dying left and right was normal to him. So he maybe didn't feel it the way others in Brooklyn did, but in 1918 there were a shitload of people dying, both in Brooklyn and Europe. Many young men were going off to war and being gassed in the trenches, but it was just as dangerous stateside where thousands of people began dropping dead in New York City. It had nothing to do with mob wars or the Black Hand or guys getting whacked. The deadliest epidemic in American history was stealing away the young and the healthy. The influenza pandemic and the Great World War had teamed up to prune the earth's human population. Not since the days of the plague had humanity so turned blue and dropped dead.

The flu was even deadlier than the war. About fifty million people died of the flu in 1918, about 675,000 of them in the U.S., and about thirty-thousand of those in New York City. The worst of it was during the autumn, when close to five-hundred otherwise sturdy people were dying of the flu every day. Hospitals were overwhelmed. Many got sick and expired at home, giving the germs plenty of time to infect the rest of the household. The pandemic caused life expectancy to drop in America by twelve years, to less than thirty-seven years for men.

The flu killed directly, of course, but it also caused mass tragedy in unexpected ways. On November 1, 1918, the dad of a little girl who'd just succumbed went to work as a substitute train motorman on the Brighton Beach line, grieving and without sleep. Approaching the Prospect Park stop, he tried to take a sharp curve into a tunnel under Malbone Street at full speed—an estimated forty miles per hour instead of the recommended three—hit the side of the tunnel entrance and derailed his train. As the cars were built of wood, they splintered into spear-like shards and impaled the passengers. Ninety-three died. Many others were maimed horribly. The disaster was so famous that the name of Malbone Street was changed to Empire Boulevard. All hospitals were full of flu patients, so triage was set up on the green lawn of the nearby ballpark, the four-year-old Ebbets Field. World War I still had sixteen days to go, and the flu, like the train approaching the tunnel, showed no signs of slowing down.

Stroll around Green-Wood Cemetery someday, in the older sections. It seems like every other poor soul died in 1918. Mass death followed Umberto from Tropea to Brooklyn.

Details of those early first days of Umberto, and later his brothers, trying to survive in Red Hook are lost in the mists of time. Maybe there was a period when they tried to go legit, threw the hook over their shoulders and went to work loading and unloading the ocean-going vessels parked at the Red Hook piers. Umberto claimed there was a period of legitimacy—but maybe he was corrupt from Day One. We do know that, if there was an attempt at making it legit, it didn't last long—a couple of years, tops.

The FBI later wrote that they could trace Umberto Anastasio's activity with dock gangs back to 1921, and—as his brothers, Tony, Jerry, and Joe came of age—he was joined by them. They each in turn took the initiation and joined a crew—a crew responsible for skullduggery on the waterfront.

Those gangs ruled their harbor empire with an iron fist, and dissent could be fatal. The dockworkers were dominated in a cruel fashion, subjected to the daily shape-up, submitting to what one reporter called "the dishonoring of daughters."

Each morning there were more men than jobs so those looking for work gathered at the morning "shape-up," where the hatch bosses decided who would and wouldn't be able to feed their families, where those willing to pay the bribe got work, bribe money that flowed efficiently into the underworld. For those who could scrounge up the bribe money during the morning, a second shape-up was held at one o'clock where men would be chosen for a half-day's work.

In most cases the ruling class in Red Hook did whatever the hell it wanted. The texture of the Red Hook social ramble was thick with shylocks, kickback extortion, and punishment to those who were tardy paying the vig. It could be an endless circle for some poor *schlubs* who lost at the track, so they paid the bribe to get the work to pay the shylock and return to the track.

The control over all money in Red Hook was obvious on a daily basis. Men knew that there was no point in even showing up to look for work unless they bought bread at the correct bakery and purchased groceries at the mob-controlled store.

Umberto was a guy who learned fast to rely on his toughness. He was embarrassed about his speech. He felt he spoke neither Italian nor English very well. But he was tough as nails, with hands straight off a Michelangelo sculpture, qualities that suited him when it came to both getting work and handling himself with his competitive and ill-tempered co-workers. He was never going to talk his way out of a jam. Better to just bust the guy's jaw.

His nickname as a kid was *"Terremoto"* or Cyclone, a reference to his quick fists, which worked not just with blinding speed, but also in crisp, well-balanced, pugilistic devastating combinations.

One of the best parts of working on the piers, Umberto thought, was that, as long as no one was looking directly at you when you did it, stuff fell off the boat all the time and managed to go home with Umberto at the end of the day.

If someone told him they didn't like it, Umberto fed him a knuckle sandwich. One of the reasons he accrued power so efficiently is that he had the looks of a leader, something in Umberto's barrel chest, in the chiseled nature of his features. The way he just laid out guys who got in his way.

He loved to gamble but he wasn't always good at it, and he was quick to assume a conspiracy against him when his luck turned abruptly. He was never one of the guys. He didn't have friends. He didn't have fun.

Umberto was too quick to turn violent for a lot of guys' taste—so they steered clear. Sometimes he had a point when he fought. At other times it was more like he was being rash or didn't completely understand the situation.

Sometimes it seemed like he woke up determined to get into a fight and then scouted around for a passable reason. You never knew what was going to light Umberto's fuse, so you tried to stay out of arm's reach.

At some point, and I'm guessing early on, Umberto discovered that there was profit in hurting, even killing people, a job designed for those who didn't feel too bad about it afterward. His fists of stone were his ladder to upward mobility. He would hurt for personal reasons, sure—but more important, he could hurt *for money.* Guys would pay to have some poor asshole hurt.

A guy who didn't do the right thing, a guy who couldn't pay, a guy who couldn't keep it in his pants. Business was business. He would go about it coldly, but sometimes allow himself a greedy grin of pleasure as he worked over a degenerate's kneecap.

"You like Sally's sister, huh? Let's see if she goes for a *gimp*," he would say. The howl of pain he heard next was like music.

Somewhere along the line he decided that he needed to Americanize his name. So Umberto Anastasio began calling himself Albert Anastasia. He moved from the hopeless drudgery of going to work with a hook over his shoulder to the hideously dangerous world of organized crime.

Albert was no historian, but he knew how things went when you got into the Life: Being a gangster came with an occupational disease for which, like the flu, there was no cure.

THREE
First Kill

UNTIL THE PASSING OF THE EIGHTEENTH AMENDMENT, a.k.a. the Volstead Act, a.k.a. Prohibition, on January 16, 1920, most mob shit was local, and battles between rival gangs were largely limited to matters of turf. You stay on your side of the street, I stay on mine, try crossing the street and there's going to be trouble. But Prohibition changed everything.

Everybody was unhappy with the new law. People thought the right to get drunk was God-given. Only two groups thrived. In the south some believed the liquor ban would keep black men from raping white women. Those assholes were happy.

And, in mob circles, it meant a fantastic business opportunity. Now an entire industry, once legal and popular, was delegated to the world of the black market. With drinking, making, or possessing alcoholic beverages against the law, an unenforceable law, booze became the ultimate earner.

Visionary gangsters like Al Capone, Meyer Lansky, and Charles "Lucky" Luciano, saw the opportunity to make a lot of money on a national, and, in some instances, international, level. (Luciano got his nickname after he was beaten up and left for dead, but survived to become kingpin.)

Albert Anastasia understood that under the new rules, a lot of guys were going to need hurting, and he was perfect for the job. He let it be known that he would do anything violent for money, and sure enough there were tough guys with rackets—including Capone himself—who were willing to pay for his services. To Albert's delight, this meant steady employment, almost none of which involved loading or unloading ships.

Albert was already astute at breaking legs and softening skulls, but as far as we know, he didn't kill anybody until May 16, 1920, five months into Prohibition and still four months shy of his eighteenth birthday.

On that day Albert and his partner in crime Giuseppe Florino argued with a guy named George Terrillo (also shown as George Terello, George Turino, George Turella, George Puerlo, and George Purello, almost never spelled the same way twice, so I've picked Terrillo as the spelling, but truth is I have no idea what this guy's name was). What we do know is that the argument took place at the corner of Union and Columbia streets in the heart of Red Hook.

Terrillo, it is said, was angry that the pair had robbed a friend of his. He demanded they give the money back. Instead, Anastasia and Florino pulled their guns and shot Terrillo, who was dead before his head hit the sidewalk, which it did with a sick thud.

Mrs. Margaret Farrera Viccio witnessed the murder. She said the thing she would never forget was the look on Anastasia's face when he squeezed the trigger. It was the face of a complete maniac, a purely evil human being who was taking the life of another and enjoying every second of it.

"You sure of who you saw?" cops asked.

"Yeah. It was Florino and his friend Albert," she said.

She explained that it was a delicate matter on account of she was a married woman but she knew Florino when she saw him because she used to be his girlfriend. Still, even with the positive I.D., it was months before Florino and Anastasia were arrested and thrown into the rat-infested Raymond Street Jail.

There are indications that the murder of Terrillo was more than just an argument. What we know is that Anastasia and Florio pulled serious backing when they bumped off the guy. They had juice. At their 1921 murder trial, extra security was present in the State Supreme Court room as there was a perpetual threat of "riot or rescue." Guards had to worry both about people trying to get out of the courtroom and those trying to get in.

You like courtroom drama? The key prosecution witness was Mrs. Viccio, who fearlessly testified. At one point, while she was on the witness stand, Anastasia caught her attention and drew his finger across his throat.

Florino—his face flushed with outrage that an ex-*goomada* would turn on him—stood up, tore at his hair, and screamed at the woman: "Shut up. You are killing your family with your lies," he yelled.

Both defendants were removed from the courtroom, and the trial went on without them. They were placed in a cell one floor below where they paced like tigers in the zoo. A roiling mob of Calabrians simmered in the halls outside the courtroom.

On May 10, 1921, Florino and Anastasia, now eighteen years old, received word that the jury had arrived at a verdict. By court order, the defendants' countrymen, who'd hovered menacingly over the proceedings, were forced out of the courtroom—and the courthouse, onto the streets with the court gates locked—before the jury entered to deliver its verdict:

Guilty, murder one.

Before Justice James C. Van Siclen announced the sentence for Anastasia and Florino on Wednesday, May 25, 1921, he allowed the convicted men to make a final statement. Anastasia was insecure about his verbal skills and chose to remain mute, but Florino talked and talked and talked. His statement lasted forty minutes. He went over every point in his defense.

"I am being sent to my death by my former sweetheart," he said. "I think I am going crazy."

"Everything you are saying was heard during the hearing, do you have anything else to say?" Van Siclen asked.

"I could talk until tomorrow morning," Florino said. But he didn't. He fell silent.

Judge Van Siclen condemned the men to death in the electric chair.

As Anastasia was being led from the courtroom, he crooked his forefinger and stuck it in his mouth and pulled a menacing face at his defense attorney.

The attorney was smuggled from the building through a secret exit. The condemned men were taken back to Raymond Street one last time to prepare for their move up the river.

Outside the courthouse was a ticking time bomb: the pack of Calabrians. With a pleasant lack of all-out violence, police defused and dispersed it. Anastasia and Florino were originally scheduled to be executed on July 3, 1921, but they ended up enduring eighteen months in Sing Sing's Death House.

In the Death House at Sing Sing, a lot of hoods got whiney, went on and on with the "poor poor pitiful me" bullshit. Not Albert. He was stoic. Sing Sing was actually a step up in accommodations from Raymond Street and besides, if he'd learned anything in his eighteen years it was that growing old was unlikely. Might as well die in the electric chair as anywhere else.

Albert's stoicism and tough-guy attitude attracted the attention of a mobster named Jimmy "The Shiv" DiStefano, a birddog scouting for talent. He watched Anastasia. Once, when Albert was lined up for food, he got into a fight with another inmate and gave the guy a tremendous beating. The beating was both efficient and enthusiastic. DiStefano was impressed. Maybe something could be done. Bigger miracles had occurred. The Shiv told Lucky Luciano about Anastasia, how the kid showed a lot of potential despite the fact that he was scheduled for the hot seat.

Anastasia and Florino came within five days of visiting Ol' Sparky when information came to the Kings County District Attorney that Mrs. Viccio's testimony was to be considered unreliable. Because of this, the men came off death row and were granted a new trial.

After a stint back on Raymond Street, they had the charges dropped entirely when the District Attorney found himself devoid of willing witnesses. Anastasia and Florio went from Death House to the streets, which almost never happened.

Anastasia returned to the piers a hero. It was like he was returning from war. Nothing like a stretch on death row in the Big House to set you apart from the crowd, especially when that crowd was in Red Hook, breathing with the tides and the comings and goings of the crucial waterfront. Everyone wanted to be on Albert's good side. The alternative was so frightening.

Lucky Luciano became a close friend and champion of the teenager.

"You're going to be my enforcer. Take care of union bullshit," Luciano said.

"Whatever you want, Boss," Albert said.

As an enforcer, Albert moved up the ranks quickly—those ranks being in the International Longshoreman's Association (ILA). When there was trouble, Anastasia was the one who put it down, and he almost always did it in the only way he knew, with his hands.

Anastasia had a reputation, one he'd never shake. Friend of Luciano, sure. But fearsome on his own, too. Anyone who tried to hurt Anastasia or get in his way was mincemeat, and it didn't matter where they hid. Juries couldn't convict you on testimony that was never given.

FOUR
The Degraw Street Murders

IN RED HOOK DURING THE SUMMER OF 1922, when Albert Anastasia returned from Sing Sing, hoods were dropping like flies—even up in the area now called Carroll Gardens, where I lived as a kid years later. The houses there were beautiful brownstones, and the front yard gardens that gave the neighborhood its name were populated by religious statuary. But that didn't keep the bullets from flying.

Anastasia and Florino were only out of jail for a couple of weeks when they were in trouble again. The instant they tasted freedom they had one thought on their minds. They were going to teach that bitch Margaret Farrera Viccio a lesson. Bumping her off wouldn't be gallant. Or maybe they just couldn't get to her. An FBI memo written decades later said the key witness against Anastasia and Florino "returned to Italy." So maybe she was gone, but her husband and her brother were still floating around the neighborhood.

First the brother: On the morning of August 15, 1922, Anastasia and Florino blew away thirty-eight-year-old Carmelo Farrera as he sat at a table in the summer garden behind his grocery store on Degraw Street. The murder occurred at a party during the three-day Feast of the Assumption celebration.

Then the husband: The *next day,* at 1:30 P.M., at the corner of Hicks and Degraw, only a few feet from the scene of the previous day's murder, Joseph Viccio was shot ten times and killed. The shots came drive-by style from three men in a six-cylinder touring car. The gunmen drove slowly up beside him and continued shooting until he was still on the sidewalk. Viccio was rushed to Long Island College Hospital five blocks to the north where he died without regaining consciousness.

There was confusion as to motive. Some said the second killing was in response to the first. Some thought Farrera was killed to keep him from testifying in Boston at the trial of Michael Scarpone—and, as it turned out, this was a happy dividend of the hit. A cop said he thought someone who yearned for the wife, the lovely and affectionate Maggie, might've killed Viccio.

By the next day the love-triangle angle had been dropped and detectives were working the theory that this was part of a bootlegger's war. No one said boo about Anastasia and Florino, but somehow they got around to arresting the pair anyway.

It was true that Farrera had been scheduled to testify on August 17 in a Boston courtroom against six men, all Italian, who were accused of murdering Michael Scarpone. Apparently working on a tip, cops scooped up fourteen thugs who were hiding out in Boston, and guess who was in that group: Anastasia and Florino. Maybe Farrera was slotted for removal anyway, and our boys volunteered to handle it on account of their own personal vendetta. The *New York Herald* described the arrested men as members of the "Italian Black Hand."

The fact that the murdered men were the brother and husband of the woman who'd put Florino and Anastasia away in 1921 was missed—accidentally on purpose, maybe. As was true of many prosecutions back in those days, cases were sometimes constructed with built-in flaws so they could fall apart at the drop of a hat.

By August 18, all but two of the Boston arrestees had been released. Anastasia and Florino were charged with the Farrera murder. They told cops they were roommates, both living in an apartment on Sackett Street just around the corner from both of the Degraw Street murders.

Now officially no connection had been made between the Degraw Street murders and the 1921 killing of George Terrillo, but on the street everyone knew what was up. The men were released for lack of evidence and witnesses.

In 1923, now twenty years old, Anastasia proved he wasn't afraid of dangerous work when he became driver and bodyguard for forty-six-year-old bootlegger Biago Giordano. The work was dangerous because the two previous bodyguards—guys named Giuseppe Stello and Gregario Lagano—were killed on duty. Stello was killed in Boston in August 1922 in what might've been part of the successful disruption of the previously mentioned Michael Scarpone trial. Lagano, his replacement, a former Henry Street pickpocket, lasted until November, when he was gunned down in the Tosca Garden on Columbia and Union streets on election night. So there was every reason to expect trouble as young Albert coolly drove the bootlegger around Red Hook in Giordano's ostentatious open-topped touring car, his hand never far from his own rod.

For all the attempts on Giordano's life, he still paraded proudly around Red Hook pretending to be a legit real-estate tycoon. There was incoming, sure, but these guys dished it out, too. On April 6, 1923, Giordano called a guy named Vincent and told him to meet him at the corner of Sackett and Columbia streets. When Vincent got there, he was shot from behind. He survived long enough to tell a Detective Denney of the Butler Street Station that the last thing he remembered was seeing Giordano and his bodyguard Anastasia standing on the sidewalk. Then he was ambushed. Vincent died and Anastasia was arrested, but quickly released because a corroborating witness couldn't be found. If you're keeping count, that was Albert's fourth known murder, and his third homicide arrest.

He was just warming up.

At 9:15 A.M., April 28, 1923, the inevitable: Anastasia was driving Giordano's car west on Sackett Street, approaching the corner of Sackett and Henry. (My co-author Mike Benson lived on that corner as a young man, above the pharmacy.) Two men, with a rifle and a shotgun, fired a fusillade through open windows of a house at 230 Sackett Street, turning the left side car doors into Swiss cheese and leaving the men bloodied and slumped in the *tonneau*. Anastasia's left side and stomach were peppered with buckshot, while Giordano took four slugs, one in the left hip, two in the shoulder, and one in the chest.

The weapons were recovered, the shooters disappeared. The next day Giordano died in the Hospital of the Holy Family without saying who shot him. His obituary noted that, at the time of his death, he had been taking care of his murdered brother's widow.

With Anastasia recovering, the Brooklyn *Eagle* said he would remain high on the hit list, along with his friend Florino.

Brooklyn cops had tried and failed repeatedly to get rid of Anastasia and Florino on murder charges, so they strategized. Snap. Maybe they could pin them on a charge for which no witnesses were necessary. Without witnesses there would be no one to hit, no one to intimidate. As long as they drew a clean judge, not a given, maybe they could give the streets of Brooklyn a break.

So, in June 1923, Anastasia and Florino were nabbed and charged with illegal gun possession. On the arrest report, Florino was reported as still living on Sackett Street but Anastasia had moved to Clinton Street, which wasn't very far away. He was still in the neighborhood.

The cops' plan worked perfectly. There were no witnesses to make disappear, just an arresting officer, and the men were swiftly tried and convicted. Florino defended himself by saying that he had a permit for his gun that had been issued to him by the police. He eventually admitted, however, that the permit was a forgery, that he'd obtained it for five bucks in a barbershop.

They were sentenced on July 14, 1923, to three years in the Blackwell Island Penitentiary on what is today known as Roosevelt Island, which sits in the East River under the 59th Street Bridge, and is best known for its fancy high-rise apartments. But back in the 1920s it was known almost exclusively for its truly spooky gothic jail.

The island has undergone a series of name changes over the centuries and was known as Hog Island in the 1600s because the Dutch put their pigs to pasture there. The penitentiary was built in 1832 of cold gray stone from island quarries and had all of the amenities of a medieval dungeon. It looked a little like a castle fortress with crenulations along the roofline and a turreted tower. In 1852, a workhouse was added. Around the time that Albert entered the penitentiary's dank walls, the island and the jail were technically both renamed Welfare Island. The name took for the land, but the jail continued to be called Blackwell. It was just so much more fitting. The jail lasted less than a decade after Albert got out. It was demolished and its inmates moved to Rikers. With Albert in stir, life went on, more guys got shot, power shifted. By the time he was released in 1925, having served two years of his three-year sentence, he returned to the extortion racket on the piers—but the power structure in Brooklyn had changed.

FIVE

A Growing Body Count

SALVATORE "TOTO" D'AQUILA may have been technically the boss but all the true power was now wielded by Giuseppe Masseria of the Morello faction, known on the streets simply as Joe the Boss.

Masseria was born in Sicily where he grew up to be a killer. When the Italian authorities started to close in on him in 1903, he fled to America where he killed and extorted his way to the top. He earned his money by selling bootleg booze, and his position by murdering his predecessor. He had puffy cheeks and squinty eyes, and brave hoods called him "Chinaman" behind his back.

"He was a pig," Lucky Luciano said about Joe the Boss in his autobiography, *The Last Testament of Lucky Luciano.* "He ate with his fingers."

Masseria also started a war in the late 1920s by ordering his crew to murder all hoods from the Castellammare region of Sicily, neophytes who were trying to chip away at his sizable turf. With the Castellammarese war still raging, Albert Anastasia returned to the streets as a well-respected professional killer. Business was brisk. More of the old guard was erased by the new.

During the early-morning hours of July 21, 1926, Carmine Cenatiempo, the mustachioed head timekeeper and "czar" of the South Brooklyn waterfront, was murdered in front of Villa Joe's catering hall on West 15th Street in Coney Island at a banquet where he had been the guest of honor.

The dinner was part of the celebration of the Feast of St. Rocco. According to police, Cenatiempo "controlled the supply of laborers" on the piers. Cenatiempo—who had himself been in prison twice under the alias Carmine Albano, once for assault in 1905 and once for robbery in 1910—had just made a speech before approximately three-hundred people when he was handed a note by a waiter that read, "You are wanted outside."

When the father of five exited the hall, he was shot dead. Police knew immediately that robbery was not the motive. They found $500 in Cenatiempo's wallet, and he was wearing jewelry worth around two grand. He died on his way to Coney Island Hospital.

Albert's name would later come up in connection with this hit, but two men were arrested almost immediately as they ran from the scene to their cars. They were thirty-six-year-old florist Clemento Foglio of Long Island City, Queens, and thirty-four-year-old Frank Russo, a restaurant owner in Dyker Heights, Brooklyn.

On July 1, 1928, Albert may have been in on the hit on Joe Masseria's underboss Frankie Yale. Anastasia's partner in crime Joe Florino was arrested in connection with the Yale hit, and though it's possible Anastasia wasn't involved, where one went the other usually followed. The hit on Yale happened at four in the afternoon, Yale was in his Lincoln, driving along 44th Street between Ninth and Tenth avenues in Brooklyn's Sunset Park section, when he was overtaken by a black sedan and blown away by a host of gunmen using pistols and sawed-off shotguns. The gunfire turned Yale's head to pulp and sent his car careening over the curb and sidewalk and into the stoop of a brownstone. Florino was arrested in connection with the hit but quickly released for lack of evidence.

On August 13, 1928, two bulldogs from the Coney Island police station came to twenty-eight-year-old Albert Anastasia's Sackett Street apartment and arrested him in connection with the Cenatiempo hit on Coney Island two summers previous. Albert had a hearing in Homicide Court before Magistrate Leo Healy where the charges were eventually dropped. Albert was the fifth man to be arrested in connection with the Cenatiempo hit, and the fifth to be released. It was Albert's fourth arrest involving murder charges.

From October 14 through 19, 1929, the stock market crashed and sank America into what became known as the Great Depression. The parks in Red Hook became known as Hooverville as they filled with the homeless living in tents. Bootlegging and skimming off the piers remained a good way to make money, but there was less of it. And keeping one's slice of the pie became more important than ever.

In 1929 the U.S. government passed the Registry Act, which allowed illegal aliens to become permanent residents as long as they registered and stayed out of trouble. If a registered alien did get in trouble, they would be deported. Albert took advantage of the act and applied for a Certificate of Registry on April 4, 1931.

"You ever been arrested?" they asked.

"Nah," Albert said. Then, under questioning, he said he had never been arrested, summoned into court as a defendant, convicted, fined, imprisoned, placed on probation, or forfeited collateral for an act involving a felony, misdemeanor, or breach of any public ordinance. He was clean as a whistle.

On May 5, during an imposition before an Immigration Inspector, and under oath, Albert added, "I have never been arrested nor subjected to criminal or civil prosecution."

His Certificate of Registry was issued, apparently by someone who never read the papers, on June 19, 1931.

Albert's old friend and Sing Sing death house mate Joe Florino was, like Albert, a man with a varied skill set. Unlike Albert, Florino knew how to use a long arm. He was a sniper. His expertise was killing like a deer hunter—not that common in urban settings, but very in keeping with every hood's not-so-secret wish to be a cowboy. In 1930, Florino still lived in the same apartment he had once shared with Anastasia on Sackett Street.

Which brings us to Giuseppe Piraino, a.k.a. "The Clutching

Hand," who lived on 77th Street in Bensonhurst. On March 27, 1930, the Hand was killed with a single rifle shot through the temple while riding in a car within view of Florino's apartment window at the corner of Hoyt and Sackett. Florino was arrested for Piraino's murder.

Piraino had been a member of the Sicilian Mafia, and came to the U.S. after escaping from prison in Palermo, where he'd been sentenced to twenty-five years. (Quick sidenote, Piraino's biggest legacy was in the deeds of his sons. Three-hundred-pounder Anthony "Big Tony" Peraino was with the Colombo Crime Family and financed the most famous porn movie of them all, *Deep Throat*. He and his brother Joseph "The Whale" Peraino ran the rackets in Bay Ridge, Brooklyn, for a while, turf that once belonged to Frankie Yale. They were around when the Five Families were formed and were charter members of the Profaci Family.)

Piraino was not the only hood in Red Hook to be known as the Clutching Hand, but the nickname on him was at its most ironic. He had a withered, twisted, and partially paralyzed left hand, with one finger bent like a hideous claw, that was hated and feared throughout Brooklyn. Soon after the Hand bit the dust, his son Carmine was also rubbed out. With the Hand dead, his crew was taken over by Joseph Manino, who was shot to death a few months later.

All of this rubbing out concerned Lucky Luciano. The situation was close to desperate. He began to think of ways to keep the lucrative organization they all belonged to from eating itself alive.

At 8:30 P.M. on July 1, 1930, another member of the Hand's crew, thirty-five-year-old Giuseppi Micello of Bath Beach, Brooklyn, was walking east, approaching the corner of East 18th Street and Avenue A in Manhattan, a tenement neighborhood long ago torn down and replaced by the Peter Stuyvesant housing project. The block was as thickly populated as any in New York, which was saying something. It was hot and everyone was outside. Women pushed baby carriages. Kids played in the street. Because of the human gridlock, there were an estimated two-hundred witnesses, many of them women and children, as two men pulled up to the curb in a roadster, also heading east. One jumped out, and approached Micello from behind with a lively gait.

"Let him have it!" the driver was heard to cry out.

The gunman did just that, efficiently pumping six bullets into Micello's back. The killer threw the gun down on the sidewalk, where it bounced and came to a stop next to the fallen Micello. As the gunman leaped into the car and sped away, an off-duty prison guard who was visiting his mother-in-law leaned out of a nearby fourth-floor window and returned fire, emptying his weapon at the getaway car. He later said he thought he might have winged the killer.

The car went onto two wheels as it turned sharply right onto Avenue A and disappeared into the twilight. Police figured they'd have no trouble finding the car, which was bullet-ridden and contained a bleeding man, but it didn't turn out to be that simple.

As was often true back in those days, a photographer from the *Daily News* arrived on the scene before the cops got there. Micello was left on his back on the sidewalk, feet toward a storefront, head toward the gutter, his hat covering his crotch.

As the Clutching Hand and his crew members were being mowed down on city streets, the Hand's wife, Grazia Piraino, managed to cash in on eight grand of her husband's $10,000 life insurance policy by threatening to claim Giussepi's death was an accident and not murder. She would have lost, of course, but the insurance company's legal fees would have been sky high so they opted to settle.

The charges against Anastasia's partner Florino for the murder of the Clutching Hand were eventually dropped for lack of evidence. Other names were introduced into the Piraino investigation, including Vergo "The Little Goat" Pisano who was then himself shot once through the heart, his body found in the middle of the street in front of a house on President Street during July 1931—at a location that no longer exists as it would be in the middle of the Brooklyn-Queens Expressway. He was DOA at Long Island College Hospital. The bullet that killed the Goat, police said at the time, either came from a passing automobile or from a nearby apartment window.

Pisano had recently been released from Sing Sing where he served five years for the murder of John Soma in 1926.

When Florino wasn't killing people, he had duties at the docks, as well. He made sure tribute money made it all the way to the top, and closely supervised the collectors and weeded out the chiselers.

Six weeks after Micello was whacked on Manhattan's Lower East Side, on August 15, 1930, Albert Anastasia, along with Frank "Wacky" Scalise and someone only identified (by Joseph Valachi) as "Buster from Chicago" murdered Giuseppi "Peter" Morello, a guy who'd been boss twenty years earlier. The hit went down in East Harlem where the target was "collecting receipts."

The torch was passed the hard way, making way for the young and ambitious.

SIX

Waiter, There's a Body in My Linguini

THE WHACKING OF JOE THE BOSS

EARLY IN ANASTASIA'S CAREER, the boss of his crew was Joe Masseria. But Albert knew and became intensely devoted to Frank Costello and Lucky Luciano. Luciano in particular. Luciano was technically on Masseria's side, but Luciano's insatiable hunger for power meant he looked out only for himself, and as soon as he thought he could get away with it, Luciano ordered that Masseria be taken out of the picture—permanently.

Anastasia conspired with Luciano to kill anyone who might challenge Luciano's plan to rule the universe. First and foremost among those guys was Masseria, and Anastasia was a part of the Coney Island quartet assigned to shuffle Joe the Boss from his mortal coil.

It was April 15, 1931, and the place was Gerardo Scarpato's Nuova Villa Tammaro in Coney Island, on West 15th Street, the current site of Banner Smoked Fish seafood market.

Masseria's reign as kingpin was challenged during the 1920s by an influx of Castellammarese. Sal Maranzano headed up the new crew. Both Masseria and Maranzano wanted to be *capo di tutti capo*. Sal was different from the uneducated thugs he was competing with. He'd been to college, spent years training to be a priest. He was a cool, calm, and clear thinker—and a visionary of sorts. He saw a world in which the various factions worked together rather than warring amongst themselves, thus increasing syndicate power ten-fold.

Masseria could have cared less about Maranzano's Big Picture. Masseria had a Big Picture of his own, one in which New York City was all his, and he shared it with no one. Joe the Boss was kingpin in New York City starting in 1920 with prohibition, and he had a bloodline and resume suitable for the job. He came from Sicily and made his bones with Lupo the Wolf of the Black Hand. The Wolf terrorized the Italian section of Harlem from 1890 to 1920. When it was finally busted, the Wolf's stable on East 107th Street contained no horses, but it did contain sixty stiffs, many of them hung on meat hooks. The Wolf's mistake was broadening his horizons instead of sticking with what he knew best—exterminating. Lupo went into counterfeiting and got caught. Masseria took over the operation and set up a system of tribute for all of Harlem. If you wanted to make your own wine or booze, Masseria would make sure cops didn't bust your stills and kegs—for a price. If you didn't pay, the Law would find and bust up your still within hours, like magic. If not the Law, then Masseria's boys would bust up your head.

The Masseria/Maranzano war raged for two years, lots of guys juked on both sides. The young rebels of those early days thought that the early bosses were stuffed shirts—Mustache Petes, they called them—and looked at them with disdain. Guys like Albert Anastasia, Lucky Luciano, and Vito Genovese thought the old bosses were exchanging raw earning potential for dignity and respect.

The notion of presenting Italian men as refined gentlemen was abhorrent to guys whose hands were still calloused from swinging a hook. "Fuck dignity. Give me money every time," Albert would say, rubbing the rough tips of his thick fingers together.

Bugsy Siegel, Meyer Lansky, and Lucky Luciano had a clandestine meeting with Salvatore Maranzano in the Bronx Zoo. There, while feeding peanuts to the elephants, they came up with a way to end the war: Joe had to go.

It wouldn't be the first time that someone tried to kill Joe the Boss. Umberto Valenti made the first attempt. And happily. He hated Masseria's guys with the intensity of vendetta.

Valenti sent thugs to squib Joe as he was leaving his apartment on

Second Avenue, on the lower east side of Manhattan. Joe was outside on the sidewalk when he saw the attack coming and ducked into a millinery shop.

Rat-tat-tat-tat, the goons opened up on the shop, shattering storefront windows. The shooters were long gone before anyone dared move. Joe the Boss was pleased to find that he was uninjured. The only damage was a pair of holes in his straw hat.

Trying to kill Masseria and failing turned out to be Valenti's fatal mistake, as he himself went down soon thereafter in a hail of bullets right after Masseria and he shared a meal in a restaurant on East 12th Street in what we today call New York's East Village. After eating themselves groggy Masseria and Valenti walked down the street arm in arm, right up until the moment Joe the Boss pulled away and all hell broke loose.

Masseria had some big names at his back: William "Willie" Moretti, Gambino, Anastasia, Costello, Adonis, and Genovese. (Adonis was born in Italy as Giuseppe Doto, but changed his name to Adonis because when he looked in the mirror, he didn't see the average attractiveness everyone else saw, and thought he looked like a Greek god.)

Maranzano had some future superstars in his squad, too: Bonanno, Luchese, Profaci, Gagliano, and Magliocco.

However, Masseria and Maranzano were equally blind when it came to the beliefs and behavior patterns of those they felt were true blue and subservient. The young turks on both sides were more interested in their own careers than in those of the Mustache Petes.

Lucky Luciano had a distinct advantage over everyone else as he was the guy with informants on both sides and made his personal decisions based on superior intelligence. Another advantage Luciano had was that he didn't buy into the pedigree bullshit. One hood wasn't better than another hood because he was pure Sicilian. It was foolish thinking, and Luciano made a lot of money by signing bootlegging deals with non-Sicilians, guys like Meyer Lansky and Bugsy Siegel, earning where the Mustache Pete's were too snobby to earn.

Luciano saw the most efficient pathway for himself to the top of the heap. First thing, he would have to take out Joe the Boss. Next he'd have to become "friends" with Maranzano, a more difficult and complicated task. At stake was control of what was still the most lucrative black market in the history of mankind: booze.

So Luciano asked Joe the Boss to join him for lunch on Coney Island. As Joe arrived smacking his lips, Albert Anastasia sat in acute anticipation in a large blue sedan around the corner on Stillwell Avenue. The car was crowded with some heavy-duty company: Bugsy Siegel, Vito Genovese, and Joe Adonis. Siegel had been donated to the effort by Meyer Lansky, who was only too eager to rid the New York mob of a Sicilian pureblood.

It was a little after noon. The owner of the joint, Gerardo Scarpato, greeted the men personally. Scarpato was one of the kings of Coney Island. In addition to the Villa Tammaro, he owned the Sea Side Inn on Surf Avenue.

Here's the meat of the mystery: where were Joe the Boss's bodyguards? Look into it, best you can find is "mysteriously disappeared." Like JFK in Dealey Plaza, Joe the Boss was uniquely insecure at the moment of his demise.

The food at Villa Tammaro was sumptuous. The men ate and ate. Masseria started the seemingly endless meal by ordering the squid, and Luciano the pork chops *al finocchio*. Both men ate spaghetti and drank Italian red wine. The feast lasted for three hours.

By the time the men were logy with gluttony and ordering espresso to sharpen things up, Albert was across the street. There were guys scattered around, keeping an eye on the restaurant entrance, back door, awaiting the signal. By now it was close to three o'clock.

Luciano patted himself on his belly, belched and left the table to go to the can. At that moment a blue sedan pulled up in front.

As soon as Masseria was alone at the table, four gunmen burst into the restaurant and aerated Joe the Boss. Sluggish from the food and wine, Joe danced, but not well enough. He couldn't avoid the path of six bullets, at least one of which hit him in the back of the head and killed him instantly. Fourteen more slugs tore up the restaurant wall behind Masseria. Luciano came out of the rest room and took a seat, a gunpowder scent getting into his suit.

For the gunmen, it was no silky-smooth getaway. They ran out the side door, which emptied into an alley and bumped into one another as they turned toward the street. There were more collisions as they tried to all get at once into the awaiting car. The driver tried to pull away and stalled the car, so Bugsy slugged him.

Everyone escaped anyway.

When police arrived at the restaurant, they found in Joe the Boss's hand an Ace of Spades, a mob symbol for "ran out of luck." Sitting alone was Lucky Luciano.

"I was in the bathroom when it happened," he told the police. "By the time I came out, still wiping my hands, the gunmen were gone and Joe was dead."

"What were you doing when the gunfire started?" a cop asked.

"I was at the urinal," Lucky said.

"You were in there a long time."

"I take a long leak."

A few days later, Masseria was laid out in a $15,000 casket with silk cushions. Engraved on the lid were the words "Giuseppe Masseria." At the funeral parlor you could hear crickets but no sobbing. His widow didn't even show up.

The papers referred to the slain Masseria as a "Harlem Overlord." Forty detectives were put on the case. Captain Ray Honan headed the investigation, which involved a lot of head scratching and shoulder shrugging.

Cops had found an odd assortment of clues outside the crime scene, including four overcoats, and five handguns, two in an alley outside the café and three in an abandoned car a few blocks away.

Despite their cluelessness, the police in New York knew that this was a big hit with major implications. They conceded publicly that Masseria was an "underworld big shot." Police Commissioner Edward P. Mulrooney faced the boys from the press and was peppered with eager questions.

"Is it true that Masseria was an enemy of Al Capone?"

"I haven't heard that."

"Did you know that several Chicago gunmen are known to be in Brooklyn and are supposed to have done the shooting?"

"No, I do not."

"Have you learned any reason for the shooting?"

"No. But we have detectives making an extensive investigation."

"What rackets was Masseria boss of?"

"Wine, fish, and beer—maybe others. He was a burglar, small time stuff until about 1920 when we believe he made a name for himself in the policy racket."

Commissioner Mulrooney somewhat understated the matter. You couldn't buy Italian food anywhere in the five boroughs without paying a sales tax to Joe the Boss.

The day after the Masseria hit, New Jersey cops pulled over a car on the State Highway, and found behind the wheel thirty-one-year-old Anthony Devers, who became increasingly hinky when he, first, gave a phony address in Jersey City, and, second, turned out to be driving a car that was registered to someone who lived on West 15th Street in Coney Island.

The Masseria hit proved to be a pivotal moment in mob history and ended the Castellammarese war. Masseria's whacking helped to put into place the mob leadership that would remain for most of the rest of the century. But that didn't mean there was no more cleaning up to do.

In addition to Luciano, there was another witness to the clipping of Masseria, and that was restaurateur Gerardo Scarpato, a man who couldn't decide if he should shit or go blind—and apparently chose wrong. He was more than willing to keep his yap shut, but he knew there was no way he could unsee what he'd seen, no way he'd convince the hardheaded hoods that his lips were sealed. Scarpato's predicament was tightened during the late summer of 1932 when he was busted for selling booze out of his restaurant. Scarpato was scheduled to go on trial on September 12 before Judge Grover M. Moscowitz, and fear was he'd cut a deal, his freedom in exchange for info regarding the hit on Joe the Boss.

Scarpato never made it to the courthouse.

On Friday, September 9, Scarpato left his home without telling his wife where he was going. His stiff was found on Sunday afternoon September 11, strangled, stuffed in a burlap sack, and left in the trunk of a car parked in front of a house on Windsor Place near Prospect Park.

SEVEN

Blood in the Streets in the City of Churches

IF THE LAW THOUGHT the rubbing out of Joe the Boss was going to halt the bloodshed in Red Hook, they were sadly disappointed. If anything, Brooklyn's deadly gunfire clicked up a notch.

On June 30, 1931, two and a half months after Joe the Boss's death, Alfred Parasi was gunned down in front of his Red Hook home on Hicks Street.

Three weeks later police arrested two friends of Albert Anastasia: Joe Florino (who may in the long run have been arrested for murder more times than Albert himself) and Anthony "Tony Spring" Romeo, who would also later become a key Murder Inc. gunman.

The Parasi hit was the first time Romeo showed up on law enforcement's radar, but not the last. By the end of 1931, the cops would be sick of his face, and sick of their inability to put him away.

It's a wonder police and the D.A. were even bothering with these "gangland-style" slayings. Witnesses turned blind and forgetful. Charges against Romeo and Florino were dropped.

On September 11, 1931, four gangsters were all in court together, charged with a series of stickups. We care, because this quartet, who managed to be simultaneously cocky and twitchy, also became Murder Inkers. They were Martin "Buggsy" Goldstein, Harry "Happy" Maione, Harry Strauss (a.k.a. Pittsburgh Phil, although he'd never actually been to Pittsburgh, a.k.a. Pep Strauss, a.k.a. Big Harry), and Abraham "Kid Twist" Reles.

They worked for Louis "Lepke" Buchalter, who ran the rackets in the Brownsville section of Brooklyn.

Goldstein was a chunky guy and known as "class clown" among his fellow hoods, cracking stupid jokes even as he was grinding a gun into a goon's goiter.

Reles's nickname—passed down from "Kid Twist" Max Zweifach, a turn-of-the-century torpedo—came because he retained a buoyant boyishness well into adulthood and his favorite way of killing was to grab a man by the head and twist until he heard that satisfying popping noise.

Maione's nickname "Happy" was one of those ironic names, like calling a midget Stretch. He had a perpetual scowl on his face, a face designed to intimidate. Happy owned a garage in Ocean Hill, just north of Brownsville.

Pittsburgh Phil was and is a member of the Pro Killer Hall of Fame. It is said that Phil alone killed upward of a hundred men. Who knows where these estimates come from? Nobody was counting. You killed a guy, you got paid, that's all.

Having Albert Anastasia in the same room with Pittsburgh Phil was like taking the field with both Ruth *and* Gehrig. It's no wonder that guys died left and right. In 1931, it wasn't odd for the meat wagon to have to pick up two, three stiffs during the same dingy Brooklyn dawn.

Like Albert Anastasia, Strauss was an artist of homicide. He didn't have a signature method of killing. Variety was the spice of life. He experimented with every brutal killing method known to man. Rope, knife, gun, icepick, bare hands, the ol' disembowel. Pittsburgh Phil had a cast-iron gut and was impatient and violent by nature.

The story goes that he once didn't care for the service he was getting in a restaurant and so, instead of insulting and stiffing the waiter like someone else might do, he stuck his fork in the waiter's eye.

On this day, the four wiseguy defendants tried to smirk their way through the courtroom proceedings, which royally pissed off Judge Lewis L. Fawcett.

The judge said he wished he could "bind them each to the whipping post with the lash vigorously applied." He was particularly annoyed because this was the second time that month that the four had appeared before him. The first time the victim said, nope, changed his mind, not them.

For the September 11 court appearance, the men were in bigger trouble—although it was still small potatoes compared to the crimes they were actually committing. In Goldstein's pocket cops found a key to a locker in the Cleveland Baths on Cleveland Street, and in the locker they found six revolvers and a sawed-off shotgun, all loaded. Strauss and Reles, along with another name that we'll hear from again, Frank "The Dasher" Abandando, were charged with auto theft. (Abandando got his nickname by being speedy on the base paths for his reform school baseball team. Dasher's speed came in handy in his line of work at least once. The story goes that he was assigned to shoot a longshoreman and approached the guy from the front on a street in Red Hook. He pulled the trigger but his gun jammed, at which point the intended target came after him. Abbadando ran around the block so fast that he came up behind his intended target, pulled the trigger again, and this time the gun fired and the mission was accomplished.)

A reporter in the courtroom recognized the men as members of the gang that wiped out the Shapiro brothers of Brownsville and their allies over the previous five years. A month later the same group was hauled in again, found in the back room of an East New York bootblack shop sitting around a vial of morphine.

EIGHT
Luciano Takes Charge

WITH JOE THE BOSS GONE, Salvatore Maranzano called for a meeting of hoods from all over the five boroughs to a meeting hall on Washington Avenue in the Bronx. Five-hundred guys showed up, biggest assembly of mobsters in American history. Maranzano declared himself Boss of Bosses. His second in command, he decreed, would be Lucky Luciano. Maranzano's self-serving proclamation received mixed reviews.

"Fogetabout," some said.

Maranzano knew how things worked in America. Few retired as Boss of Bosses. Most exited like knights in the olden days, carried out on their shield. So he decided to make a series of strong preemptive moves. He made a list of guys who might threaten his power and therefore should be removed from the board like a chess piece. All the biggies made Maranzano's list: Capone, Luciano, Genovese, Adonis, Costello, Moretti, Dutch Schultz!

Schultz's real name was Arthur Flegenheimer, a Bronx boy known for being a psychopath. He was also a cheapskate and was reputed to have kept every penny he ever stole—or earned smuggling foul black-market beer.

Besides threats from competing mobsters, Maranzano had other problems, as well. He was under surveillance by the Department of Justice and under investigation by the Internal Revenue Service. The government investigation had led authorities to a farm for which

Maranzano held a lease at Hopewell Junction in Dutchess County, N.Y., where two 2,500-gallon stills, hundreds of gallons of mash, and redistilled alcohol were found. On the seventy-five-acre farm was a pond, which was found to contain the body of a man, weighted down with stones and pieces of metal.

Maranzano's plan was to start by bumping off Luciano and Genovese. With that powerful pair out of the way, he could regroup and maybe take his time executing the others. The plan never got off the ground. It was thoroughly unreasonable to suppose it would.

"I'll just kill everybody" was a common sentiment in power-hungry guys who came unhinged. Joey Gallo was like that, and look what happened to him.

Maranzano's plan was to have an Irish gunman named Vincent "Mad Dog" Coll hit Luciano and Genovese at Maranzano's office on the ninth floor of the New York Central Building overlooking Grand Central Station.

But things did not go as planned. Tommy "Three-Finger Brown" Lucchese caught wind that Luciano and Genovese were being targeted and informed Luciano. And so the tables were turned. Lucky called Albert Anastasia.

"Albert, I need you to intervene with Maranzano," Luciano said.

"Anything you want, Boss," Albert said.

"Visit Maranzano's office before the Irish gun gets there."

Albert assembled a team and before they headed out, he handed each of them a brand-new fedora.

"After we whack the guy, throw down the hat," Anastasia said.

"How come?"

"Just do it."

At 3:45 P.M. on Thursday afternoon, September 10, 1931, the men arrived at Maranzano's Midtown Manhattan office and began to pound authoritatively on the door, proclaiming loudly, "Open up! We are the police!"

Inside, Maranzano was fretting. He knew that knock came from a pro-gun, and Luciano and Genovese were yet to arrive. In Maranzano's office, eleven men were working. Someone answered the door. The invading men had handkerchiefs over their faces and the broad brims of their hats pulled down.

"Line up against the wall!" one of the gunmen said. Maranzano went pale and felt cold sweat soak through his shirt. This wasn't an Irish gunman from out of town. They had their faces covered, but one of them had those big gnarly hands like Albert Anastasia.

The office workers did as they were told. Maranzano made a move to join them.

"Not you!" the guy with the Michelangelo hands said.

With their target isolated, they fired a volley of bullets that killed Maranzano instantly. No one else was injured. The killers were in no hurry. They threw down their hats and sauntered out the door.

As Albert and the other gunmen left the building and stepped out into the hubbub around Grand Central, on his way in was Mad Dog Coll, who'd been paid $25,000 to whack Luciano and Genovese.

Coll arrived upon a scene of chaos, targets not there, his client already dead, killers taking flight, cop cars screaming toward the scene. The pro killer pulled up his collar, did a quick about-face and disappeared into the stream of pedestrians.

Maranzano's murder was witnessed by a thirty-one-year-old professional boxer from Brooklyn named James Santuccio, who claimed to have been in the building for innocent reasons, and probably should have told cops he kept his eyes shut because they immediately took him into custody and held him as a material witness.

Another witness was a telephone operator named Grace Samuels who, smart girl, said she didn't know nothing about nothing because everyone spoke Italian, and she didn't.

Investigators picked up the fedoras that had been left beside the body. They all bore a label that read "Made in Chicago." Cops told the press that the hit was done by "guys from out of town."

For prohibition-era detectives, the files in Maranzano's office turned out to be a gold mine, listing the ritzy clients and establishments along Park Avenue that received their booze from Maranzano.

They also found Maranzano's diary, which contained the names of politicians, lawyers, and immigration officials with the Federal Nationalization Bureau. The book was found on the sidewalk outside the building, dropped or planted by fleeing gunmen.

When the customers listed in Maranzano's diary were questioned, none of these people had any idea why that guy they hardly knew would have their number in a book.

To give you an idea of how things were back then, Maranzano was one of *four* mobsters to be offed *that day* in the area. There were others in Manhattan, the Bronx, Long Island City, Queens, and Orange, New Jersey.

The Manhattan victim was shot to death in a back-room speakeasy in the garment section. The Bronx victim was killed by gunfire in drive-by fashion on Arthur Avenue, while the victim was beaten into unconsciousness with a lead pipe, thrown upon a rubbish heap and set afire.

On the evening of December 30, 1931, a guy named Michael Mestreberti got offed. It barely made the news, largely because it happened at the same time that a mad bomber sent mail bombs to members of the Fascist Party in New York City, killing two and maiming three. A plain old whacking couldn't compete.

Cops didn't ignore the shooting, however. Tony Romeo was among those arrested for the murder (along with Michael Cappola and Samuel Farrera). As usual, the arrest turned out to be a minor inconvenience for the detainees. The most memorable thing about this arrest was the interrogation of Romeo by Assistant Chief Inspector John J. Sullivan, which featured this exchange:

"What do you do for a living, Romeo?"

"I'm a delegate of the longshoreman's union."

"They have an office?"

"Yeah, at 13 President Street."

"What happened to the man whose place you took?"

"He was shot and killed."

"And what happened to the man whose place he took?"

"He was shot and killed."

"Well, what do you think is going to happen to you?"

"I don't know."

Although he had another decade to live, Romeo went out just the way Sullivan thought he would.

NINE
Five Families, One Murder Inc.

WITH MARANZANO OUT OF THE PICTURE, Luciano was at last at the top of the heap. He said that what organized crime in New York needed was a major reorganization, that all the killing back and forth was doing nobody no good.

It was time to stop the madness. Instead of having one guy in charge of all the crime families, a system that would lead to the new boss getting whacked again and again, Luciano proposed a system where New York turf would be divided five ways, into families, each ruled by a godfather. The godfathers would form a commission, and the commission would resolve disputes between families, whenever possible without violence.

Luciano instituted what you might call Lucky's Rules of Etiquette, do's and don'ts for mobsters, designed to keep hot heads from destroying the entire body. Killing civilians and politicians was forbidden, the thinking being that such crimes would bring too much attention to the mob, which worked best underground and away from the spotlight.

He also developed a framework whereby families could work on their own or in conjunction, depending on the circumstances. Some major cities with significant Italian populations would be ruled by a single family. New York would have five families, just as it had boroughs.

Each family would have a boss, an underboss, a *consigliore* (a man of wisdom who would give advice to the boss), and capos—a hierarchy based on the old Roman Guard.

Those families would be:

The Lucky Luciano family, with a lot of the nitty-gritty work being handled by Luciano's underboss Vito Genovese.

The Lucchese family, run by Tommy "Three-Finger Brown" Lucchese, who like the baseball pitcher Mordecai Brown, only had three fingers on his gun hand.

The Joseph Bonanno family, with underboss Carmine Galante.

The Joe Profaci family, underboss Joe Magliocco.

And Vincent Mangano, underboss Albert Anastasia. This made sense. Luciano figured Mangano and Anastasia were both waterfront guys, and their polar opposite styles complemented each other.

Although the names changed, the five-family system lasted well into the twenty-first century.

At first, at least, being Mangano's underboss was a nice place for Albert to be. There was power but no target on his back. He could squeeze the piers dry and maybe every once in a while his head didn't have to be on a swivel.

Plus, it was legit. Mangano was *Sicilian* and still maintained ties with the actual Sicilian Mafia. He came with the Sicilian guys' stamp of approval, and that carried a shitload of weight. His rackets included booze, dope, and the smuggling of illegal aliens from Italy. He'd been in the U.S. for less than four years, yet here he was a godfather. Mangano was aloof, a rich man with clean fingernails, having little or no contact with the sweat and grime of the piers that buttered his considerable bread. He left the sweat and grime to Albert.

Even in that world of homicidal psychopathic whackjobs, Mangano was a bit of a character. He fancied himself a cook and prepared large meals for his crew. What did he cook? Fish, of course. On the piers all he had to do was turn around and there was fish.

Albert liked being Mangano's underboss a lot more than Mangano liked having Albert as his number two. There wasn't much good will between the men. They had a physical dislike for one another, and discussions deteriorated into pushing, shoving and, at least once, punching.

Mangano didn't want Albert, didn't trust him, but Albert was appointed by the Commission—that is, Luciano himself—so Mangano had to put up with it. Luciano had a guy in Mangano's crew. He would just have to deal with it.

Truth was, it was more than Mangano just not liking Albert. Anastasia made Mangano nervous. Mangano knew that Anastasia was a favorite of Luciano and Costello, and he couldn't help but fear that Anastasia's presence just below him in the pecking order meant that decisions would bypass him.

His worries were real.

As it turned out, Anastasia was more than a threat to Mangano's power. He was a threat to Mangano's life. As Albert's power grew, Mangano would be Boss in name only, with Albert calling the shots for the *brugad*—especially on the waterfront, where Albert's brothers had his back.

So, for a while at least, Albert Anastasia killed only the guys that Vince Mangano told him to kill. Guys like John Bazzano.

Ostensibly, Bazzano made his living as proprietor of the Rome Coffee Shop in Pittsburgh. However, he lived in a mansion, which made authorities think maybe he was serving something out of that coffee shop other than coffee.

It was well known that Bazzano was the King of Booze in Pittsburgh, and if you wanted to sell alcohol in western Pennsylvania, you needed Bazzano's okay or bad things would happen.

Things were looking rosy for Bazzano until July 29, 1932, when three Pittsburgh hoods—brothers "Prince" Johnny, James, and Arthur Volpe—came into the Rome Coffee Shop and were sipping some coffee.

The Volpes were allied with Vincent Mangano of Brooklyn, so it didn't really shock anyone when three gunmen entered and blew the

Volpe brothers away. John died in the gutter. James was shot once in the back of the head as he attempted to flee. Arthur was shot in the back of his head as he ate a meal in the shop's back room. John was shot three times, the wounds making a perfect triangle in his chest. One of the bullets penetrated his heart and another severed a large blood vessel. The Volpes died instantaneously.

The killers fled in a Ford sedan. On the floor of the shop, police found several loaded shells and five empty .32 caliber bullets. A witness took down the license plate number on the fleeing vehicle, which was traced to a false name and address.

All three guns were recovered in the street a few blocks away. Two were turned over to the police immediately, while a third came in later after the man who discovered it became frightened and threw it in a garbage can.

Detectives quickly learned that, although John Bazzano's brother Sam was in the shop hiding under a chair, John himself was nowhere to be found. Asked where John was, Sam shrugged. John's wife said John left town.

Asked when he would return, she said simply, "Not for a long time."

Prohibition agents said they were aware that the Volpe brothers had been treading on dangerous ground, trying to expand their turf, and were not surprised that they'd been taken out. At the Volpes' funerals, Al Capone himself sent flowers.

Bazzano, as it turned out, had really fled the Steel City and was staying in Brooklyn until the heat back home cooled off. Out of the frying pan . . . The heat in Brooklyn was just as bad.

On August 5, 1932, Bazzano was invited to dinner with Albert Anastasia and some of his boys. Eager to be wined and dined, Bazzano filled his belly with good food and wine, and then Albert inserted an ice pick below his occipital bulge.

Albert didn't know what the bulge was called, but he knew where it was. Shoved the ice pick all the way in to the handle, severed the spinal cord. The others went to work at that point, and it was a slaughter. Gruesome shit. Three days later Bazzano's body was found in a sack, cut up into pieces of varying sizes and dumped in a Red Hook gutter like the cat's meat guy had dropped it.

Brooklyn cops knew the Bazzano hit was connected somehow to the murders of the Volpe brothers. But was it another in a series of hits, or was it an act of revenge? Just like at Ebbets Field, you couldn't know the players without a scorecard.

Detectives said they had information that the killers were going to have a party on August 17, 1932, in Manhattan, at which time those who whacked Bazzano were to be paid five grand each. The party was raided, and cops busted Albert Anastasia and thirteen other hoods—nine of them from Brooklyn, four from Pittsburgh.

Some of the others were: John "Johnny Bath Beach" Addo, Antonio "The Chief" Bonasera, Sam di Carlo, Peter Lombardo, Michael Russo, Angelo Colizza, and Paul Palmieri. All fourteen were charged with murder, all pleaded not guilty before Magistrate George H. Fowell.

Defending the men was Samuel Leibowicz, who was ridiculously good at his job. Coming into this case he had defended seventy-seven men in murder trials and earned seventy-six acquittals. He was like Perry Mason. (Leibowicz went on to become a judge and presided over a few gang trials, sentencing hoods to long stretches. Asked how he could defend gangsters during one part of his career and send them up the river in another, Leibowicz shrugged and said it was just a job.)

Leibowicz's winning streak continued and all fourteen were released. Anastasia was re-arrested under the public-enemy law but that didn't stick either. Albert was discharged on September 1, 1932 in the Adams Street Court after Magistrate Casper Liota said there wasn't enough evidence to hold him. Regarding the way the authorities had treated Albert, lawyer Samuel Leibowicz said, "The man's re-arrest was a contemptible outrage, committed just to help the police make a record."

On August 1, 1932, a stocky racketeer named Isidor Juffe was kidnapped. Joe Adonis was later indicted for the kidnapping, but Juffe initially named Albert as one of his kidnappers. (A guy by the name of Samuel Gasberg was tried in 1940 for the kidnapping. Authorities said Gasberg was trying to "frighten Juffe into a settlement of certain unspecified obligations." The *Daily News* specified the obligation as payback of a $5,000 loan. The prosecution said Juffe was frightened because he was taken to a house near Prospect Park, repeatedly beaten, and held overnight before being released. Part of Gasberg's defense was that he might have kidnapped Juffe, but later Juffe kidnapped Gasberg, so they were even. On the stand Juffe admitted to bribing cops. Gasberg was acquitted by a jury.) An FBI memo on the kidnapping of Juffe reads, "It was reported that Juffe recognized Albert Anastasia as one of his assailants but that Anastasia was never prosecuted for this crime." According to FBI records, Anastasia was never indicted because three state witnesses were found slain.

Luciano wasn't done with his reorganization. He didn't want each of the five families in New York doing their own hits. That was how wars started. He was going to cop a riff from the old Sicilian mob, and mold from clay a *sette,* a gang of killers—like the *Stoppalieri,* the *Fratenanza di Favara,* the *Fratuzzi,* or the *Fratelli Amorosi*—a *sette* that would work for the Commission. Hits would be approved by the Commission and carried out by a small group of pro killers.

Guys who did the wrong thing could be whacked, of course, guys who failed to pay the appropriate tribute or couldn't pay back a loan, but the *sette*—a secret organization of professional killers functioning outside the mob family—was not to be used by power-hungry men to get rid of everyone above them so they could more easily climb the ladder to wealth and power.

"Less disruption but more profits," Luciano said. "Less blood, more money. Fewer shots, more silence."

As it turned out, "Less blood" turned out to be a false prophesy, as there was no era in Brooklyn bloodier than the one that would follow.

The godfathers agreed that a *sette* was called for, but who would be in it? Luciano wanted the guys to be outside the five-family framework, non-Sicilians who if caught wouldn't lead police to anyone's front door.

"Jews," Luciano said. "I know just the guys. But we need to have one of our own in charge. I propose Albert Anastasia. He is the best killer I know." No one disagreed, and so it was done.

Luciano told Albert that the new job was going to cut into his time on the waterfront. "You have your brother Antonio to watch the piers for you, so that will be okay," Luciano said. "And you will remain underboss to Vince Mangano, a position of great power."

Luciano and Anastasia shook hands. There was a glint in Anastasia's eyes. Running his own *sette* was going to be fun.

The Jews that Luciano knew were the bloodthirsty crew of Louis "Lepke" Buchalter, out of Brownsville, Brooklyn, a gang of killers that he'd himself gotten from Abe "Kid Twist" Reles. Lepke, which is Yiddish for "Little Louis," was born in 1897 and had been wild since he was a kid when his dad died and his mom ran off. He teamed up with another kid out of juvie, Jacob Shapiro, and they worked as a team, stealing and extorting. Lepke did a stint in Sing Sing for robbery, but otherwise his rise to the upper echelons of the underworld went unchecked.

Unlike Kid Twist and Albert Anastasia, Lepke wasn't a guy you'd figure to be a hood. He was happily married, didn't fool around with women, and wore conservative suits. But he had one quality that made him perfect for Luciano's *sette*. He was a sadist.

Lepke had three brothers: a rabbi, a dentist, and a pharmacist. He was a kid from the East Side of Manhattan, a mugger and a pickpocket, a guy who breathed extortion. As a teenager he had a gang called the Gorilla Boys.

He always had plenty of craps money by levying tribute from pushcart peddlers. He developed a nice eclectic record with crimes involving furs, garments, baking, trucking, drug smuggling—and murder.

Albert's kind of guy. Lepke liked to stay in the background and for many years wielded great power without publicity. Lepke and Anastasia already knew and respected one another. To round out the hit squad, Albert mixed in a few of his own guys.

The team of killers had no name, although Albert sometimes called it *cosa mia*.

Albert and Lepke cross-pollinated their crews. Lepke would send guys to take care of waterfront issues, and Albert would use his men to police Lepke's garment industry in Brownsville. Police saw a pattern in which Jewish guns killed Italian thugs, and vice versa, and they couldn't make any sense out of it. It looked like the Jews and Italians were at war. It didn't occur to them until years later that their bosses were in cahoots. A killer or team of killers would be given a place and time. When they reported, they'd meet with a finger man who would point out the individual to be whacked, and the job would be done without the actual gunman knowing who or why.

If a gun was caught and asked who he worked for he could honestly say he didn't know. That gave both Anastasia and Lepke an extra layer of plausible deniability and became one of the secrets to the murder racket's notorious success.

Plus, these killers were the best in the business. Albert taught them icepick tricks, how to leave a wound so small that the hapless coroner might say the guy died of natural causes. Others excelled at making corpses disappear so the coroner never got into the game to begin with. No *corpus delecti*. Nothing for the widow to bury.

So there were made guys mixing with unmade guys, Jews and Catholics, guys from the city, the Bronx, Brooklyn, Queens. They only had one thing in common, they could dispatch another human being and disappear into the night again and again without losing any sleep over it.

Albert's crew would include Pittsburgh Phil, Kid Twist, Happy Maione, and Mendy Weiss from Brownsville, plus Anastasia's own guys, Angelo Catalano and Frank "Dasher" Abbandando.

And Louis Capone. No relation to Al, Louie reminded Albert of himself in ways. He was versatile. He could kill with a rope, kill with a tommy gun, kill with an icepick. He could kill with a grin on his face and, though he was arrested many times, he hadn't been convicted. He lived on Stone Avenue in Brownsville, same neighborhood as the Jewish guys. He was short, stocky, dark-skinned, and made out of nails. Like Albert, Capone enjoyed looking sharp, wore tailored suits and silk handkerchiefs. His jewelry was "heroic-sized," and he always smelled strongly of hair oil. When his name came up in the papers, the ink-stained wretches of the press called him "dapper."

Albert liked Capone's cover, too. Part owner of the Oriental Danceland Restaurant on Stillwell Ave. in Coney Island—now Riviera Catering. (Which just so happens to be where I married Emily in 1979. My Uncle Joe had a connection with the place dating all the way back to Louis Capone.)

As Albert became increasingly reclusive, stuck inside by his notoriety, Louis Capone became very important as a liaison between Albert and the trigger boys who were doing all the work.

Another crewmember was Vito "Chicken Head" Gurino, a behemoth of a man who could kill you up close or from afar. He was an expert marksman. Asked how he got to be such a good shot, Vito said he used to practice by shooting the heads off of chickens.

There were dozens of other killers that time has forgotten. Guys who killed and were killed, their bodies lost in Jamaica Bay or in a landfill. Albert picked up a nice piece of change for each hit, but if the fish wasn't big enough, he'd get a kid, a wannabe, to do the actual icing, and sometimes he got away with an overhead as light as thirty bucks.

Headquarters for the crew was set up in the back room of the Midnight Rose Candy Store in Brownsville. It was an ordinary-looking storefront at the corner of Livonia and Saratoga avenues, underneath the elevated portion of the Number 3 subway train. There was a window in the front so you could buy candy without going inside the store.

Most customers didn't go in. The ones that did slunk like coyotes. The dark green awning read:

~ CANDY~

CIGAR

Stationery & Toys

SODA ~ CANDY

Yes, candy was up there twice. There was a movie theater on one side and a shoe-repair shop on the other, ten paces from the Saratoga Avenue subway stop. Also on the block was a Jewish deli, hosiery dealer, barbershop, and a pharmacy where the back-room potions of cocaine and opium guaranteed regular customers.

After a while, Brooklyn cops noticed that only guys who looked like hoods ever went into the corner store, so they kept an eye on Midnight Rose's. Sometimes they'd brace a guy as he came out.

"What you doing in there?"

"Buying a stick of gum," the wiseguy would say.

If a cop asked Anastasia for identification, he would pull out a business card that stated he was a salesman for a mattress company.

"Midnight Rose" was a hit song from 1923, then a Broadway musical five years later, but in this case referred to Mrs. Rose Gold, proprietor. Rose was a racketeer in her own right—numbers, there were girls upstairs—and she knew how to keep her mouth shut.

Asked to testify regarding goings on in her back room, she said she had no idea what her boys were up to. That was their business. (The building that held Midnight Rose's place is still there and houses Ftawa Mini Market, a twenty-four-hour corner store bodega. The guys that run the place had no idea that it used to be Midnight Rose's, at least not until a writer wandered in one day and ratted out the building's history.)

Although there can be little doubt that mayhem and violence continued without interruption, Albert Anastasia stayed out of trouble for almost a year after the Bazzano hit. His streak of good luck ended on August 2, 1933, when he ordered a hit on fifty-four-year-old laundry owner Joseph Santorio in a grocery store on Manhasset Place in Red Hook, right in front of the man's wife and ten-year-old son.

Don't try to find Manhasset Place on a map. It used to run parallel to Hamilton Avenue but was destroyed to make way for the Brooklyn-Queens Expressway. Santorio lived around the corner from his business, on Hamilton.

The victim owned coin-operated machines and hadn't paid or underpaid the skim. Santorio was trying to run a Laundromat and was sick of mob muscle leaning on him all the time.

The hit was a Murder Inc. gig, probably paid for by "czar of the laundry racket" Jacob Mellon, who regularly visited laundry owners throughout Brooklyn and told them that they had to pay up or their laundry would be wrecked, burned down, and their life would come to a sudden end.

Choice was theirs.

The dues owed to Mellon could be as high as $30 per week per laundry. He attempted to make the skim appear legitimate by setting up an organization called the Neighborhood Laundry Association. If you wanted to know who didn't pay up, you just had to ask the fire department, which knew even before the police.

Anastasia was arrested at eleven o'clock on the night of August 9, 1933, at Brooklyn's St. George Hotel. He told police that his occupation was baker and his residence was right there in the hotel. He was taken to Raymond Street, which by now must've seemed like a home away from home.

The day after Anastasia's arrest, District Attorney William F.X. Geoghan took the case before the grand jury. Geoghan's stint as head prosecutor in Kings County was haunted by stories of corruption and negligence. The fact that Geoghan was involved in his case must've warmed Albert's heart. (Geoghan was eventually removed from office and replaced by William O'Dwyer.) Assistant D.A. Bernard J. Becker called six witnesses, one of whom was the medical examiner.

Also arrested on August 14, 1933, for the Santorio murder were Frank Panetta and Tony Romeo, who denied participation in the crime. A check of their records revealed that Panetta did time on liquor charges, and in 1931 was discharged on charges of kidnapping, felonious assault, and attempted extortion. Romeo received a suspended sentence for assault in 1929 and twice was arrested for murder for victims Alfred Parasi and Michael Mestreberti.

For the Santorio hit, Romeo was discharged in Magistrate's Court for lack of evidence. Anastasia, however, was indicted.

On August 15, Albert Anastasia appeared in Kings County Court. According to one observer, he was "dressed in the height of sartorial elegance." *The Daily News* called him a "dandy." Along with his co-defendants, he was ordered held without bail.

Albert's trial began in October, Judge Franklin W. Taylor presiding. Attorneys Leo Healy and Sam Leibowicz defended Albert. As was now getting to be predictable, witnesses for the prosecution became inexplicably squirrely as soon as they were administered the oath.

Take for example, Michael Luisi, who ran the store where Santorio was shot. Luisi said he was there when it happened, there were two shooters, in overalls and wearing caps. He didn't get a good look at their faces. But neither of them was the defendant, of that he was certain.

Luisi's testimony at Anastasia's trial differed so severely with his grand jury testimony that he ended up doing thirty days in City Prison for contempt of court.

The victim's widow and son were sometimes genuinely confused and sometimes they were faking, but either way they couldn't keep their story straight, and by the end of October the court had seen enough. Judge Taylor dismissed the case against Anastasia on the grounds of insufficient evidence. It was at least the seventh time Anastasia had been arrested for murder, and every time he walked away free. It had to be some kind of record.

* * *

Because history only remembers the hits for which Anastasia or one of his boys was busted, we get a skewed view of just how slick they were at what they did. Anastasia's killing unit was unrivaled by any group outside the military. They worked quickly and almost always left no clues. They worked mostly in the New York area, but they traveled well, too, and were known to hit guys in the country. All you had to do was pay the fee and your enemy was no more. They killed many hundreds of men. Some of the guys had a "strictly business" attitude. Anastasia admitted that he enjoyed killing.

Even before the feds knew that "Murder Inc." existed, they realized something was up. Albert's crew was so prolific that it caused a *national* rise in the murder rate. The spike was especially spectacular in Brooklyn, where multiple hoods were turning up dead every morning.

On November 16, 1933, Albert took further legal steps to chuck his illegal alien status. He filed an application for a certificate of Arrival and Preliminary Form of Petition for Citizenship.

There was a question on the form that read: "Have you ever been arrested of or charged with violation of any law of the United States or state or any ordinance or traffic violation?"

He answered, "Yes. Convicted of misdemeanor in 1923. Traffic tickets but do not recall dates."

On March 1, 1934, he gave to the U.S. government a sworn affidavit in which he admitted that he had lied about his criminal record on earlier applications in the citizenship process.

That would be the last step he would take toward being granted citizenship for another decade—by which time the circumstances of his life would be drastically different.

TEN

A Thriving Business

IT WAS RAINING STIFFS. Nine days after Albert filed his citizenship application, a concerned party paid for a hit on a nineteen-year-old "safe and loft burglar" turned stool pigeon named Alex "Red" Alpert.

Alpert, of Belmont Avenue in easternmost Brownsville, was just out of jail. His yellowbellied squealing had resulted in his crewmates walking into a police trap, with one of the robbers being shot dead. As far as hits went this one wasn't a big one. Just a former juvenile delinquent who didn't know how to cork his yap and ended up getting a guy killed.

One of the tricks to running Anastasia's thing was knowing who was around. Pittsburgh Phil, for example, was just as apt to be on Raymond Street as at Midnight Rose's. By 1934, Phil had been arrested *eighteen times* without a conviction, despite a well-deserved rep as a paid assassin. For the Alpert hit, Albert sent Buggsy Goldstein and Anthony Maffetore to do the job.

Around five in the morning on November 25, 1933, Red Alpert was gunned down. His body was discovered two hours later sprawled in the front yard of a Brownsville house on Van Siclan Avenue near Sutter Avenue.

He'd been shot elsewhere and dumped in that spot. His body was positioned so that it was half inside the gate, half out, feet toward the street. The stiff looked like a drunk sleeping it off.

A hundred pedestrians passed by before anyone bothered to report it. Then a beat cop, Officer Lindholtz, arrived.

Every cop in the neighborhood knew the kid, who was always in trouble. Alpert had been in the Miller Avenue police station the previous weekend accused of cutting a guy. Alpert was put in the cooler, but it was the victim who developed cold feet and refused to press charges. Alpert went back out to the street.

There were no signs of violence, but it wasn't like Alpert to pass out on the street like that. Officer Lindholtz nudged the body with a toe a few times.

"Come on, Red, time to wake up, good morning, sleepyhead."

Nothing. Alpert didn't wake up so Lindholtz called a doctor from Trinity Hospital. When the doc arrived, he lifted Red's upper body and looked underneath.

"Now we know why he's unconscious," the doc said. "There's a bullet hole under the left shoulder. This man is dead."

Still, there was no sign of blood, leading to the conclusion that the body had been dumped. The medical examiner estimated time of death about 5:00 A.M.

In December 1933, Prohibition ended and mob wars petered out. New rackets would need to be created. Old smaller rackets would have to be expanded, but in the meantime there was a period of peace. A good time for a legendary gangster's mind to turn to . . .

Romance. It was in 1934 that Albert fell in love. He courted a teenager who had recently moved to New York City from Canada. He wed the nineteen-year-old Elsa Bargnesi, and in 1935 they had a son, Albert Jr. Eight years later they had another son, Richard, and in 1949 there was another surprise when Elsa gave birth to twins, Gloriana and Joyanna.

Indeed, happy days were here again, but after a while business for Albert's Brownsville crew picked up. On September 30, 1935, Joseph Amberg, ostensibly the head of a laundry supply firm, and his chauffeur Morris Kessler were whacked in the Blake-Christopher

Garage on Blake Avenue in East New York. They were lined up against the wall and practically bisected with machine gun fire.

Three of the shooters were disguised as mechanics, and a fourth wore an expensive suit. The gunman in overalls escaped in a car while the well-dressed man escaped on foot.

Four of the Amberg boys were bad, bad guys. How bad? Their mom changed her name to disassociate herself from them and lived in seclusion. After Joseph was killed, police feared that his brothers would retaliate, but that wasn't what happened.

A few weeks later, early in the morning of October 23, Joseph Amberg's brother, "Pretty" Louis Amberg was found, skull crushed, hacked to death by nine blows from an ax, his body left in a burning 1935 sedan in front of a home on North Elliott Place in Vinegar Hill, Brooklyn.

Pretty's nickname was in reference to him being not-so-easy on the eyes with a face that could stop a sundial. So it was particularly ghastly when his body was found nude with his dick severed and shoved head first into his mouth. Nearby in the street was an empty ten-gallon gas can.

Pretty was the third Amberg brother to meet a violent death. The first was Hyman who was gunned down during an attempted escape from The Tombs in November 1926. Louis had survived a previous attempt on his life. He was seriously wounded by gunfire in 1932.

The brothers used to work for Kid Twist, with the emphasis on the *used to*. Pretty had fifteen arrests on his record dating back to 1914, including three for murder, but only served three and a half years up the river, and another short stint in Elmira, both for weapons charges.

Anastasia, the story goes, sent Louie Capone to dispatch the brothers, and the killings were done as fearsomely as possible, to not only rid the world of enemies, but to scare the living shit out of every hood who even thought about stepping on Twist's toes. The dismemberment was probably administered posthumously, but the survivors didn't know that.

On November 19, 1935, Louie Capone turned himself in accompanied by his mouthpiece Walter R. Hart. He surrendered to Assistant D.A. Bernard Becker. Capone, thirty-seven years old at the time, was taken to police headquarters where the commander of the homicide squad questioned him.

"You friends with Amberg?"

"No."

"Know him?"

"Met him once or twice."

"Where'd you meet him?"

"Tailor shop on Pitkin Avenue."

"Where were you when Amberg was hit?"

"The track."

"Where were you when you heard Amberg was dead?"

"The track."

"How's that?"

"I spend a lot of time at the track."

Capone was booked for murder and held without bail. Things looked pretty bleak for Capone there for a few days, but before the week was over, he was out. His lawyer produced four witnesses—the owner of the East New York garage where the murders occurred and three of his employees—who said they'd seen the shooters fleeing the scene, and nope, Louis Capone was not one of them. Under questioning, the witnesses were quite insistent. These guys were lanky, wiry guys, drinks of water, and Capone was what you call compact.

ELEVEN

Death of Dutch Schultz

YEARS EARLIER, DUTCH SCHULTZ had survived being on Maranzano's hit list, but now he was out on $50,000 bail and facing tax-evasion charges. Schultz walked out of the Hudson County Jail on October 1, 1935. There had been an attempt to bribe the judge in the case. Judge William Clark announced on October 22 that, despite demands by the defendant, he was not going to step aside and let another (presumably bought and paid-for) judge take over. The point was moot, as Schultz didn't have long to live.

Because of his legal woes, Dutch Schultz found U.S. Attorney Thomas Dewey to be a pain in the ass. Dewey was hell-bent on busting up the rackets. Dewey, a Midwesterner with a mustache, would turn out to be the mob's greatest enemy of the 1930s. He was a man of great ambition—ran for president twice, almost won in 1948—and one of the ways he made a name for himself was by going after the rackets. He started out as assistant to the U.S. Attorney for the southern district of New York in 1930, became the U.S. Attorney in 1933, and in 1935 was named by New York State Governor Herbert Lehman as special prosecutor for a grand jury investigation into vice and racketeering in New York City.

Before Dewey was done, he'd put seventy-two hoods behind bars, out of seventy-three tries.

Up until the mid-1930s, the authorities weren't that interested in combatting organized crime. Smart cops knew certain things were hands off. Mob and Chinatown were two of them. Best to not do anything. Ever. Trying to prosecute mobsters only got the state's witnesses killed.

But when Dewey declared war, instead of chipping away at organized crime by arresting and prosecuting mob soldiers, he announced in a very public way that he was going after the bosses. Take off the head of the beast, he said, and the entire thing will die. Dewey was to the New York mob what Elliott Ness and The Untouchables were to Chicago.

Dewey didn't just piggyback on investigations being run by other organizations. He knew that organized crime had tentacles like an octopus, tentacles deep into the fabric of the city's lifeblood, its influence everywhere. So he hired his own investigators, guys he knew he could trust. He soundproofed his office, and what was said in that room stayed in that room. He wasn't bribable.

The standard of the day was to bring in gangsters one at a time for questioning. Dewey said to hell with that. He scooped up all the gangsters he could find and interviewed them one after the other, playing one off the other. He had some early success, nailing beer baron Waxey Gordon on tax charges, which worried the top guys.

Schultz came to Albert Anastasia with a job offer. He wanted Dewey clipped. Things would improve for everyone if Dewey was out of the picture. Whoever replaced him would understand that there were some guys you just didn't prosecute. It went against Lucky's Rules of Etiquette, but Dewey was a special case.

"I'll look into it," Albert said.

So Anastasia slapped a shadow on Dewey. Albert handled the job himself, pulled the brim of his fedora down over his eyes and pushing a baby carriage down the street. No one paid any attention to him. He followed Dewey day and night.

What Anastasia discovered was that Dewey was a man of habit. He left his home every day at the same time and went directly to a nearby drug store where he'd change a dollar and close himself up in the phone booth in the back to make a few calls, calls he apparently didn't want to make from home.

Albert understood this. He often did the same thing. You don't want your wife knowing your business. So he went back to Schultz and said the job would be easy.

"Every morning Dewey makes phones calls from the same phone booth in the back of a drug store," Albert said. "We hit him, hit his bodyguard, hit the guy behind the counter, and get the hell out of there."

"Great," Schultz said. Albert could barely look at the slob. There were spit bubbles at the corners of Schultz's mouth and stains on his shirt. Anastasia held out his palm. He took Schultz's money and instead of hitting Dewey he went to Luciano and told him of Schultz's plans.

"That's bad business," Luciano said. It was simple wisdom, he explained. "Hit Dewey and the heat comes down." His eyes became hard black marbles. "I got a better idea," he said.

Lucky's idea was to clip Schultz instead. He never liked him anyway. He was a slob, unclean, and sloppily dressed. Luciano would say, "Asshole's worth a few million and he dresses like a pig."

Plus, Schultz was German, and kind of an ass-kissing wannabe from Luciano's point of view. He'd converted to Catholicism because he thought it would make the Sicilian mob guys like him better. The Earth would be better off without him.

It came down on October 23, 1935, carried out by men with machine guns, and took place in the barroom of the Palace Chop House on East Park Street in Newark, New Jersey, while Schultz and his friends were having dinner. At 10:15 P.M. a car pulled up in front of the restaurant. Three men got out. One, the driver, a guy known only as Piggy, stayed with the car, while the other two took soft steps into the eatery.

The gunmen were Mendy Weiss and Charles "Bug" Workman. Bug was like lefty pitchers. He had a screw or two loose upstairs.

Schultz and his men were in the restaurant's back room counting receipts.

Schultz had just gotten up from the table and had gone to the men's room when the gunmen entered with their machine guns hidden under their coats. Opening his coat to flash his longarm, Weiss calmly told the waiters and the bartender to lie down on the floor so they wouldn't get hurt. The employees complied without a sound.

Upstairs was a dance hall, where a handful of aroused couples were shuffling around cheek-to-cheek, talking with their hips, grinding the beat, a moment of slow rhythmic pleasure interrupted by the roar of automatic weapons downstairs.

Shultz's accountant, Otto "Abbadabba" Berman, his chief henchman, Abe "Misfit" Landau, and bodyguard Bernard "Lulu" Rosencrantz, forty years old, were killed instantly.

The targets managed to get their own guns out and fire a couple of shots in return, but they missed everything, and might've been dead before they finished pulling the trigger. Several .45 caliber bullets that missed their mark were found lodged in the front door.

Rosencrantz was shot in the right wrist, the center of his chest, in the arm, and in the neck.

Wounded was Leo Frank of Newark who took a bullet that ranged from his right shoulder to his lower abdomen. While most victims fell where they had been standing, Frank managed to stumble out the door and into the street before he collapsed.

Weiss shouted at the bartender, "Where's Schultz?"

The bartender gestured toward the men's.

"I got it," Workman said. He entered the john and found Schultz still at the urinal. Workman shot Schultz in the back, and the slovenly man, dick still out, stumbled out of the men's room and back into the restaurant.

At that moment the owner of the joint, a guy named Jacob Friedman, came out of his office to see what the commotion was, and was just in time to see the final moments of Schultz's life.

Friedman later said, "Schultz was reeling like he was intoxicated. He had a hard time staying on his pins and he was hanging on to his side. He didn't say a cockeyed thing. He just went over to the table, put his left hand on it, so to steady him. Then he plopped into a chair, just like a drunk would and said, 'Get a doctor, quick!'

"Count to a thousand and then you can get up," Weiss said to the owner standing in the doorway and the employees who were still on the floor. The employees did as they were told but the owner ducked back into his office to call for an ambulance.

Schultz was rushed to Newark City Hospital, where he lingered long enough for a priest from St. Philomena's in Livingston, New Jersey to be summoned—an indication his conversion to Catholicism had been sincere.

A police sergeant came to Schultz's bedside and asked who shot him.

"Who shot me? No one!" Schultz replied.

Although many of Schultz's vital organs were unharmed in the attack, his liver was grooved and, these being the days before instant surgery and antibiotics, infection killed him. Schultz died at age thirty-three, and was buried in Gate of Heaven Cemetery, in Hawthorne, N.Y.

For the gunman, the getaway did not go smoothly, at least not for Workman. He was the last out of the restaurant and was horrified to find that Weiss, the driver, and the car, were gone. So he tucked his gun back under his coat and wandered the streets of Newark for the better part of the night. His anger grew and grew at being abandoned and when he took his beef to Lucky, Lucky patted him on the back, told him he'd done real good, handed him a big roll of cash and told him to take a well-deserved vacation in Florida.

About an hour and a half after the shooting in Newark, gunfire erupted in Times Square, Manhattan. Two of Schultz's associates, Marty Krompier, former Schultz bodyguard and chauffeur, and Sammy Gold, a minor underling who was probably in the wrong place at the wrong time, were shot in the Hollywood Barber Shop at 7th Avenue and 47th Street, beneath the Whelan Drugstore just off the stairway of the BMT station at the southeast corner near the Palace Theater. The victims had just finished having their hair cut when the attack came.

A porter was helping Krompier into his coat when the shooting began. The porter dove out of the way, but Krompier had his back to the door and was slow to react. A bullet hit him in the back, causing him to reel around, at which time he was struck again in the left arm, left chest, and abdomen.

Police burst into the tonsorial chamber. Krompier twitched on the floor yelling, "Do something for me! Do something for me!"

In all of the shooting, only one gunman was identified, that being Albert Stern, who at the tender age of twenty-one was already wanted for eight gangland slayings.

Also in the barbershop was press agent Monte Prosser, a smart man who was busy playing the bagatelle machine and couldn't see the faces of the shooters.

It was noted that many of the victims on that record day of bloodshed must have been relaxed, perhaps thinking they were far enough from the battle lines to be safe, and had not followed rule number one of mob safety: They turned their back to the door.

Schultz had a pretty twenty-one-year-old wife who was being interviewed by police. Her story kept changing, but the bottom line was she had delivered to her husband a few hours before he was shot a sheath of papers pertaining to racing, loans, and numbers for rackets covering Upper Manhattan and the Bronx.

Schultz was off the board, but Dewey remained, and number-one on Dewey's Most Wanted list was Luciano. Dewey quickly learned that his dreams of sweeping up the mobsters and making the streets of New York safe again were highly optimistic. Luciano was smart and knew how to avoid successful prosecution.

Dewey understood that the biggest problem was keeping witnesses safe. Just a whisper that an individual was planning to testify against a hood, and his life was worthless. Dewey tried keeping witnesses anonymous, but eventually, because of the Constitution, hoods had the right to face their accusers. Also, the newspapers, believing in the people's right to know, would print the names and addresses of witnesses. There was no Witness Protection Program.

Dewey tried arresting and holding witnesses as material witnesses, but this served to discourage potential witnesses from coming forward. Smart people saw nothing, knew nothing.

In 1936, Dewey finally came up with a case against Luciano. It wasn't for multiple murders as Dewey had dreamed. The best he could manage was a case against Luciano involving New York brothels.

Dewey simultaneously hauled into his office every piece of street scum he could find. He asked them where they lived and who paid them, and by the time he was through, he was able to charge Lucky Luciano with sixty-two counts of white slavery.

Luciano was not only brought down for small-time crimes, but the witnesses who testified against him in court were small-time hoods and aging whores. A professional hotel thief! It was humiliating.

The stool pigeon's name was jailbird Joe Bendix, who took the oath and stated in public that Luciano was the brains behind "compulsory prostitution." Bendix was a repeat offender, doing fifteen-to-life, and eager to do anything that might shorten his sentence.

The jury was told that whorehouses in New York made $12,000,000 a year and that Lucky took a skim off every penny of it. How did Bendix know? He said he knew Luciano personally, had had sixteen or eighteen conversations with the guy over eight years. He said he met Luciano in 1928 at a joint called the Club Richman.

"He gave me a job, and some tips," Bendix said.

"What sort of tips?" Dewey asked.

"He said that when I was around collecting and got wise, I could make some extra dough from the madams."

The other damaging witness at the trial was twenty-three-year-old Shirley Mason. She said that Luciano and the other boys from the syndicate were palming off damaged goods on unsuspecting clients. What she meant was that she had a venereal disease, failed a Wassermann test, and had been banned from the houses of Atlantic

City. But that didn't stop her from working at a house on the Upper West Side of Manhattan, a house run by one of Luciano's nine co-defendants.

The final witness against Luciano was an aging veteran named "Cokey Flo" Brown, whose ravaged appearance alone told the jury everything they needed to know about what prostitution did to women.

Bottom line: Luciano was convicted and was sentenced to thirty years in Dannemora. Albert Anastasia's best friend, his champion, was behind bars.

During the summer of 1936, Louie Capone, Buggsy Goldstein, Blue Jaw Magoon, and a couple of other guys were having an argument in Midnight Rose's, loud enough to annoy the neighbors. Someone called the cops. At the scene police found racing forms. The gang was hauled in, frisked, charged with disorderly conduct, and then released for lack of evidence before their lawyers could arrive. Legally, it turned out to be no big deal, but it pissed Anastasia off.

"Don't shit where you eat," he said. "You want to fight, go someplace else. You brought the cops to us, stupid."

TWELVE
Murder of Joseph Rosen

"WE GOT TO SEND DEWEY A MESSAGE," Albert said. And so at 6:30 A.M. on Sunday, September 13, 1936, he and his Brownsville crew fought back against Thomas Dewey's anti-racketeering campaign with a hit that was both targeted and timed to make the motive crystal clear. At the time it seemed like a bold stroke, but it ended up kicking the shit out of Murder Inc.

Forty-six-year-old Joseph Rosen was a former owner of a trucking firm that hauled garments. He'd been slapped around plenty by the boys and, fed up, had the balls to tell the Law about the skim gangsters were putting on his industry.

Up until 1933, Rosen had been a partner (with Morris Bluestein of Garfield, New Jersey) in the New York and New Jersey Clothing Trucking Company. He'd been head of the garment industry's trucker's union, but lost his control and his business to Lepke.

In fact, one of the first things Lepke did upon gaining control of the union was to take over Rosen's company and force Rosen to be his employee. When Rosen didn't like that, Lepke got him a job as a truck driver, but like most hoods, Rosen found real work to be out of the question.

Lepke told Rosen to get the hell out of town, go someplace else, there wasn't room in the New York Metropolitan area for both of them. Rosen left briefly, but returned. Rosen opened up his candy store in Brownsville dressed like he sold a shitload of candy.

To open the store, Rosen had to borrow money from a guy, so now there was that leaning on him. Unlike others who'd been bullied by goons and took it quietly, Rosen was royally pissed off and when he heard that Dewey was holding anti-racket hearings in April 1936 he volunteered to sing and sing loud—a fatal mistake.

"I want to get even," Rosen told Dewey's right-hand man, Deputy Inspector John J. Gallagher.

Lepke heard it on the grapevine. Rosen was going to squeal. "He's got to go!" Lepke said.

The Rosen gig went to Pittsburgh Phil and Mendy Weiss. Also in on the mission was a guy named Sholem Bernstein, a car thief, and Louis Capone, who was to keep an eye on the car thief to make sure he didn't develop a yellow streak at the wrong time. All four ended up participating in the actual hit.

Rosen was scheduled to testify for Dewey on September 14, but came up a day short.

On the morning of September 13, he was leaving his Brownsville, Brooklyn, home on Wyona Street as he did most mornings, on his way to open his stationery and candy store for business. The store was only a few feet away, around the corner on Sutter Street.

Rosen opened his store, opened a box of new magazines and was in the process of placing them in their racks with his back to the door. The rest of the story we only know because a butcher named Louis Stanner and his daughter Julie across the street happened to be looking out their front window.

Four men entered Rosen's store together, pulled their guns at the same time, and opened fire. Rosen was struck fifteen times, all in the chest. Rosen barely had a chance to turn around and face the shooters. He fell onto his back, his head striking a stack of newspapers sending copies sliding across the tiled floor.

Stanner began to scream, "Murder! Murder!"

The witness continued to watch as, with precise timing, the four men ran from the store and piled into a Chevrolet sedan that pulled up just at that moment. (Of course, the witness's name and address were printed in Monday's papers.)

Rosen had a wife and two daughters, twenty-three and eleven years old. At a nearby police station, a detective tried to get Rosen's widow—a large, soft woman in a flowered housedress—to talk but she was having none of it.

As Mrs. Rosen sat in a chair with her elder daughter standing beside her, she responded angrily: "There has been enough talking! You want me to talk, give me $50,000 so my family and me can leave the country, then maybe I talk! I can't tell you anything, not anything. My life wouldn't be worth two cents if I talked. Out of the country, that's where I'd be safe. I'll take my girls with me. You've done it with others. I've seen you do it with others. Why don't you give me a break?" she screamed as her daughter Sylvia held her head against her bosom and tried to soothe her.

"We'll protect you here," authorities said.

That got her started again: "I don't want any of your phony promises. The whole police force couldn't give me enough protection! I told him not to talk to Dewey!"

And there it was. In her hysteria, she'd blurted out the truth. Worse, police captain John J. McGowan jotted down the quote and later told a reporter verbatim what Mrs. Rosen had said.

The police knew Rosen had had powerful enemies, hoods who'd forced the victim out of the trucking business. Thomas Dewey, however, denied that Rosen had been or was scheduled to be a witness in his rackets investigation. Now, no one believed him.

Dewey's investigation was seriously wounded. Who would want to testify regarding the rackets after what happened to poor Mr. Rosen?

Dewey was incensed that the cops had let slip that Rosen was one of his witnesses. The leak seemed designed to discourage others from talking. The leak resulted in Police Chief McGowan's demotion.

The hit was very professional. No bullets missed. All of the shots struck Rosen between the neck and the waist. All of the bullets went in the front and came out the back. One reporter commented that the bullet holes could have been covered by a hat, but that might've been an exaggeration.

One of the reasons for the tight grouping of wounds in the body was that Pittsburgh Phil had shot Rosen four times after he was down and still. Four bullets were found imbedded in the floor.

The day after the Rosen murder, Albert paid Lepke a visit. Lepke was sitting in his office and Mendy Weiss was there. Both were in a pissy mood.

"Everything go okay with that thing?" Albert asked.

Mendy said, "Yeah, except for Phil. I gave him orders not to do any shooting. But after the guy is laying on the floor, he shoots him." (Significantly, Allie "Tic Toc" Tannenbaum overheard this conversation and would later relate it word-for-word to authorities.)

The only noteworthy thing about this hit over all of the other hits Lepke was involved in, and there were hundreds, was this was the one that would bring about his downfall.

Police found the getaway car later on the Sunday of Rosen's murder. It had been stolen from a Bushwick man, and abandoned at the nearby corner of Livonia and Van Sinderen avenues, about three-quarters of a mile east of Midnight Rose's. The license plates found on the car had been stolen from a separate vehicle.

Also on that Sunday, a pedestrian at the corner of Ralph and Church avenues found a .38 pistol and turned it in to police. It was believed to be one of the rods used on Rosen.

Outing witnesses was not the only odd journalistic touch to come out of New York's highly competitive tabloids. *The Daily News* printed a picture of Rosen's eleven-year-old daughter, looking curious and a little steamed, standing next to a bullet hole in the wall of the hat store next to the victim's establishment.

According to the shaky stats of the time, Rosen's was the thirteenth gangland murder of 1936, none of which had resulted in an arrest. Six weeks passed before District Attorney Geoghan, notoriously ineffective in mob cases, opened grand jury hearings into Rosen's murder. Asked if the murder might have something to do with racketeering, Geoghan said he had no comment.

Despite her early histrionics, Esther Rosen did talk. She was joined by one of Rosen's ex-partners, a bar owner from Elizabeth, New

Jersey, named Martin F. Kelly. "I'm not afraid of those racketeers," Kelly said. "They can get me and I won't care. They ruined a $50,000 trucking business I had for twenty-four years. I fought in the war, I'm not afraid." Kelly testified that in 1931 he and Rosen were partners in a trucking company, seven trucks carrying loads of unfinished clothes from New York factories to a variety of locations in Jersey. Business was good, but then plummeted. Contractors told him one after the next that they couldn't do business anymore. They'd been forced to use another company that was twice as expensive. Before long he and Rosen were out of business. Now Kelly was under twenty-four-hour guard.

Nobody was saying names out loud, but there were whispers about who the killers were: Anastasia. Lepke.

After the cops broke up the fight at Midnight Rose's they had a list of guys who hung together, guys who were getting popped for this and that and needed to be watched. This was their first inkling that all of the hits in New York were coming from a single source, that they were dealing with a "murder-for-hire racket" and not just an epidemic number of individual beefs. Midnight Rose's cover had been blown, and in a strong sense it was the beginning of the end for Murder Inc.

Police soon had a source who'd talked to Louis Capone and had the inside scoop on the Midnight Rose operation. Capone had reportedly discussed how murder-for-hire worked and how the Brooklyn organization sometimes shared or swapped work with other such organizations like the Purple Gang in Detroit.

So, after the Rosen murder, police raided the Coney Island restaurant Oriental Danceland, where Louie Capone was part owner. He was also on the premises when the raid took place and was one of eleven men taken to the Coney Island precinct house, booked for vagrancy, and thrown in a cell. Capone was held on Raymond Street as a material witness, bail set at $100,000.

Raymond Street might've been the mother of all shitholes but part of Capone was pleased he was there. That's because outside was growing into a dangerous place. He'd talked to a guy who talked to the Law who talked to the press. That kind of thing could be fatal. The idea of professional killers banding together as their own crew might've been old hat in Sicily, but in New York it was new and exciting and sold tabloids by the shitload.

Capone's existence on Raymond Street went about according to norm. He learned to have a lifelong dread of rats, and developed a cough that sounded like the last grips of consumption. On Raymond Street, you didn't get to choose vermin or pestilence, you got both. Busted in connection with the Rosen hit, Capone was being held as a material witness in the 1933 murder of Alex "Red" Alpert, a murder for which Kid Twist and Buggsy Goldstein would eventually be indicted.

Rosen wasn't the only Dewey-cooperator to meet an ugly death. On May 25, 1937, a thirty-two-year-old stool pigeon by the name of George Rudnick found himself in a Brooklyn garage with some of Albert Anastasia's star killers: Kid Twist, Happy Maione, Pittsburgh Phil, and Frank "The Dasher" Abandando. Rudnick had been caught talking to people from the Dewey investigation. They not only killed Rudnick, they overkilled him, stabbing his body sixty-some times. They sliced him deep and often with a meat cleaver. They left a bloody pulp still wearing clothes.

There were a couple of reasons for the overkill. One was they were having fun, and sometimes when you start hacking up a guy and filling him with holes it is hard to stop. The other was they wanted to send a message.

After pulpifying Rudnick, they stole a car and left the ghastly remains inside the trunk in front of a home on Jefferson Street between Evergreen and Central avenues in the Bushwick section of Brooklyn. They could have put the body someplace where it would never be found, but again they sent a message.

Police found the body the next morning. In the only one of Rudnick's pockets that hadn't been shredded by the frenzied attack, police found a bloodstained note that read, "Thanks for the information you gave me. Come over and see me soon again." A lawyer on the staff of Thomas Dewey signed the note.

The killers had smashed Rudnick's skull but left his face unmarked, so when his wobbly-kneed mom came down to the morgue she was able to identify her boy.

During autopsy the medical examiner discovered that this was not the first time someone had tried to kill Rudnick, and police files verified this to be true. In 1929, he had been stabbed in the chest so severely that his scarred lungs developed chronic tuberculosis. He was also shot during a previous hit attempt at the corner of Powell Street and Pitkin Avenue.

The murder turned out to be important because it would result, three years later, in the downfall of two of the four men who participated. A third would merely fall down.

During the summer of 1937, Anastasia dispatched killers Jacob Drucker and Irving Cohen from Midnight Rose's to the Catskills where they murdered Walter Sage, a former gunman for Kid Twist turned pro gambler. They took him for a ride, stabbed him thirty-two times with an icepick—or perhaps an upholsterer's instrument, Coroner Lee Tompkins wasn't sure—then tied his body to a slot machine and a rock and dumped him into Swan Lake near the town of Liberty, New York. The weight failed to keep the body from bobbing to the surface, however, and it was found on July 31. Tompkins said he estimated the body had been in the water for about two weeks. Police had no trouble IDing Sage's body because his fingerprints were on file from when he was twice arrested for murder in Brooklyn a few years back.

The killers kept their mouths shut, even after they were caught and put on trial. Cohen was acquitted, but Drucker drew twenty-five years and died in Attica in 1962.

Dewey was prosecuting mobsters for whatever he could dig up. Lepke's many arrests had resulted in no convictions until 1937 for a fur case—and even that verdict was reversed in an appellate court and a retrial ordered. Lepke was released on bail and skipped.

On July 15, 1937, a hood named Samuel Silverman was found murdered in his automobile in front of a house on East 91st Street in the Canarsie section of Brooklyn, a favorite neighborhood to dump bodies for many decades. Canarsie was the most remote section of Brooklyn, and a body found there might make the Brooklyn papers, but by Manhattan standards it might as well have been found in Timbuktu. Canarsie was like another world.

While many fine people, salt of the earth, came from Canarsie, it was not a prestigious community. It was like Red Hook in that sense. In fact, in a New York City that is and always has been Manhattan-centric, Canarsie was the outer edge of an outer borough, in southeast Brooklyn, farthest from the skyscrapers in the city.

It was pressed up hard against the uninviting waters of Jamaica Bay, with East New York to its east, Brownsville to its north, and East Flatbush to its west. The name is that of a Native American tribe, the original inhabitants, meaning (in the Lenape language) "fenced-in city," or fortress.

The neighborhood's biggest defense was that few had the time to go there. During the first half of the twentieth century it was the butt of jokes, symbolic of a circuitous route, going the long way around. If someone arrived late, people said, "What, did you go by way of Canarsie?" It fetched an automatic laugh. I remember hearing it on TV as a kid.

During the Depression, immigrants—legal and illegal alike—from Sicily and the southern part of Italy, clustered in Canarsie along Jamaica Bay where they lived in shacks, fished to eat and raised chickens. There were empty lots with spiky vegetation sticking up like whiskers from a witch's nipple.

For the first few decades of the past century, Canarsie made a play for being a destination spot, and its most popular attraction was

"Golden City," an amusement park and "beach resort" that the 1939 WPA Guide to New York City called "forlorn." Others called it unwholesome, its nocturnal dance halls and transient hotels populated by fresh-off-the-boat drunks and whores. A fellow could go there seeking action and come home with the clap and without a wallet. Golden City mildly competed with the conglomeration of seaside amusement parks in Coney Island until the 1930s when it burned down.

Silverman was twenty-five years old and was awaiting trial for a stickup. He was found in a car with his body trussed and three bullet holes in his head. He had been bound in such a way that the more he struggled the tighter the rope around his neck became. He was killed during the morning of the 15th, a Thursday, and his body discovered later the same day by children who were playing in the area.

Canarsie was so popular for dumping bodies that Silverman was only one of two stiffs found in that neighborhood that day. The other was found at 2:00 A.M. burned beyond recognition—and never ID'd—in a gasoline-soaked and blazing sedan in a parking lot on East 95th Street between Avenues A and B. The murder, police noticed, was very similar to the 1935 castration slaying of Louis "Pretty" Amberg, which we've previously discussed.

While Silverman was held following his stickup arrest, he furnished info that resulted in the arrest of Nathan "Little Natie" Kaufman. Kaufman gave Albert Anastasia an envelope to take care of Silverman.

In November 1937, Pittsburgh Phil was arrested and charged with manslaughter after running down a seventy-five-year-old woman with his car as she crossed Kings Highway at East 96th Street in Brownsville. His buddy Kid Twist by this time was known as the top hoodlum in Brownsville.

Lepke called a meeting to announce his intentions and among those in attendance were Albert Anastasia, Meyer Lansky, and Bugsy Siegel.

"I'm going underground," he said. "Only Albert will know where

I am. My rackets will be run by Mendy Weiss, who will be under my orders."

There was a massive manhunt for Lepke. He was spotted in the Caribbean, in several countries in Europe, but it was all bullshit. For two years Albert hid Lepke in plain sight, right in Brooklyn.

With Lepke in hiding, Albert set out to destroy the case against him. Seven witnesses against Lepke were rubbed out by contract. The papers did their best to make Lepke legendary. They said he pulled in a half-million dollars a year. They called him "the country's bloodiest racketeer."

In 1938, Isidor Juffe, the guy once kidnapped by Albert Anastasia and Joe Adonis, caused a major fuss when, following an arrest for running a fur racket, he told his interrogators that he didn't get it; he'd been paying big bribes to avoid prosecution for years, how come this time it didn't take?

The comment got Mayor LaGuardia's attention. A massive internal investigation ensued. Sketchy cops scurried like roaches in a tenement basement when you flick on the light.

During the overnight of October 18–19, 1938, sticky fingered gremlins went to work. Drawer after drawer of police files were snitched from the Bergen Street precinct house in Cobble Hill, Brooklyn. The files contained info on more than seven-thousand cases in the precinct for a two-year period. It was a disaster.

The investigation into the burglary was massive, the cover-up glaring yet effective. The D.A. was not allowed to participate as he was too close to the action. An assistant D.A. was charged with accepting $800 from Juffe to shield Juffe from criminal prosecution. So a special prosecutor was appointed by New York State Governor Herbert H. Lehman. Big names fell hard. It was like dominoes. Friends of politicians. Society ladies.

On October 22, during the early hours of the morning, in what was called a "pre-election move," there was a roundup of well-known hoods in Brooklyn. Nothing much was accomplished by the arrests, other than it made it look like authorities were doing something to combat organized crime that had turned the 1930s into New York City's bloodiest decade.

Among those arrested were Albert Anastasia and one of his top gunmen, Tony Romeo. Albert gave his address as 387 Clinton Street. Both were charged with vagrancy. It was Anastasia's ninth arrest—but considering five of those arrests had involved murders, this was small potatoes.

Since the "don't shit where you eat" incident two years earlier, activity inside Midnight Rose's was peaceful enough. The boys drank sometimes, and they could get loud, but they took the brutality outside.

During the summer of 1938, Kid Twist got into fisticuffs with an affiliated New Jersey bookmaker named Mortimer Levy. The bookie had taken from Twist a $300 loan, this despite the rule that said a gang couldn't lend money to its own members. Reles grabbed Levy by his coat lapels and gave him a good shake. Levy pushed Twist off and then punched him in the face, sending the tough guy onto his ass. Levy eventually paid back the loan, but under re-negotiated terms. (There was no doubt plenty of room for negotiation as the regular interest rate on a $300 loan was 267 percent.)

At least this time no one called the cops. That would have made Anastasia's head explode.

THIRTEEN
Morris Diamond Is Iced

WHICH BRINGS US TO THE END STORY of one Moishe "Morris" Diamond: witness. Diamond was the fifty-three-year-old office manager of Local 138 of the International Brotherhood of Teamsters and Chauffeurs who once campaigned for the election of rackets buster Thomas E. Dewey.

To Diamond's union, violence was nothing new. The president, Billy Snyder, had recently instructed his men to vote in favor of a strike halting the movement of baking supplies in the city. He was shot dead on September 13, 1934, in a restaurant on Avenue A. Police questioned Diamond afterward. The public was familiar with the Snyder slaying because Dewey himself had used it during his campaign, even presenting a pre-election radio drama about the kill. Diamond's fatal flaw was that he'd blabbed about Lepke. That witness-status put Diamond on Albert Anastasia's short list.

Diamond was on his way to work, stepping out of his house on 68th Street between 17th and 18th avenues in Bensonhurst, stepping into the fresh air of May 25, 1939, where he was gunned down. The victim was rushed to Israel Zion Hospital at 7:15 A.M. He only managed to identify himself, but not his killer, before he croaked. Word on the street was that Albert Anastasia personally handled this one for his pal Lepke. Eyewitnesses weren't sure what they saw. Although one did tell authorities that the gunman had escaped in a car occupied by two men. Some eyewitnesses had been far enough away so that their inattention and lack of observation could be believed, but there was one witness who was having trouble convincing anyone that he hadn't seen anything. That was an unnamed street-cleaner who had been approximately ten feet away from the gunman when he blew Diamond away. The shooter and the street-cleaner had made eye contact, and the worker was so afraid that the police had placed him under guard.

The killing furthered Anastasia's plan to take complete control of the Manhattan garment district.

Irving Penn was not a gangster. He was in fact a music publishing company executive. But, unfortunately for him, he lived in the same building as a gangster on East 178th Street in the West Farms section of the Bronx. On the morning of July 25, 1939, Penn left his house on the way to work and walked right into a gunman who pumped five bullets into his body. Oops. Wrong guy.

Earlier that morning neighbors had noticed a car cruising up and down the block. As Penn left his home and started down the sidewalk the car pulled to the curb. While the driver stayed behind the wheel, the man in the passenger seat (most likely tailor-turned-gunman Jack "The Dandy" Parisi) got out, shot Penn, got back in, and sped off.

Penn was rushed to the hospital and as he lay dying, Assistant District Attorney Arthur Carney sat at his bedside and asked again and again, "Who did it, Irving?"

Irving was in bad shape but managed to say, "No reason . . . anyone . . . would want . . . to shoot . . . me." He died three hours later.

Police got a good description of the car and located the vehicle abandoned about two blocks away. In the car were two pistols, one recently fired and empty, the other cold and fully loaded. Both the car and its license plates proved to be stolen.

Right away detectives figured Penn had been shot in a case of mistaken identity. By all accounts he was legit, no mob ties, and happily married with two daughters, fourteen and ten. Within days, police had polished that theory and concluded that Penn had been mistaken for henchman Philip Orlovsky, who lived in the same building.

It was a ghastly mistake, one that could mean nothing but trouble and Albert was furious. The rules were simple: I.D. the target, learn his habits, shoot the correct guy. He hadn't been so mad since the boys brought the cops to Midnight Rose's.

Speaking of Rose, it was around the time of the Penn murder that the boys' landlady got into trouble. During the summer of 1939, Rose—a sixty-seven-year-old grandmother, several times married—was busted for racketeering and perjury. Cops said she ran a brothel upstairs, kept a policy bank, gave out loans to suckers, and helped distribute the locations for a floating crap game. She had a bail-bond racket going, and business was so good that she sometimes farmed business out, for a fee, to other bondsmen.

The indictment for Mrs. Rose boasted seventeen counts, and the old lady was facing a prison sentence of eighty-five years and fines of $85,000.

It was only after Rose's arrest that some of the other shop owners on Mrs. Gold's block tentatively spoke about the comings and goings at Saratoga and Livonia. It was, you know, shady. One proprietor said she was afraid that the public would think the whole block was involved in the rackets, and that would be bad for business.

Luckily for Mrs. Rose, she knew people. Powerful legal aid rushed to her rescue.

Midnight Rose was at first held on $50,000 bail. That was cut to $10,000. And then she was suddenly just released. The official reason was that she was old and sick, and the justice system had been unnecessarily harsh on her. In jail her health grew worse. They gave her some tonic but mostly she was sick in bed. Organized crime prosecutions were complicated and took months to prepare. So they let her out, and her health improved dramatically.

Her case went on for years. Also indicted was Midnight Rose's son Sam Siegel. At her indictment hearing, her son caused a hubbub when he fainted in court, and the defendant ran to comfort him, sobbing, "My son! He has a weak heart!" She ended up pleading guilty to eight counts of fraud, and was given a suspended sentence.

As this was going on, Chief Justice Frederick Kernochan of Special Sessions told a U.S. Senate Sub-Committee that racketeers were protected by district leaders and that those leaders put so much pressure on the NYPD that woe be the cop who didn't know which way the wind was blowing.

Justice Kernochan—a veteran of New York City politics and a buddy of FDR, who was the president—said that racketeering could not be checked until politics and municipal government were divorced. He said, "Racketeering is a new word but what they do is very old. The guerrillas of thirty years ago are the gangsters of today. Gangs existed then as now because they had some useful connection with district leaders."

At that same Senate Sub-Committee hearing at which Brooklyn D.A. O'Dwyer was accused of refusing to prosecute labor racketeers (the same accusation that had gotten his predecessor fired), an international unionist was accused of having sole control of employment at the Rockefeller Center development, and labor unions were accused of being run "by bullets, not ballots."

During the summer of 1939, Lepke might have been hiding, but he wasn't suffering. In fact, he was a picture of comfort: gaining twenty pounds, mostly on Nathan's hot dogs, growing a mustache, catching rays on the Coney Island beach, and living in an apartment in Louis Capone's Oriental Danceland on Stillwell Avenue.

Lepke was however the only comfortable hood. With Lepke on the lam, law enforcement clamped down on mobsters, harassing with a maddening, steady pressure. It got to a point where a hood couldn't scratch his own ass without a beat cop asking him why he had an itch. The message was clear: Give up Lepke and everything goes back to nice.

Lepke got to a point where his friends were few and far between.

He was fat and tanned but lonely. Only Albert Anastasia remained trueblue—or so it seemed.

Every post office in America had a wanted poster for Lepke with the ominous words, "WANTED DEAD OR ALIVE: $50,000 REWARD." Anastasia told Buchalter to remain out of sight for as long as he wanted. To hell with the hoods on the corner who got the heat up their ass. Why give yourself up for those assholes? Would they do it for you?

That loyalty caused Albert grief. Now the assholes on the corner were mad at him, too. And their bosses. And their bosses' bosses. Buchalter was bad for business. Give him up or face the headache.

Every man has his breaking point, a point where survival instinct overpowers all loyalty. Albert decided that maybe the best bet for everyone all around was to turn Lepke in and then work to destroy the case against him.

Perhaps, Anastasia's biggest accomplishment during the 1930s was in keeping his two lives separate. His wife and kids did not worry about the dangerous world their husband and dad lived in, for the simple reason that—in theory, at least—they didn't know it existed.

At least Elsa claimed she knew nothing about Albert's other life. Some might wax skeptical. She knew he was out all night. She knew the types of men he consorted with. She knew the reasons his name was sometimes in the newspapers. She must have suspected something close to the truth. Many believe that Elsa's ignorance, if it existed at all, was focused and purposeful.

Albert's Jekyll-Hyde life was performed with great skill. He was a regular in church—the mass still said in Latin in those days. Elsa wore white gloves, and the kids dressed in their Sunday best in church. That night he'd go out and dispatch some degenerate who did the wrong thing. Then he'd carefully wash his hands and go home to his loving family.

There was nothing Albert Anastasia loved more than killing a man. It was his true joy, and he often didn't assign any of his boys to go out on a hit. He took care of it himself. He was careful. Identified the target, learned his habits, etc., chose his time and spot carefully, but he did it himself. It was a habit that bothered his friends.

"I know you love it, Albert, but it's too dangerous. You are too important for us to lose you because a stupid beat cop turned a corner at the right moment and got lucky," said Luciano, who knew about luck.

Lepke seconded the idea. "Let the crew paint the houses. If they get caught, who cares?"

Albert said OK. He couldn't promise that he'd give up killing cold turkey, but he'd try to cut back.

During that era, there was no more powerful media figure in America than Walter Winchell, whose radio broadcasts reached every ear with a radio. On August 24, 1939, Winchell during his broadcast called for Lepke to surrender.

"It's either that or be gunned down by the G-Men, just like Dillinger," Winchell said, a reference to bank robber John Dillinger who was whacked by feds outside the Biograph Theater in Chicago in 1934 as he exited the movies with that most-famous *femme fatale*, the Lady in Red.

Lepke heard the broadcast. After, Lepke and Albert had a talk and decided that surrender would be the best solution.

"You'll be out before you know it," Albert said. "Take my word for it, the witnesses against you are going to disappear."

"You sure?"

"Yeah, yeah, yeah, the deal is done," Albert said. "You just have to deal with the feds. You'll get five years and be back on the streets. I fixed it so that O'Dwyer and Dewey can't touch you."

"Thanks, Albert."

Albert just smiled. "I'll drive you myself," he said.

Lepke and the feds agreed on a rendezvous near Manhattan's Madison Square Park. Albert drove, Lepke sat shotgun, and in the back seat was Louie Capone's sister-in-law holding a baby she'd borrowed from a neighbor.

With both Walter Winchell and J. Edgar Hoover watching, G-men put the cuffs on Lepke. The lady with the baby moved into the shotgun seat and Albert drove surreptitiously away. And that was the last Lepke ever saw of freedom.

The deal Albert had discussed didn't exist. Lepke would never be free again. Albert understood this. "Once they get their hands on him, all the deals in the world can't save him," he said privately.

Lepke went down initially on the fed charges for drug trafficking, fourteen years. Then Dewey arrested him and charged him with extortion. He lost that trial and they added thirty more years to his sentence. They still weren't done. He was arrested a third time and the charges against him were again upgraded, this time to murder.

Thirty-year-old Irving "Puggy" Feinstein was a clothing salesman with quite a past. His youth was spent in the ring, where a disappointing boxing career resulted in the flattening of his nose—and his nickname. He'd been a small-time crook, a smash-and-grab guy, but he was trying to put all of that behind him. His efforts were of fluctuating success.

Puggy was a bachelor who lived with his parents in Borough Park. He'd recently had his heart broken. He'd fallen in love with a nice girl from Flatbush. They were engaged. He'd purchased the furniture. Then some neighborhood creep, a real asshole, told the girl that Puggy was an ex-con and they broke up.

Feinstein soothed his broken heart by gambling. He would lay out odds on daily occurrences, an over/under on the subway's arrival time, whether the next guy to come around the corner would be smoking a cigarette, whatever it was. Parlay on the next three brands of smokes sold at the corner stand. At the track or a backroom parlor, he was coming in his pants.

Sure, he owed some money here and there, but he liked to gamble, and he liked to host parties in which there was a lot of gambling going on. They were like orgies for him. Trouble was, he did it in the Borough Park section of Brooklyn where all gambling was under the auspices of Vince Mangano, Albert's boss.

"Al, he's got to go." Mangano handed Anastasia an envelope.

"I'm on it," Albert said.

It was September 4, 1939. Albert did his usual research into the predictable movements of his target and learned that once a week like a clock Puggy went to Brownsville to pay off a loan. He sent out Twist, Pittsburgh Phil, and Buggsy Goldstein to do the dirty work—yeah, he sent Buggsy to hit Puggy. And in this case the work was legendarily dirty. They created a crime scene that made hardened beat cops stagger and vomit.

"Here's the plan," Pittsburgh Phil said. "We pick him up in a stolen car and we take him to Twist's house."

"My house!" Twist said.

"Don't make no difference," Pittsburgh Phil replied. "I can do the job silently."

Twist knew this to be true. "Okay," he said with a shrug.

When they got to Twist's house, which was on East 91st Street in Canarsie, he was horrified to find his wife there. He gave his wife fifty bucks and told her to take a hike.

"You mother is asleep in the other room. Don't wake her up," Mrs. Reles said, and sashayed out the door.

Feinstein started to squawk but Pittsburgh Phil got him from behind, arm against his throat. Twist could tell that this wasn't going to be exactly silent, so he turned on the radio loud so if his mother woke up she'd think it was a party.

Feinstein thought this was because he was behind on some payments. He had, after all, been on his way to visit his shylock when he was kidnapped.

"Don't hit me, I got the money," Feinstein said.

He was horrified to learn that these guys didn't care about the money.

Twist fetched a rope and returned to the couch area where Pittsburgh Phil was pissed off.

"He just bit me! Now I'm gonna get lockjaw."

Pittsburgh Phil got on top of Feinstein so he couldn't move much, and Goldstein punched every one of Feinstein's accessible body parts to punish him for biting.

Using teamwork, Pittsburgh Phil pulled Feinstein's chin away from his chest, while Goldstein and Twist, each holding an end, slipped the rope over Feinstein's Adam's apple.

The men then exchanged ends of the rope and made two loops around his neck. Pittsburgh Phil was a whiz with knots, what a boy scout he would've been, and he rigged a rope so that Feinstein's feet were bound to the back of his neck, and the more he tried to struggle, the tighter the ropes got around his throat. The men stood around and watched as Puggy Feinstein strangled himself to death, taking a big dump in his pants as he did so.

"You got something for this?" Pittsburgh Phil said, holding out his bitten hand. Feinstein broke the skin in a few places. The teeth hadn't gotten as far as the bone but it looked like it hurt.

Twist went to the bathroom and pulled some first-aid shit out of the medicine cabinet. Iodine, cotton ball, adhesive tape, and Pittsburgh Phil was all set—although he was still bellyaching about needing a tetanus shot.

Twist's mom hadn't woken up—or if she did, she stayed quiet about it.

They turned their attention to the corpse whose shit was stinking up the room. Goldstein fetched a can of gasoline. They put the aromatic stiff into the stolen car and drove it to a vacant lot at Fillmore Avenue and East 52nd Street in the Flatlands section of Brooklyn. They poured the gas over the car and struck a match. The fire burned spectacularly for a time and then slowed. It didn't destroy the evidence the way the men had hoped. No one called the fire department and the fire was down to a smolder before the crime scene was discovered.

The grim and noxious discovery was made by Louise Maurer, a ticket-taker on the BMT subway who was on her way home. The feet and Feinstein's rings were intact. Feinstein's brother Hyman identified the body by the rings, some of which had fallen off while others stayed on the bone.

Assistant Medical Examiner George Ruger attributed death to strangulation. He could tell the body had been doused with gasoline. His hands, feet, and neck were bound with sash cord, and then burned entirely, except for his shoes, which were untouched by the flame. Best guess was he was killed elsewhere and dumped in the lot. Perhaps the murder took place in Feinstein's car, which police couldn't locate.

FOURTEEN
How the Twist Turns

THE YEAR 1940 BROUGHT DEWEY'S big crackdown on Murder Inc., which as of March 21 had a name thanks to the boys from the press. According to the *Brooklyn Eagle,* a pair of canaries named Abraham "Pretty" Levine and Anthony "The Duke" Maffatore first broke the shroud of silence around Albert's crew. According to the *Daily News,* Maffatore sang about thirty murders. NYPD Detective Lieutenant John Osnato asked Maffatore what Murder Inc. did in its spare time. The canary said it was funny. Scams sometimes got domestic. There were ops run by Midnight Rose and members of the Brownsville crew setting up rich housewives who liked to play cards. When a woman would get in debt, she'd get money from a shylock. If she couldn't pay back, she was tricked out. If she wasn't a desirable trick, she'd be given an opportunity to rat out rich-blooded card games where the thugs could then raid, rob and/or skim. Pretty and the Duke sang, but it did them no good. They simply joined the caravan up the river.

As all of this was going on, Albert's brother Tough Tony who jumped ship in 1924 when he was eighteen, quietly went through the process of being naturalized as a U.S. citizen.

The first big Murder Inc. arrest was of thirty-seven-year-old, two-hundred-pound Irving Cohen—alias Jack Cohen, alias Big Gangi. Originally from Brooklyn, Cohen had become a bit player in Hollywood movies such as *Golden Boy*. Cohen was arrested and charged with the murder of Walter Sage, who was found during the summer of 1937 in Swan Lake tied to a slot machine. Cohen was a memorable defendant as he wept throughout his trial, which apparently did the trick as his jury acquitted him after less than two hours of deliberation.

Soon thereafter the quartet of Twist, Happy, Buggsy, and Pittsburgh Phil were arrested together in 1940 and charged with vagrancy. Police knew all four of them were killers, but at least they were off the streets for a while—and into The Tombs, a.k.a. City Prison, Manhattan's version of Raymond Street, at Centre and White streets. On the inside, the Tombs were known for rats and drippiness. On the outside it was known for an impressive architectural feature, the "Bridge of Sighs" that connected the jail at fourth-story level with the Manhattan Criminal Courts building. Conditions were so bad that the building was torn down in 1941 and replaced by a new jail across the street.

That spring, Kid Twist received a visit in jail from his lawyer. No one listened in but after the mouthpiece split, Twist had a new attitude, a complete about-face. He sat and contemplated for a few hours and then summoned a guard.

There is an alternative version of Twist's turn: Twist's very pregnant wife Rose was called in by O'Dwyer and told to visit her husband in jail. "Tell Abe that hoods in trouble are talking about him and it don't look good," O'Dwyer said. His best bet was to talk about them right back, and maybe he'd be able to cut a deal. Besides, he had a kid, a little boy, and another on the way; they needed him home where he belonged.

However it was delivered, the message was received. He wasn't going to skate as he had in the past. Being home where he belonged aside, his only chance of seeing the light of freedom again was to squeal, and then move to Mongolia under an assumed name.

"Tell the D.A. I want to talk to him," Twist said.

O'Dwyer had Twist brought to him.

"You let me walk out of here clean as a whistle and I'll give you everything you need," Twist said.

"Deal," O'Dwyer said, "Let's do this."

And that was how it started. O'Dwyer called for a stenographer, and Twist began to yakety-yak. He was one of those guys who remembered every guy he ever whacked, every guy he'd seen whacked, remembered in detail, with dates and places. He knew, as they say, where the bodies were buried.

He said that he, Goldstein, and Pittsburgh Phil were childhood friends in Brownsville. They had stolen from the same pushcarts. He ran down his impressive criminal resume. Sure, he'd been the guy to give the icepick to George Rudnick in a Brooklyn garage on May 25, 1937. Then he told the story of how he helped Buggsy and Pittsburgh Phil Strauss kill Irving "Puggy" Feinstein on September 4, 1939. Puggy was shot, stabbed, and his body set on fire.

"That kill was special to me," Twist said. "It happened in my home, my mother's home."

He squealed on Maione, on Goldstein, on Weiss. He squealed on *Anastasia*. There must have been a part of him that knew they were better at killing than he was at hiding. Maybe he thought that he'd bring them *all* down and there wouldn't be anyone left to whack him by the time he walked. Maybe he knew he was dead either way, and the last thing he wanted was to give the government the satisfaction of executing him. A bullet was better than the hot seat. Maybe. We don't know. But whatever the reason he took a life filled with gangster honor and respect and flushed it down the toilet. Now, on the street, he would be thought of with nothing but shame and disgust.

He sang till he was hoarse. O'Dwyer kept count. Twist confessed to *eighty-five* murders. One of those murders was the grotesque butchery of George Rudnick. Happy and the Dasher were arrested. He said Albert Anastasia personally offed thirty guys, but he was the "finger man" who "ordered all of the hits." He said that Albert was "the boss," and that no murder could take place without Albert's okay. He said that he had personally carried out many hits that had been ordered by Albert, including that of Morris Diamond. He said that, as far back as 1934, Albert ran just about all of Brooklyn. He was friends with Luciano, friends with Adonis. In the parlance of the day, the entire combination was in his cartel. The whole mob was in his family. He said, "In Brooklyn, we are all together with the mob on the docks."

How powerful was Anastasia?

"Albert Anastasia, who is our boss, is the head guy on the docks," Twist said. "He is the law."

Asked the parameters of complete control, Twist said, "The area of mob control includes five miles of Brooklyn waterfront, and it takes in two to five blocks from the water, too. It has a lot going for it."

Every ship-line operator to every corner candy store operator had to pay tribute, he explained. Every man who got work on the docks had to kick back a portion of his earnings. They spoke in code. "We got to go to the boss's house tonight to buy wine," they would say. In other words, the boss got a cut of everything.

The D.A.'s stenographer filled almost a hundred notebooks with the squiggles and doodads of shorthand.

It is said that no news in the history of the United States—the bombing of Pearl Harbor, Dodgers winning the World Series, the assassination of JFK—moved as fast as the news that Twist had sung. The Gangland Grapevine was lightning quick.

A lot of guys went into hiding before they could be scooped up. Dandy Jack Parisi. Tony Romeo. Vito Gurino. They all took a powder. A nation-wide BOLO (be on the lookout) was broadcast for Albert Anastasia.

"He is very dangerous," the police alert read.

But Albert, too, was not home. He disappeared from Red Hook and, when there were no cops around, was spotted here and there, usually living it up in a swanky Manhattan hotel. Then he disappeared altogether, and no one knew where he was.

* * *

Not long after Twist blabbed, Bronx District Attorney Samuel J. Foley interrogated a twenty-seven-year-old dice-game hustler named Lazarus Black with a Bronx Grand Jury listening in.

Black had been persuaded to talk by his wife who showed him clippings indicating that Kid Twist was blabbing his face off in police protection, so it was best for Black to cut a deal or risk being hung out to dry.

Black turned himself in. Cops took him on a tour by car, and the cooperative man pointed out key Murder Inc. locations, places used by Twist and Buggsy. He pointed out a sewer where hitmen disposed of the license plates off the stolen cars they used during hits.

Irving Penn's death, Black said, was a mistake. Black pointed the murder car out during the ride around, and the rightful owner had to give it up while it was processed as a possible crime scene. Black's info was so good that Foley proclaimed the Penn murder solved. As a result of Black's grand jury testimony "Blue Jaw" Magoon and Buggsy Goldstein were indicted. Buggsy, Anthony Maffetore, Abraham Levine, and Louis Capone were also charged with the 1933 murder of Red Alpert.

Magoon and Goldstein were also indicted for grand larceny, charged with stealing a car from the Manhattan Beach Garage in Brooklyn and using it to kill Penn. It all depended on the testimony of Black.

Magoon was not sent to Raymond Street, but rather to the much nicer West 53rd Street Jail, which was known on the street as the "Singing Jail." Trouble was, when you got out of the Singing Jail, it was best to lay low. Police theorized that Blue Jaw and Buggsy were clowns and this wasn't the first time they'd set out to shoot one guy and ended up shooting another.

It was believed that they went out in 1940 to shoot a recent parolee named Matthew Kane and ended up killing a financial district investigator named O'Hara. Those kinds of blunders didn't make you many friends. (Kane was returned to Sing Sing and promptly killed in prison.)

* * *

Murder Inc. was being massacred. Albert went to the war chest to see they got the best lawyers, but there was only so much that could be done. Frank "The Dasher" Abbadando and Max "Maxie the Jerk" Golob were busted for the killing of John "Spider" Murtha in Brooklyn on March 3, 1935. Murtha was an ex-con who'd been out for a stroll with his twenty-eight-year-old sweetheart Flo when the Dasher and "Maxie The Jerk" Golob told her to step aside and pumped eight slugs of hot lead into him.

Also under arrest was forty-four-year-old Joseph Daddona, for kidnapping Joe "The Baker" Liberto and taking him for a ride to Long Island, and for owning a car involved in the killing of Charles Brown, a black guy who was shouting about a black labor union.

Cops had Happy Maione in stir, and Albert was pleased at reports that Happy was snarling like a caged beast when approached by peace officers of any sort.

Not that the cops had solved all of the murders. They were still looking at Murder Inc. for a nasty rough kill in Connecticut, November 20, 1933, in the town of Somers. A forty-year-old hood named Albert Silverstein with ties to both Lepke and Twist was found dead dressed only in a Navajo rug, and dangling on a barbed-wire fence. Silverstein had been punctured with eight stab wounds and his face had been beaten beyond recognition. That's the touch of gruesome that made Murder Inc. so effective.

Midnight Rose's was raided—which pretty much put an end to the joint as headquarters of anything. Cops found a stockpile of guns hidden in the cellar, along with many sets of brass knuckles and blackjacks for administering the hurt.

For Blue Jaw Magoon, things went from bad to worse when cops questioned his *goomada,* Evelyn Mittleman—a woman with a kiss-of-death reputation. Turned out Mittleman, who was only twenty-five, got around pretty good, and seemed to be affectionate toward hoods in general. *Three* men had been murdered over her, it was said. They followed a pattern. She would be a guy's summer date at a resort in the Catskills, and later he'd get squibbed off. She eventually was caught because she frequently visited the Raymond Street

Jail to talk to another of her beaus, Pittsburgh Phil. Her arrest brought headlines and instant notoriety. Miss Mittleman hadn't had a job in five years yet wore a fur and $100,000 in jewelry.

Singing turned out to be contagious. Another rat, a hood who lived (it was specified in the paper) at 1419 West Third Street in Brooklyn, named Charles Workman, linked Lepke with the murder of Joseph Rosen, and when he went home he stayed away from the windows.

On April 7, 1940, O'Dwyer announced that he was bringing the hammer down on Louis Capone. The district attorney said, "Capone was a contact man for this murder ring. His fingers are dipped in the blood of every murder committed by this mob. He is one of the higher ups but is not the top man in this murder ring. He was in on the know of every crime committed by these bums."

O'Dwyer didn't want to take Anastasia to trial on Twist's word alone. He needed corroboration, or else it turned into a *he said/he said* case and Anastasia would walk, and they'd never get another shot at him because of double-jeopardy laws.

On April 15, Capone was removed from his cell, interrogated for twenty hours and then thrown back into his cell. The newspaper articles are very telling. The names of the bigwigs in Murder Inc. are mentioned regularly, all except one, all except Albert Anastasia, and that was the name they wanted Capone to say, and that was the name Capone refused to say.

By the end of April, O'Dwyer announced he was seeking to arrest Gesuale Capone, Louis's brother, for the attempted garroting of Calorgaro Verruse, who bellyached about shape-ups in the Hod Carriers union.

In May, Louis Capone's charges were upgraded to murder one for the 1936 murder of Joseph Rosen. Also charged in that hit was Pittsburgh Phil, Lepke (who was already a resident of Leavenworth), Mendy Weiss, and Jimmy "Dirty Face" Ferraco.

By December, Capone had also been charged with the 1939 murder of Irving Penn in the Bronx. In 1941, Lepke himself was added to the list of those accused in the Rosen murder, and he got to move from the penitentiary back to The Tombs so he could attend his own trial.

The pre-trial preliminary court hearings began in June 1941, at which time Assistant District Attorney Burton B. Turkus—Brooklyn-born and the son of an immigrant seamstress—told the court that Louis Capone was guilty of "at least six" murders.

Jury selection began that fall. After a month, only eight panelists had been chosen. Everyone was terrified of being on this jury. During the selection process, there was argument over Capone's nitro pills, which he carried for a heart condition. The judge was concerned that Capone carried enough pills with him in court to commit suicide.

By this time the average New Yorker knew that there was danger in being associated with the Murder Inc. boys in any way. It took the parties twelve monotonous weeks of voir dire to pick a twelve-man jury.

The trial took many weeks and in early December Lepke and Capone were convicted. Reporters said that Capone had remained cool during the trial and didn't show signs of stress until the jury entered the courtroom at which time he broke out in a flop sweat.

Lepke became the first boss ever to be convicted of a murder he ordered rather than committed himself. Lepke, Capone, and Mendy Weiss were scheduled for execution on December 10, 1942, but there were the usual delays, and the men lived in the death house until 1944. Sometimes the reprieve came late. In February 1944, the men got as far as eating their last meals before their execution was postponed.

FIFTEEN
Phil and Buggsy on Trial

IN THE SPRING OF 1940, D.A. O'Dwyer announced that his Murder Inc. roundup had led him to the murder of Puggy Feinstein, and presented evidence to the grand jury in the case. He got his indictment. Pittsburgh Phil and Buggsy Goldstein went down.

Pittsburgh Phil bugged out while in jail. He stopped bathing, stopped grooming. He gripped the bars of his cage and screamed all day and night. He wasn't the most popular inmate. He chewed on things. He chewed his bars. In court he chewed on his lawyer's briefcase. Maybe he was looking for an insanity plea. Backfired. By acting like an animal, he became that much easier to fry. During testimony, he could be heard mumbling to himself.

At one point, Judge John J. Fitzgerald asked Phil what day it was.

"Same as any day," Phil replied. At least he understood the question.

Leo Healy, a veteran Murder Inc. lawyer, who'd successfully defended Albert Anastasia for the murder of Joseph Santorio, defended Goldstein. Back then, however, Healy had been opposed by D.A. Geoghan who routinely pulled his punches. Those days were over. Now they had to deal with Burton Turkus, pure as the driven snow.

Pittsburgh Phil was defended by a guy named Daniel Pryor, whose job was to convince the jury that his client wasn't a malingerer and actually was the drooling mentally defective idiot they saw in court.

One of the key witnesses was Murder Inc. turncoat Blue Jaw Magoon, who testified that his pal Buggsy Goldstein had told him all about the killing of Puggy Feinstein. The weird bondage, the sleeping mom, the shit on the floor, the gasoline. They asked about Anastasia, and he said he'd rather not talk about it. Betraying Anastasia was about the stupidest thing a guy could do. "You cross Anastasia, you cross the *national combination*," Magoon said solemnly.

"I went to dinner in Sheepshead Bay with Mr. Strauss and Mr. Goldstein, and the *moida* of Mr. Feinstein was discussed in some detail," Magoon said, having memorized his lines.

"Did Mr. Strauss show any visible wounds?"

"He had a bandage on his hand."

"Did he explain what the bandage was for?"

"He said Feinstein bit him while he was mugging him, and he thought he might get lockjaw."

Magoon said that, while they ate their fish, Strauss and Goldstein argued. The killing had been sloppy, and they accused each other of being responsible for that.

On Monday morning, September 16, 1940, Kid Twist took the stand for the second time that year at a murder trial in Kings County Court, this time against Phil and Buggsy.

"How many men have you killed, Mr. Reles?" Burton Turkus asked.

"Eleven."

"Do you remember their names?"

"Yes, sir." Twist listed the names: George Rudnick, Irving Shapiro, Jake the Painter, Rocco, Greenblatt, Joey Silvers, Pug Schulman, Whitey Friedman, Jack Paley, and Pug Feinstein.

"That's ten."

"There was one more, but I can't think of his name right now. Wait, yes, it was Monk Bosco."

After some back and forth it was established that Greenblatt was

Moe Greenblatt, a plasterers' union delegate, Rocco was longshoreman Rocco Morganti, and Jake the Painter was Israel Goldberg.

"Before you mentioned Pug Feinstein. Was that Irving 'Puggy' Feinstein?" Turkus asked.

"Yes, sir."

"Who helped you with that murder?"

"I was helped with that one by Harry Strauss and Martin Goldstein," he said, using the given names of the defendants.

"Do you see those men in the courtroom today?"

"Yeah, they right over there at the, uh, defense table," Reles said with a gesture.

"What else do you remember about the killing of Puggy Feinstein?" Turkus inquired.

"It was a job we did for Albert Anastasia," Twist said. He turned and made eye contact with the blue-ribbon jury. "Albert was our boss—the big guy in the gang. I met Strauss in a crap game in a lot behind a fence. He told me he was over to Albert's house for supper and Albert gave him a contract to wipe out a guy named Puggy. I asked him, for what? And he said Puggy double-crossed Vince."

"And Vince is?"

Twist turned and looked at County Judge John J. Fitzgerald, who coolly returned his gaze. Reles returned his eyes to the courtroom gallery and said, "Vincent Mangano."

Boom, he'd named the top two guys in what would one day become the Gambino Crime Family. As they listened, Pittsburgh Phil looked toward the ceiling. Buggsy quietly wept.

"Tell us about how the crime occurred."

"Well, me and the defendants was part of a good earning business in bookmaking, loan sharking, and other pursuits. We was standing . . ."

"When was this?"

"Evening, Labor Day night, last year."

"And where were you?"

"Standing outside Midnight Rose's candy store. A guy who looked like he might've boxed a few too many rounds came up, said he was looking for Louis 'Tiny' Benson."

"Who was Benson?"

"A collector for us, collector and pay-off man, both bookmaking and loans, traveled with money because he was a big guy, weighed 450 pounds. He'd cash a hundred-dollar check for you, charge you five bucks. He brought his own little folding chair to crap games, extra-wide I guess."

"What'd you say to the punchy guy?"

"We said Tiny's not around and the guy introduced himself as 'Puggy from Borough Park.' Strauss nudged me and said that this was the guy we were looking for."

"Looking?"

"Yeah, guy we had a contract for. We agreed to get Puggy to my house and to kill him."

"Your house was . . . ?"

"On East 91st Street in Canarsie. I said we should use my house because I was going to move out of there anyway. Later that night Puggy was brought to my house by Goldstein and Duke Maffetore. To ready the joint, I sent my mom to bed and my wife went for a car ride. I had a hell of a time finding a rope and an icepick. Then we turned the radio up to kill the noise and Strauss mugged Feinstein."

"Perhaps you could explain for the jury what you mean by mugged."

"Sure," Reles said, and with appropriate hand gestures, explained that it meant choking him between your forearm and chest, applying maximum pressure onto the victim's neck. "The guy kept on fighting and kicking so I turned the radio on even louder and got the rope. I gave Strauss one end of the rope and we put it under Puggy's head while Goldstein held the other end. Then we looped it twice around his neck, pulled on it until he was shaped like a ball and then tied both ends."

After Feinstein was tortured to death in this bizarre fashion, Twist said they were worried about fingerprints, not theirs but the victim's. It would be better if cops couldn't ID the body, and so they decided to burn it. They put the body in the car and drove to a nearby vacant lot.

"Who drove?"

"Maffetore." The witness explained that Maffetore was Murder Inc.'s primary car thief.

"Where was Goldstein?"

"He was there. He went to the Esso station and had a can of gasoline and saturated the body with it. Then we lit the body and left."

"Where did you go?"

"Mr. Goldstein, Strauss, and Blue Jaw Magoon drove to Sheepshead Bay for dinner."

There had been bickering in the car. Strauss accused Goldstein of being useless because "he couldn't handle a rope right." Goldstein shot back that the rope wouldn't have been necessary if Strauss had known how to mug a guy.

Twist finished his testimony and went back into hiding.

The next witness was the car thief Maffetore, who corroborated much of what Twist had said. Turkus again did the questioning. He admitted to being present at the Feinstein killing but insisted that he had stayed out in the house's hallway during the actual killing, although he had heard the cries of the victim as he was tied up into a ball and allowed to suffocate. He drove the car with the body in it, and was at the vacant lot when it was doused with accelerant and incinerated.

"I went back to our corner later," Maffetore testified. "Strauss gave me thirty bucks and told me to keep my mouth shut if I knew what was good for me.

After that, the defense pretty much threw in the towel.

Pittsburgh Phil actually chewed on a towel that his mouthpiece gave him to keep his sloppy mouth off of his briefcase. The jury was out for an hour and a half. Guilty. Guilty. Pittsburgh Phil stopped chewing. But he did trace patterns on the linoleum-topped desk in front of him with his fingertips.

Buggsy raised his hand like a kid in school who, for once, knew the correct answer.

"Yes, Mr. Goldstein?" the judge said.

Buggsy stood and turned toward the jury. "Could I say something? Don't we deserve a little word?"

"No statement at this time," Judge Fitzgerald said sternly, banging his walnut gavel.

Buggsy kept talking anyway. Who cared if he was in contempt of court now?

"We want to thank the jury for what they come up with. With that kind of testimony you had to come up with what you did."

Later, when the men were returned to court for official sentencing, which didn't figure to be a surprise, Buggsy gave his official statement: "I want to thank the court for the charge he made that is sending us to our death. I only wish it applied to you, judge."

"What's that?" Judge Fitzgerald said.

"I would like to piss up your leg, judge."

"The sentence of this court is that you be put to death," Judge Fitzgerald sputtered.

"I will take it tomorrow and be satisfied," Buggsy said.

The men were escorted in cuffs to a car outside the courthouse. On the way they walked past a pack of boys from the press.

"It's Ol' Sparky, Buggsy. How do you feel?" one shouted out.

"I would die happy if I could knock off Turkus and take care of Judge Fitzgerald. Just tell that rat Reles I'll be waiting for him—in hell! I'll be waiting and I'll bet I got a pitchfork. Pity I can't sit in the chair holding Reles's hand. Reles in one hand and Magoon in the other!"

The men were driven to Grand Central Station where they were loaded onto a train that took the scenic route along the Hudson—"up the river"—to Ossining, N.Y. and the death house. Buggsy and Pittsburgh Phil were executed at Sing Sing on June 12, 1941.

SIXTEEN
The Perforation of Peter Panto

DURING THE SUMMER OF 1940, even as Murder Inc. was being torn apart, Albert Anastasia remained a busy man. He was still underboss of the Mangano Crime Family and czar of the waterfront, and in that theater of action the killings continued unabated.

That summer, there were a series of unsolved murder cases near the Red Hook piers, the most dramatic of which was the disappearance and presumed murder of Peter Panto . . .

On the evening of July 14, 1940, twenty-eight-year-old longshoreman Peter Panto was talking to his fiancée in her dreary Red Hook kitchen. There was a scrub board and the washing machine had a crank.

"I got to go meet some men," he said. "About union business. I don't trust these guys."

"Don't go," the girlfriend pleaded.

"I'll be back in an hour," he said putting on his hat. "Then I'll help you make sandwiches."

The sandwiches, which would go uneaten, were for a picnic they were planning for the next day.

From Albert Anastasia's point of view, guys like Panto were a royal pain in the ass. Panto didn't like conditions on the piers, and he was noisy as hell about it. Panto was the rank-and-file leader in the longshoreman's union who'd led the dockworkers in a revolt against the hoods in charge. That kind of thing could get a fellow killed, and did.

Panto had been actively opposing the ILA control by Emil Cararda, his brother and several lieutenants—including Albert's contact man in the union, Tony Romeo. He was the sort of guy who, if left alone, could start a revolution, with strikes and demands and scabs and violence.

Better to just scratch him off the face of the earth. So Albert sent the moose-like Mendy Weiss and some guys to take care of it. Weiss's days of freedom were numbered.

Mendy was a kidnapper and choker by trade. Because of his size and strength, he usually offed guys without sustaining personal injury but Panto fought back. During the attack, Panto bit down so hard on Weiss's fingers that he reached the bone in several places.

It was Panto's last act of aggression. He was thrown in a car, garroted till dead, and buried in quicklime at a chicken yard in what today is known as Lyndhurst, New Jersey.

The battle between management and labor in Red Hook had never been a happy one. For generations guys were clipped or disappeared for yapping instead of zipping. Same ol' same ol'. But lately the pace had picked up. Life was cheaper than ever. Street cleaners found stiffs almost every morning, a pain in the ass as they had to stay with the body, and the cop who came almost always had stopped to get his breakfast first. The corpse wasn't going nowhere.

This Panto business had Anastasia's name written all over it. Getting a guy whacked was a lot cheaper than a strike. Most of what happened in Red Hook was considered none of the cops' business, by both the hoods and the cops, but in the case of Peter Panto, union agitator and troublemaker, the Brooklyn powers-that-be saw a political need to do something.

Albert was hard to find, but not so much his brother Antonio "Tough Tony" Anastasio, who was taken by police and held on

$100,000 bond. On the BOLO list was Giuseppe Florino. The Sing Sing Death House boys, still at it almost twenty years later.

The killers and the Law had been on this merry-go-round before, and the only real question was how would the old Sackett Street roomies get off the hook this time?

On the stone sides of the Montague Street ramp, where it led down to Furman Street and the docks, someone wrote in chalk, "Where is Pete Panto?" The answer wouldn't come until January 1941 when his body was pulled from its quicklime Lyndhurst grave.

Even as thousands showed up for Panto's funeral, the investigation into his murder sputtered to a halt.

SEVENTEEN
The Sette Is Kaput

WHEN WE LAST SAW KID TWIST he was singing his brains out in exchange for his freedom. Trouble was, the government needed to keep Twist alive long enough for him to finish testifying in court.

After that, they could turn him loose and take bets on his life expectancy—which would have been measured in minutes. Never before had a get-out-of-jail-free card been issued to a guy with a record as long as Twist's: forty-three arrests, everything from juvenile delinquency to murder.

Now wanted for murder because of Twist was Vito "Chicken Head" Gurino, a guy with a record of twenty-seven arrests for drugs, guns, burglary, grand larceny, vagrancy, bookmaking. Police searched Gurino's home and found a pile of travel brochures, which led them to believe that he'd fled the country. Truth was, he'd stayed local, got as far as Jersey City, and when he found police had searched his home, he tried to find sanctuary in Manhattan's Church of the Guardian Angel. Turned out the priests didn't want him either, and they dropped a dime on him. Gurino was a nervous prisoner. Who knows if he blabbed? Word on the street was he had confessed to a couple of hits.

His wife Gertrude did her part to keep him alive, screaming that her Vito was no squealer and her wish was for him to *not* die a squealer's death. He ended up pleading guilty to three murders, was sentenced to eighty years, and died in 1957 of a heart attack in the Dannemora Hospital for the Criminally Insane. Gertrude got her wish.

The news got worse. Allie "Tic Toc" Tannenbaum also turned, became a blabbermouth, hoping the justice system would throw him a rebate in return. Word leaked out that the government was methodically constructing a case against Anastasia, one they hoped would stand up in court, one that couldn't be wiped out with a couple of disappearing witnesses.

Authorities believed Anastasia blew it when he killed Morris Diamond in Bensonhurst, that he'd left a visible trail that could be presented convincingly to a jury. The government, in fact, was building a small army of men to testify, men who'd make it clear that Albert Anastasia was the real deal, as big as they came.

Because an accomplice's testimony is not considered corroboration, Twist's statements about the murder of Morris Diamond were thought to be particularly damaging because he was not an accomplice in that murder but had merely heard Anastasia talking about it. Twist said he was visiting Anastasia's home and had heard Albert and Mendy talking about whacking Diamond.

Twist quoted Albert as saying, "As soon as you give me his address, we will take care of him."

With that piece of info, the district attorney felt he finally had a case against Anastasia that would stick. The only problem was finding Albert. Many police believed that he never got too far from home, like Lepke when he was on the lam, but others thought Albert had fled, and so the search for him traveled as far as Italy and Cuba.

For a year and a half, Twist lived as a virtual prisoner, moving from hotel to hotel, always under armed guard, being "kept safe" so he could sing in court the same way he sang for the D.A. Every fifteen minutes a cop would poke his head into his room to make sure he was OK. You could hardly blame the guy for going stir crazy. He could get room service and take a shower, but he couldn't leave.

To be honest, Twist could take a shower whenever he wanted to, but he didn't. Want to, that is. He enjoyed punishing his guards by filling the room with his own stink.

What he did like to do was eat. He packed on the pounds, which made him seem even more like a hog rolling around in its own slop.

The most dangerous time for Twist, it was thought, was when he was taken to a Brooklyn courtroom to testify. On March 19, 1941, in the Kings County courtroom of Judge Franklin Taylor, Reles was on his third day on the stand to talk about murders committed by defendants Harry "Happy" Maione, and Frank "The Dasher" Abbandando—including the meat cleaver killing of George Rudnick.

Both Happy and the Dasher dressed in blue suits, the Dasher standing out because he was wearing a fire-engine red tie. Twenty cops patrolled the courthouse hallways to make sure the witness got to and from the witness stand safely. The prosecutor was Burton Turkus, the man Albert had taken to calling Mr. Arsenic because he was poison for the rackets, who was described as "slim and debonair."

During earlier court sessions, the medical examiner had testified as to the state of Rudnick's body when it was found. There had been sixty-three separate stab wounds, and his skull had been shattered like an eggshell.

While Twist was testifying, Happy leaped to his feet from behind the defendants' desk. He grabbed his full water glass and hurled it at the witness stand like the Dodgers' Cookie Lavagetto throwing to first base. The glass narrowly missed assistant district attorneys Sol Klein and Louis Joseph, and whizzed by the head of court stenographer Julia McGowan before smashing against the top rail of the witness box. Mayhem ensued.

Judge Taylor banged his gavel, and the bailiffs puffed out their chests until order was restored. The judge declared a brief recess while the mess was cleaned up and the hysterical stenographer composed herself. When the session resumed, the water glasses on the defense table had been replaced with paper cups. The defense asked for a mistrial, the judge said no way, and the direct examination of Kid Twist resumed.

"You observed the murder of Rudnick?"

"Yes."

"Could you describe for the court the murder, please, Mr. Reles."

"Pittsburgh Phil used an ice pick, and Happy used a meat cleaver," Kid Twist replied.

"By Pittsburgh Phil you mean . . . ?"

"Oh, yeah, Mr. Strauss."

"And Happy?"

"That's Mr. Maione."

"Mr. Reles, do you expect immunity from prosecution in exchange for your testimony here today?"

"I do not."

The jury was only out for two hours when it came back and gave Happy and the Dasher the thumbs down. The pair had their executions delayed a few times but finally fried on February 19, 1942.

Twist and the others turning songbird was the sort of thing that the Commission could not overlook. Here was something that could come back to haunt. It was strike one against Albert, who if picked up could have been considered a candidate for singing lessons himself. One thing was for sure. It was time to disband Murder Inc. It had outlived its usefulness. The *sette* was kaput.

EIGHTEEN
The Canary Could Sing, but He Couldn't Fly

ABRAHAM "KID TWIST" RELES put up with his role as material witness for as long as he did because at least he was safe. His life wasn't worth a plugged nickel on the streets (and probably not worth much more in jail). His only hope of staying alive was to remain in an undisclosed location. Trouble comes when sometimes even the most undisclosed locations get disclosed.

Twist thought being a material witness was OK at first, but it got old quick. He was rooming with Tic Toc Tannenbaum to keep him company. That got to be maddening. They argued about who got to tell who to shut up.

Twist was scheduled to testify against Anastasia on November 13, 1941, but he didn't make it.

On the eve of his testimony he was under heavy protection. Six NYPD detectives were guarding him. They had him holed up in the Half Moon Hotel right up against the boardwalk in Coney Island, Room 623.

None of that protection did any good. Twist, it was said, attempted to escape and "fell" out the hotel window, plummeting sixty feet, six inches to his death. He landed in a sitting position on the deck below, fractured his spine at C4 and C5, and ruptured his liver and spleen.

Twist's guards said it must've been a sort of accident. Twist had been spitting up blood and believed he was dying of lung cancer. He was attempting to escape from custody when he tragically fell to his death.

The Medical Examiner at Kings County Hospital found that Twist had benign yet "remarkable cysts" on his lungs. No cancer. A piece of the stiff's liver was sent to the city toxicologist, who found no drugs or poisons.

Police told tabloid reporters Twist was believed to be headed for a hidden cache of mob money, a sort of buried treasure for which only he held the map, at the time of his demise. Police theorized he was hoping to retrieve the money for his kids, but he never made it to X marks the spot. Didn't even get close.

The money for Twist's kids was theoretically one and the same with that referenced by Buggsy Goldstein who was in the van on his way to Sing Sing's death house when he said he had a secret regarding Twist that he didn't feel like keeping anymore: "He has $60,000 of mine and the other boys. He was minding plenty of money for the mob because we thought he was the smartest guy of all and could keep it where nobody could get it until maybe some of us were in trouble. But we never got it," Buggsy said.

Another theory was that Twist was found by three pro guns from California who'd been brought East for the express purpose of taking him out.

Twist was married and the father of two. His eight-year-old boy, Abe Jr., was known as Little Kid Twist. There was also a baby. His wife Rose had been the last person to visit Abe at the Half Moon before he decided to get the hell out of there, Amazing Spider-Man style. Between the time his wife left and his Great Leap, Twist played cards with his fellow witnesses, Tic Toc Tannenbaum, Sholom Bernstein, and Myer Sycoff.

Following his death, a pair of cops grabbed the widow, gently, at her home on 79th Street in Bay Ridge, Brooklyn, and she was taken downtown to the district attorney's office where she was interrogated for close to eight hours. The D.A. wanted to know what she and her Abe talked about. Her answers couldn't have been more vague. The best she could come up with was that they'd discussed "general matters."

The reasonable probability that someone grabbed Twist and tossed him out the window received very little play. They wondered why he climbed out the window, how he managed to pull it off while under armed guard. There were three detectives and two patrolmen on the scene supposedly watching, and yet he was able to die in such a dramatic fashion, right under their noses.

Police Commissioner Valentine ordered a complete and thorough investigation. The working theory was that Twist had tied two bed sheets together sometime before 7:30 A.M. Evidence was noted that supported that theory. He'd left shoe scuffs on the sill. To one end of the bed sheets, he'd tied an insulated radio wire. He tied the other end of the wire to the radiator and out he went, out the West 28th Street side of the hotel.

It sounded like a decent plan for escape, until you did the math. The bed sheets and the wire put together was eighteen feet long, while it was sixty-two feet from Twist's sixth-floor window to a cold, hard, sundeck-roof atop the building's second-floor extension.

Additional footmarks indicated that Twist had made it down as far as the fifth floor when the wire slipped off the radiator up above and he fell the rest of the way. There was an eyewitness to the fall, William Nicholson, secretary of the Coney Island draft board, who was looking at the hotel through his office window when Twist plummeted. Nicholson noted the time as precisely 7:30.

Troubled by the fact that Twist was on Albert Anastasia's hit list and died on the eve of testifying, New York's little mayor Fiorello LaGuardia ordered a special investigation, which determined that Twist's armed guard had over the course of its eighteen-month task become lax.

Some said they checked in on their prisoners every fifteen minutes, some said they slept in chairs right in the room with the men they were guarding. Whatever. As a result of the mayor's investigation, five of Twist's guards were arrested and charged with neglect of duty. In addition, the three detectives and two plainclothes men were demoted and put back on patrol duty.

At Abraham Reles' burial, a small group of mourners gathered. As a workman was shoveling dirt into the hole atop Reles's coffin, a small furry animal appeared out of nowhere and ran between the feet of the gathered.

"What was that?" a woman asked.

"That was a chipmunk," her husband replied. "The rat is in the grave."

Kid Twist had stayed alive long enough to do tremendous harm to Albert Anastasia and the Brooklyn mob. Because of his statements regarding Albert's grip on the Red Hook waterfront, the leaders of the ILA were rounded up and their books and records seized.

The raids and seizures were not as effective as they might've been because a little bird told the union heads that a raid was coming, and books were burned or switched out in the nick of time. Cops expecting evidence found men shrugging their shoulders and claiming to speak less English than they actually did. Much of the seized paperwork was found to be inadequate or falsified.

Investigators tried to look into the union elections through which the leaders gained power, and found that those were sketchy as well. Cops came to the conclusion that union elections in Red Hook were a scam. You voted for the right guy, if you knew what was good for you, and everyone knew who the right guy was. Tony Romeo. Dandy Jack Parisi. All guys who answered to Albert Anastasia.

In addition to the feds, the city became way too interested in Red Hook. Chief Assistant District Attorney Joseph Hanley publicly quantified the corruption: The squeeze on dockworkers amounted to as much as ten dollars per man. That was the direct skim. Indirect skims were harder to trace but just as lucrative. Each worker was compelled to patronize the same barber. If you wanted a bottle of wine you went to the right store. If you wanted to buy a shirt, you went to the right shop. The bottom line had to be in the hundreds of thousands of dollars.

It wasn't just the skim, either. There was outright theft to add up, too. Steamship lines, truck outfits, and stevedoring firms were routinely robbed. Hanley learned that Albert Anastasia had "more to say about the movement of freight than the ship owners."

Hanley learned that there wasn't much left in the union funds after the skim, and it wasn't an overstatement to say that the unions existed solely to pad Anastasia's pockets and the pockets of his friends.

Hanley was blunt: "The money is turned over each month to a notorious gangster. That notorious gangster is Albert Anastasia."

Predictably, just as Hanley's investigation was beginning to make headway, O'Dwyer shut it down. (In 1945, a grand jury would censure O'Dwyer for doing this.)

According to grand jury findings, published by the pure Burton B. Turkus, "William O'Dwyer testified that his chief concern and paramount object was a conviction for murder of Anastasia, because Anastasia was the leader and most prominent gangster in the Brooklyn underworld, that not a single murder in organized crime was committed in Brooklyn without Anastasia's permission and approval . . .

"We find every case against Anastasia was abandoned, neglected, or pigeonholed.

"We find that William O'Dwyer as District Attorney . . . failed and neglected to complete a single prosecution against Anastasia . . .

"We find there admittedly was competent legal evidence sufficient to warrant indictment, conviction, and punishment of Anastasia for murder in a case described by William O'Dwyer as 'a perfect murder case.'

"We find negligence, incompetence, and flagrant irresponsibility whereby Anastasia was permitted to escape prosecution, conviction, punishment for murder and other vicious crimes."

Kid Twist's singing ended up sending six to the chair, but not Albert Anastasia, boss of Brooklyn. Anastasia had moved surreptitiously for the past year and a half. Now with Twist dead he no longer had to worry about being hauled in for questioning the instant he poked his nose out of his house. Somehow his troubles had lifted in one fell swoop.

Albert could move more freely, appear in public places. Instead of phoning in his bets, he once again went to the racetrack—Belmont, Aqueduct, Jamaica, Saratoga in the summer. He went to restaurants and though he always sat facing the door, he didn't hide his face. Of course, the police weren't the only danger in his life, so he always traveled with a bodyguard.

On December 7, 1941, in a sneak attack, Japanese dive-bombers torched up Pearl Harbor, incinerating 2,403 U.S. sailors. FDR declared war on Japan, and from New York to California American men lined up to enlist. In Europe, Hitler had conquered Europe with his Nazi storm troopers, so we went to war against him, as well. The only country on Hitler's side was Italy with fascist Benito Mussolini in charge. Everything changed.

NINETEEN

Burning of the Normandie

AS 1942 BEGAN, with American participation in WWII still in its infancy, Albert Anastasia failed to immediately take in the whole incredible scope of the global conflict. He was still focused on making money and helping his friends, especially Luciano who was doing time for bullshit crimes. The war effort needed the docks and Albert ran the docks. He would need to be accommodated.

The U.S. government had been playing hardball with gangsters, so Albert said, "I can play hardball, too." To the feds, he said, "Release Luciano or bad things are going to start happening on the docks."

The government told Albert to take a hike so he gave them a taste of what he could do.

It was January 3, 1942, less than a month after Pearl Harbor. The French ocean liner *Normandie* was in an ice-clogged Hudson River dock, Pier 88, off West 48th Street in Manhattan. The ship was being converted in the "largest naval auxiliary in the world," with a name change to the U.S.S. *Lafayette*.

Two million dollars' worth of luxury equipment and fittings were removed and stored in a warehouse. A couple of coats of battleship gray were applied. Portals were covered with steel casings to protect against gunfire. The intended use of the ship was kept quiet but it was assumed it would be used to transport troops to Europe, 12,000 at a time.

Some of the guys working the *Normandie* job were under the control of Tough Tony, so getting a job done was easy. Albert told them it would be okay with him if they were careless with matches.

"Make a little fire, just enough to let them know what we could do if we wanted to," Albert said. He envisioned guys rushing in with fire extinguishers, the sprinkler system would turn on—and he'd again demand Lucky's freedom.

Trouble was, Albert's guys had some really, really good matches—in the form of oxy acetylene torches, which were being used by union welders. At 2:30 P.M. on February 9, a worker torched bales of deflated lifeboats and kapok-filled life preservers inside burlap sacks and covered with tarpaper. In seconds, the fire was off and running.

But the fire-fighting equipment aboard the ship turned out to be a joke. Almost nonexistent. There wasn't even a sprinkler system. The fire department wasn't called right away as workers tried to battle the growing flames themselves. By the time the pros arrived, it was out of control.

What followed was the largest amassing of fire-fighting apparatus, both land and sea, in New York City history—a record it held until 9/11. One man was killed and more than a hundred more sent to the hospital while fighting the fire.

It took firefighters seven grueling hours to put the fire out. With its hull filling up with water from the fire-fighting effort, the *Normandie* settled into the soft mud of the berth-bottom.

The vertical and horizontal fire doors had all been locked to prevent the spread of the fire to the lower decks, but now those locks were hindering efforts to pump water out and keep the ship upright.

It turned out to be a losing battle. The incoming tide pushed the ship over, starboard side up. At midnight the ship was listing at a critical twenty-five degrees and the order went out to abandon ship. All fireboats were moved away from the ship to keep them from being squashed, and the pier and bordering West Street were evacuated.

With a deafening moan of surrender, the *Normandie* capsized, rolling over onto her side, at 2:30 A.M. on February 10. The Navy ended up purchasing Pier 88 from New York City to cut down on the red tape involving salvage operations. Lampposts and a catwalk were built on the side of the ship, so work could continue twenty-four hours a day.

The government at first made a public statement that saboteurs were suspected for the devastating fire, but they backed away from that statement almost immediately. The message changed to: no evidence of enemy spies being aboard. The official explanation of the fire was changed to negligence on the part of workers. An order to move the flammable bales away from the welding area had been inadequately followed. The bales were supposed to have been moved to another area entirely, away from the sparks, but instead had been moved only a few feet.

But they knew what had happened. Albert Anastasia had said bad things would happen and a really, really bad thing had.

Albert was torn. He wanted to use the *Normandie* as a bargaining chip, but he didn't want anyone to think he was on Mussolini's side, either. So he was quiet about it. Considering the size of the mess he'd made, he never bragged.

In the months that followed the U.S. Navy, New York State, and Luciano worked out a deal. In exchange for his promise that his boys would keep the New York docks free from sabotage and enemy infiltration, Luciano was moved from the middle of nowhere—a.k.a. the Clinton Correctional Facility in Dannemora within pissing distance of the Canadian border—to Great Meadow prison closer to New York City where it was easier for him to do business.

One of the last things Albert Anastasia did before transitioning his life into the war effort, was to take care of another guy who, like Kid Twist, was under arrest and ripe for turning rat. Murder Inc. vet Tony Romeo was a guy who'd beaten two murder raps and became a delegate in Local 929, ILA, AFL. The police had Romeo listed as Anastasia's "contact man" in the union. He was in on the Panto murder, as well as many others. He could blab like Twist so he had to go.

It is unknown exactly when Romeo was whacked, but on June 28, 1942, a set of men's clothes were discovered in a thick wooded area near Wilmington, Delaware. In the pants pocket was a wallet containing cards that indicated the clothes belonged to Romeo. Police still didn't know where the missing Romeo was but wherever he was there was a good chance that he was chilly.

Romeo's body, bullet-ridden and badly decomposed, was discovered two days after his clothes, on the shore of the Brandywine River, near Newcastle, Maryland. The man's jaw had been broken. Newspaper reports noted the connection between Romeo and Anastasia, and said that, though he was a delegate in Local 929, he made his real money as one of Anastasia's pro killers. Romeo had been questioned extensively regarding the Peter Panto murder in July 1939, when Panto disappeared, and again at the end of January 1941 when Panto's body was discovered.

On July 1, the widow Romeo and a detective from the Brooklyn Homicide Squad drove to Wilmington to I.D. Romeo's body.

TWENTY

The War Effort

JUST BECAUSE A GUY IS A HOOD don't mean he ain't no patriot. On July 20, 1942, Albert Anastasia enlisted in the U.S. Army. He wasn't much for soldiering, being a middle-aged man, but he made it clear he had a few ideas that the top brass might find interesting.

Anastasia told the generals even while the U.S. was still battling its way across Northern Africa, that Lucky Luciano could be very influential in the war effort. He had deep connections in Sicily and the boot of Italy, and a single word from him could prepare the locals for the invasion, emphasizing the benefits of cooperating with the Americans and discouraging the Nazis and Fascists as much as possible.

In Sicily and Italy, the ports were mob controlled. Mussolini was a powerful leader but he'd never done the Mafia any favors. In the 1920s he appointed a sick-o bully named Cesare Mori to put down the Mafia by systemically humiliating Mafia families.

Mobsters could be counted on to be anti-Fascist. A coordinated effort by the allies and New York's top hoods could create a tender spot, creating what Winston Churchill would call the "soft underbelly," where the invasion could establish a beachhead. The Pentagon called the mob/army partnership *Operation Underworld*.

Luciano was eager to be to World War II what Sgt. York had been to World War I, the number-one hero. He sat in a prison cell and dreamed of parachuting behind enemy lines, of using his contacts with organized crime over there to skew the battlefield for the Allies. He was happy to find that the Army took his ideas very seriously, and soon enough he was briefing the heads of counter-intelligence.

"You guys should invade at *Golfo di Castellammare*," Luciano said. "It's a favorite Mafia drug-smuggling spot."

The Army's policy regarding mobsters remained unwritten, but they clearly thought the strategic benefits offered by men of organized crime far outweighed the unsavory nature of their backgrounds.

Luciano gave them the names of guys who knew Sicilian geography like the backs of their hands. He said, "If you run into any Sicilians who won't go along, tell them Lucky Luciano won't be pleased to hear they were not helpful."

So much goodwill was established between the Italians and the Italian-Americans that weapons were smuggled to mobsters in Italy and used to attack important Axis railroads and bridges.

There was a big strategy room, with a map of Sicily and southernmost Italy, with specific characteristics marked, all intelligence gathered from the men of organized crime, all used to the advantage of the Allies as they executed the Allied invasion of Sicily during the summer of 1943. During the Sicilian and Italian campaigns, the U.S. seemed to be fighting downhill, and G.I.'s learned that the magic words were "Lucky Luciano." Say it and doors opened.

Anastasia was stationed at Indian Town Gap Military Reservation in Indian Gap, Pennsylvania. The Army gave Albert a job befitting his age and experience. They needed longshoremen, there were military cargo ships out there that had to be loaded and unloaded, a process that Albert understood all too well. So the army created a longshoreman school at Indiantown Gap, Pennsylvania—called just The Gap by the locals—and made Albert the teacher.

"Here's how you throw the hook," he'd say. Guys from middle America marveled at his accent: *"Trow da hook."*

You might think that longshoreman school would be at a fort that was on a body of water, since the shore is in the name and everything. But Indiantown Gap was between Reading and Harrisburg, just north of Hershey, in the center of Pennsylvania. Land locked for hundreds of miles. So the boats were simulated. The loading and unloading was real.

Now that he was part of the war effort, Albert took advantage of lenient rules regarding soldiers to rejuvenate his efforts to become a U.S. citizen. On December 30, 1942, a rule was passed that servicemen could become naturalized citizens by filing a Preliminary Form for Petition for Naturalization.

After asking for permission from his commanding officer, Albert did just that on March 18, 1943. He filled out a ten-page questionnaire, which included a "Personal History Statement." On it he disclosed that he had a police record.

His C.O. OK'd the application, which was sent to the Chief Examiner of the Immigration and Naturalization Service in Philadelphia for approval. Albert's application got special attention. Apparently his reputation preceded him.

A query was sent to the Immigration and Naturalization Service (INS) at the Port of New York and a crew list was found for the ship upon which Albert had arrived in America. At that time, it was discovered that Albert had been a deserting Italian sailor and that there was no record of "admission for permanent residence."

In April, Albert was issued a Certificate of Arrival, and his INS Chief Examiner, a fellow named George C. Reich, located the file regarding Albert's 1930s naturalization proceedings that had been abandoned. He also acquired from the NYPD a copy of Albert's arrest record, which might've been written on a scroll.

On June 29, 1943, Reich traveled to The Gap, to interview Anastasia in person. It turned out to be an important point that Reich knew that Albert had deserted, had a police record, and that he had at one time lied about that record. Yet he nonetheless approved Anastasia's application.

* * *

Boss Vincent Mangano still didn't get his hands dirty, but he did try to help the Allied effort. He had an import-export business and used that capacity to become the Army's number-one liaison between the American and Italian Mafias.

In the meantime, Luciano was deported, transported from his prison cell to a small cage on Ellis Island. From there he was put onto the freighter *Laura Keene*. Albert was allowed to travel east from Pennsylvania to attend Lucky's farewell banquet on board, and there they enjoyed a feast with the upper echelon of organized crime while Immigration cops stood by armed to the teeth. On the other side of the pond Luciano was greeted at the pier by agents with the U.S. Office of Naval Intelligence and wasn't heard from again until after the war. His dreams of going behind enemy lines came true.

Deportation was a happy ending of sorts for Luciano, but Anastasia wanted to remain stateside. He remembered nothing of his homeland that would make him want to return. Albert thought his worries of being deported went away on June 29, 1943, when the Common Pleas Court of Lebanon County, Pennsylvania, entered an order admitting Albert to citizenship, i.e., he was naturalized as a U.S. citizen. He was officially an American.

While some mobsters were helping win the war, Lepke Buchalter was awaiting execution. In the same fix were Louis Capone and Mendy Weiss. There were the usual delays—six of them. One of the cruelest features of the Sing Sing death house was that, when another prisoner was fried the lights dimmed and flickered in the cells. Even the toughest hoods winced at the sight of the flickering light.

In March 1944, the men, the former backbone of Murder Inc., started their final countdown. They began to receive visitors, folks coming to say good-bye. Lepke was visited by his wife Betty and twenty-year-old son Harold. Capone had a long talk about eternity with Father Bernard Martin.

Capone hadn't been feeling well—a bad heart, a doctor said—a health issue that went untreated because, well, why? He spent most of his last days flat on his back, did not participate in prison exercises, and hadn't ventured outdoors in a long time.

Lepke had one visitor that got reporters covering the death house excited. He was Frank S. Hogan, the New York County District Attorney, and his arrival led to speculation that Lepke was finally going to name names, names like Albert Anastasia. But the D.A. left disappointed. Lepke claimed in his last hours that the government had offered him a deal, his life for the names of the bosses. He told them his secrets were going with him to the grave.

Several of the delays had come at the last second, and the trio had had their share of last meals. On March 4, 1944, the reprieves and delays ran out.

A reporter asked Lepke's wife how he was holding up. "He is fine," she said. "When a man is innocent, he doesn't go to pieces."

That night, around eleven o'clock, the three men took the long walk. Lepke was last to go, pronounced dead and still smoldering at 11:16 P.M. Capone and Lepke were stoic, tight-lipped, and silent. Lepke glanced briefly at the gallery of thirty-four spectators when he entered, sat in the chair without assistance, and kept his eye on every movement as he was strapped in—right up until the moment they pulled the hood over his head. Mendy was a mess. Chewing gum, accompanied by Rabbi Jacob Katz, he entered screaming, "I'm innocent. This was framed up! I'm innocent and Governor Dewey knows it! The only reason I am going is because I am a Jew. I've been framed because I'm a Jew!" And then exhausted, "Give my love to my family and everybody else. I am innocent."

Each hood got four jolts of juice, after which Dr. Charles Sweet opened their shirts, listened with a stethoscope and said, "This man is dead." Capone, it was said, was the 500th person to be executed in Sing Sing's electric chair. Quite an honor.

One by one the stiffs were gurneyed off to an anteroom where autopsies were done right away while the meat was still warm.

Many miles away, in Indiantown Gap, Pennsylvania, Technical

Sergeant Albert Anastasia raised his glass in a toast to his friends who had passed on.

Mendy and Lepke were buried within fifteen minutes of each other on March 5, both in Mount Hebron Cemetery in Flushing, Queens. Lepke was buried on the western edge of the cemetery, Weiss a few hundred yards to the east. Two days later, Louis Capone was eulogized at Our Lady of Solace Church in Coney Island and buried in Holy Cross Cemetery in East Flatbush.

Lepke still holds the U.S. record, richest man to get the chair.

On November 22, 1944, after twenty-eight months in the service, Technical Sergeant Albert Anastasia was honorably discharged as over age. The event made the newspapers a couple of weeks later. The killer Albert Anastasia was returning to the streets.

In the years following World War II, there was a lot of press to the effect of, if everyone knew Albert Anastasia was the boss and a killer, how come Anastasia was still wandering around? Nobody had an answer.

Murder Inc. was a thing of the past, but Albert, through brother Tony, maintained control of the waterfront, was raking in the dough, and kept himself away from the fray. He needed a fortress that could provide him comfort and keep him and his family safe, so he set about making one. In Fort Lee he built his dream house, a white stucco Italianate-styled mansion on 1.3 acres of landscaped and manicured lawn at the end of a long, gated drive off of Bluff Road amidst a park-like setting. The location was at the brink of the Jersey Palisades near the George Washington Bridge on the other side of the Hudson from Manhattan. The place had the paranoia of a great military fortress. There was a ten-foot fence around it, and two killer Doberman pinscher dogs roamed the grounds with a foamy snarl.

At the same time, Albert shored up his cover as a legitimate businessman by purchasing a piece of a dressmaking factory in Hazleton, Pennsylvania, a town about sixty miles from the fort where he had been stationed in the army. Albert put his old heavy-lifter, Jack "The Dandy" Parisi, in charge of things in Hazleton and holed up with his wife and kids in Fort Lee.

Albert looked at the big picture. What was the number-one obstacle between him and his dreams? Easy answer. Vincent Mangano. With the manicured fingernails. He had to go.

TWENTY-ONE
Death of the Mangano Brothers

To tell this part of the story I've got to jump ahead a little bit. When I was about sixteen in 1972, I was hanging out at home with my best friend Anthony Goombadiel. We were making ourselves a couple of quick cocktails off of my mom and dad's rolling bar before we drove to the daily number pickups in the all-black East New York section of Brooklyn.

The joints we were to visit that day were funky but friendly. The brothers loved Joey Gallo because he sided with them in prison and they continued to give us their business. Crazy Joey was a real tough guy, fearless and smart, our boss, and he'd just been murdered in front of his family because he was his own man.

We were still in shock.

"Joey was one of the all-time greats," I said—and so we poured more Dewar's on our ice, toasted to Joey, and talked about the greats: Capone, yes. Luciano, of course. And Anastasia.

Goombadiel said, "His mug should be chiseled in rock on the Mount Rushmore of this Life."

"Where is that mountain?" I asked.

"Canarsie," Goombadiel said. We laughed and drank some more.

"Uncle Joe told me a story . . ." I said.

In the story, Uncle Joe was drinking in a bar called Hanley's on Court Street and Third Place in Red Hook, 153 years old. Anastasia had his own stool in there. Sat in the same place every time he came in.

One day Albert came in and went into a rage because someone was sitting on his stool. The owner of the place, who was tending bar, tried to diffuse the situation: "Albert, how can you be sure that's your stool?"

Anastasia gave him an elaborate, "Huh?"

"You know I move them around when I clean up in the morning, right?"

"I know my stool when I see it," Albert said and shot the bartender a look.

My uncle said he'd never forget it. They say, "If looks could kill."

The bartender almost pissed his pants. Albert had always been nice to him, but things were never the same after that.

While Goombadiel and I were sipping our drinks, my uncle Joe Schipani came over to pick up my dad Rick.

Uncle Joe, who was called "Joe Shep" on the street, was a made man in the Genovese family. He was born in Manhattan, a juvenile delinquent on the Lower East Side. When he was eighteen, he moved to Church Avenue just off of Flatbush and later he lived on Ocean Parkway in Coney Island.

He started out as a petty thief and a stick-up man. He was arrested for the first time at the age of twenty (with two other guys) in April 1932 for holding up eleven men and three women in an apartment on South Third Street in Williamsburg. They got away with about $160 in cash and were arrested within minutes of leaving.

Uncle Joe went away for a while after that, but while he was inside, he did some quality networking, and by the time he got out he was on the good side of some big boys. One of them was Albert Anastasia.

He knew them all. Not just Anastasia, but Joe Adonis, Lucky Luciano, Frank Costello, Vito Genovese. Uncle Joe started out as a driver for those guys, going out on scores, making getaways.

Joe said he liked driving but he was more of a people person, so they let him be in on making the scores. That was when he got the nickname "Gentleman Joe" because he would kiss the women's hands and never take their wedding rings.

Although not stealing wedding rings was probably a smart bet all around. They could be melted down for their gold if you had enough of them, but you couldn't get anybody to fence them. They were usually engraved with mushy bullshit and nobody but the most desperate bride would want one used.

Uncle Joe got turned over to Joe Adonis and put in charge of running the gambling and shylocking out of Joe's Italian Kitchen in Brooklyn. After Lucky Luciano got his prostitution sentence commuted and was deported to Italy my Uncle Joe starting running with Frank Costello. Luciano at one point left Italy and went to Cuba, via Argentina, where he worked with, among others, Santo Trafficante, to turn Havana, Cuba, into a gambler's paradise, a project later realized in full in Las Vegas, but destined for failure in Cuba on account of Fidel Castro who didn't want mobsters or reptilian American tourists in his country. Anyway, Uncle Joe went to Havana with Adonis and met Lucky in person. By 1940, he was listing his address as on President Street between Fifth and Sixth avenues in Park Slope. That's the other end of the street from where the Gallo crew hung out. In March of that year he was busted again, for shaking down bookmakers who were taking bets on someone else's turf, which was South Brooklyn. Also arrested in that incident were his younger brother John (who gave the same address) and Alfred Attaniese who lived on First Street, all Red Hook. Since hassling guys over taking illegal bets wasn't on the statutes, the men were charged with vagrancy. A detective named John McMahon found them in a car parked in front of 1 Hamilton Avenue. According to the police report, the men "couldn't give a good account of themselves and either couldn't or wouldn't disclose a means of support."

Most of the time, Uncle Joe got away with whatever he was doing, and we knew that he didn't need to exaggerate. In 1946 and into the 1950s, he did a ton of work with Genovese captain Frank Galluccio, a big Brooklyn bookmaker.

Uncle Joe went over to the Genovese crime family where he was bumped up to capo. That was when he started to make his move in the unions. He was Costello's right-hand man for years and dealt with the labor unions.

He became a union negotiator. Every contract went through Joe. The feds said in a report years ago that Joe Shep was one of the most powerful hoods in labor in New York. He was also in control of private carting—that is, the garbage association in the five boroughs.

No one's private garbage got picked up without paying a fee, and the fee was whatever Uncle Joe said it was going to be. If you didn't pay the fee, your garbage didn't get picked up.

Uncle Joe got involved in the restaurant biz. He had a piece of the great Italian joint called Casa Bianca. It was on Fourth Avenue and 100th Street right near Fort Hamilton and the Brooklyn side of the Verrazano-Narrows Bridge. He also had a piece of Gurney's Inn out in Montauk, at the very easternmost tip of Long Island. His partner out there was Monte from Carroll Street, owner of Monte's Restaurant. And, last but not least, he was partner with my father Ricky in our bar, the Dis and Dat Lounge, in the Mill Basin section of Brooklyn.

Joe was very close with my dad. They would hang out together at the Gondola Hotel in a restaurant owned by Joe Morola. They played cards once a week, legendary games with some big pots. After cards, they'd go to Sheepshead Bay to the old Randazzo's Restaurant. They'd bring the wives, my mom Dee, and Joe's dear wife Ann who looked like Carol Channing and was a very classy woman. My family loved Joe.

He had been involved in dozens of sit downs with Frank Costello, the Prime Minister of the Underworld, right up until the day Frank died in 1973 at the age of eighty-two.

I had lunch with Uncle Joe and Costello near the end of Costello's life. It was at the time when the Columbos and the Gallos were shooting at each other. Joe set the meeting up on Woodhull

Street, in Red Hook, near where the Battery Tunnel feeds into the Brooklyn-Queens Expressway.

The sit down was designed to figure out how to stop the shooting, but it didn't work out. A few weeks later, Funzi Tieri came with Joe to settle it. Tieri was called "The Old Man" and was boss of the Genovese crime family.

Sadly Tieri is known as the first guy to go down under the RICO Act. Tieri couldn't stop the shooting either, and six months later bullets were still flying all around Red Hook.

He had been there and done that—and some of his stories involved guys who'd later be inducted into the mob hall of fame, guys like Anastasia.

On this day, while Goombadiel and I were in East New York, Uncle Joe and my dad were on their way to President Street for a meeting. The boys were restless. They wanted to break from the Gallos with Joey gone. Uncle Joe was there to calm them down.

Uncle Joe came over and kissed us.

"I just told Goombadiel your story about Anastasia having his own stool," I said.

"You know I was with Albert in the old days with Costello and Lucky," he said.

"We know, Uncle Joe."

"Smart ass kids. You know the history books say Albert ordered the hit on Vincent Mangano, but that's a load of bullshit."

"Who ordered it?" we asked, stunned.

"No, you squirts, Albert killed Vincent Mangano *himself.* His days of doing the dirty work were long past. He could have gotten anyone to do it, could've been miles away, keeping his hands clean. But that wasn't what he wanted. He wanted to do it himself, just so he could see the expression on Vincent's face."

The notion filled Uncle Joe with great joy. He told us that Albert and Vincent could never get along, argued about everything. Albert heard that Vincent was going to have him killed, and so killed Vincent first.

"Albert did the right thing," Uncle Joe said, "he got the okay from

Frank Costello and Lucky Luciano. He had to get word to Lucky in Italy, and Lucky sent back his blessing. Lucky said Mangano was not whacking up to him like the old days.

"Albert set up a meet with Vincent on Columbia Street at a warehouse." The location was on Red Hook's main drag and just around the corner from the Woodhull Street meeting. There was no Battery Tunnel, no BQE, so Red Hook felt less like it had a wall running through it.

Uncle Joe said, "Vincent was to pick up some gambling money that Albert was whacking up to Vincent. 'That's not the only thing getting whacked,' Albert said."

It was April 18, 1951. Uncle Joe said there was no chitchat, no dramatic dialogue. Albert shot Vincent as soon as he walked into the warehouse. Vincent had a smile on his face and his arms outstretched when Albert shot him.

"How come they never found Vincent's body, Uncle Joe?" I asked.

"They didn't even look for him for a long time. They thought he was hiding."

"Where was he?"

"He was taken out to sea, gutted, and fitted with concrete shoes. He looked like the mummy," Uncle Joe said.

Obviously, they never found Vincent Mangano. Not so the body of his brother Philip. At ten o'clock in the morning on April 19, 1951, the day after Anastasia iced Vince, a Brooklyn fishing-boat owner and operator named Mrs. Mary Gooch was on her way to work. Running late, she took a shortcut across the Bergen Beach marshes. She feared going that way. During the spring of 1949 she had the misfortune of discovering a body in those marshes, and on this day her worst nightmare came true. It happened again. Partially hidden in a clump of weeds was the prone body of a man whose trousers and shoes were missing, bare-ass dead.

Mrs. Gooch didn't stick around. She ran the rest of the way to her marina where she called the police. When cops came, they discovered that the man was wearing a huge diamond ring on his pinky and had three holes in him, one in his neck and two in the face, later determined to have been caused by .45 caliber bullets.

The stiff was ID'd as fifty-one-year-old Philip Mangano, a "laundry-owner." His cover, in addition to folding shirts, was that he was the treasurer for a Brooklyn ship-painting company, a place where he'd never reported to work.

It was big news because he was the brother of the boss, but Philip Mangano was well past his prime and had seen his day. He wasn't a fella people thought about much anymore.

Back in the old days, Philip had been an enforcer, and when Vince told him to hurt people he went out and did it. Now, however, he was a man defined mostly by his weaknesses: women and gambling.

Philip liked women with loose morals and tight technique. He liked his gambling parlors exotic, airless, without humor, and frequented those in Lower Manhattan. According to one street snitch, Philip had just come down a staircase lit in only blue light and had been on his way to see his bookie when he was corralled by a couple of guys who led him by the elbows into an impatiently waiting car.

It was a world where getting into trouble was so easy. In addition to his no-show job, he was a card-carrying member of the City Democratic Club, with headquarters in Red Hook. It sounded political but in reality, the place was a hangout for hoods.

He had a record of eight arrests including a murder charge—the murder being that of a Manhattan bootlegger in 1923—which was dismissed. Also on Philip's resume: worked a hitch as Frankie Yale's bodyguard.

In 1940, the *Brooklyn Eagle* published its list of the top hoods in town. Albert Anastasia was three, behind Adonis and Vince Mangano. No surprise there, but Philip Mangano was listed as number seven, the reason—he was Vincent's brother. On that list anyway, he outranked Tough Tony Anastasio.

* * *

In the Bergen Beach weeds, cops took photos of Philip Mangano's body from every possible angle, and then had it carefully wrapped and transported to the Medical Examiner's office for autopsy. When the crime scene investigation was complete, police concluded that Mangano had been dead for about twenty hours, shot elsewhere and dragged by rope to the location where Mrs. Gooch found him. No telling what happened to his pants.

According to the victim's wife, he had been shopping with her in Bay Ridge when he announced that he was going to get a cup of coffee. He walked away, and she never saw him again.

The NYPD Homicide Bureau rounded up some bigwigs, feeling that there had to be power behind the hit, a small-time beef wouldn't be handled this way, Mangano's pedigree was too deep.

Hauled in for questioning were Albert Anastasia, Adonis, Costello, Gaetano Ricci, and Jack Sparacino. All expressed deep sorrow over the disturbing demise of their dear friend.

Top theory on motive was that Mangano was erased to silence him. Later, when it was realized that brother Vince was missing, the theory switched to a coup. Anastasia. He'd gotten rid of Vince to become boss, and got rid of his brother to stifle potential *vendetta*.

That was what people whispered in the shadows. In public they said the Philip Mangano hit was a small-time thing: the missing pants, maybe it was some kind of sex thing. If not sex, personal in some way. A jealous husband, a bill collector, a guy who Mangano was squeezing. Something like that. Nothing *organized*.

Someone put out an order that there were to be no flowers, nothing fancy, nothing to draw attention to Philip's funeral, which came and went like a whisper in the fog. Philip Mangano was buried in Holy Cross Cemetery in East Flatbush.

As for Mrs. Gooch, who had now twice found a stiff while taking the shortcut through the marshes, she decided to take the long way around from then on. And with the Mangano name off the chessboard, Albert Anastasia became a full-fledged and recognized Boss of one of the Five Families.

* * *

But for the Commission this was strike two against Albert. They knew what happened to Mangano, and they called Albert in for a sit down. Albert broke Lucky's rules. It was forbidden to take power by killing the man above you. Lucky made Mangano boss, and it wasn't up to Albert to undo that.

"But Mangano had a contract out on me," Albert said. "Even if I did it, which I didn't, it was kill or be killed. What could I do?"

They believed him, many of them had seen Mangano and Anastasia fight, actually hit each other, so Albert Anastasia lived a while longer. But he couldn't be trusted. You can't trust a guy like that, a guy who will shoot his way to the top.

TWENTY-TWO

The Era of Government Committees

FOR A TIME ANASTASIA ENJOYED the good life. Then the feds went to Hazleton and scooped up former Murder Inc. gunman and current Hazleton dressmaker Jack "The Dandy" Parisi, and told him he was suspected of being the triggerman in the murder of Morris Diamond.

In Hazleton, Parisi dwelled in a luxury apartment. When the D.A.'s office came to pick Dandy up, they found him sleeping in what was called "a hand-carved bed." Very la-dee-dah. In case trouble came to the front door, the apartment had a secret exit into an adjoining house, but Dandy never heard them coming.

They asked him what he did for a living. Frustrated, he said he was a garment company executive: "I'm just a tailor. That's what I was when I was a kid, and that's what I am now. I started with nothing but a needle and a thread and now I run two dressmaking factories. It's the American Dream."

Befitting his nickname, and his real-life skills as a tailor, Parisi looked great in court. He wore a form-fitting suit and large silk tie. The suit was double-breasted and boldly pinstriped—boldly ignoring the courtroom superstition against pinstripes, as they could resemble prison uniforms.

Parisi pleaded not guilty. On the second day of the trial, a juror asked to be excused on account of he was Joseph Rosen's nephew, and Murder Inc. had bumped Rosen off so . . .

Judge Harry Stackell was pissed that this fact didn't come out in voir dire, but let the juror go. It made no difference. The defendant was close with Albert Anastasia, and the prosecution's case fell apart.

The case against Parisi was dependent on the testimony of one witness, a nervous butcher's daughter named Julie. She told the D.A. that she'd seen Parisi shoot Rosen—but when push came to shove, she decided that she really didn't recognize the shooter and her eyesight wasn't that good anyway and never mind.

While on the witness stand, Julie looked to the high and ornate courtroom ceiling as if searching her memory.

"I am recanting my previous statement," she said, apparently by rote.

The defense moved for a dismissal, and Judge Stackell sadly agreed. "I am convinced in my heart that Mr. Parisi is guilty, but I have to dismiss the charges," he said.

From the early 1950s on, the feds started in on Anastasia and never let up. Not that they ever accomplished their goal, which was to send Albert to the chair, but he couldn't relax either. He endured a steady rain of incoming from the feds.

Albert evaded wave after wave of Justice Department investigations. Senate and Congressional committees formed and did their thing. Albert had hoped his stint in the army would wipe the slate clean, but he was sadly mistaken.

During this time, Albert picked up a new nickname: Lord High Executioner. The name was first coined in the late nineteenth century in the lyrics to the song "Behold the Lord High Executioner" from Gilbert and Sullivan's operetta *The Mikado*.

The phrase popped up occasionally during the first decades of the twentieth century in descriptions of vigilantes who appointed themselves "judge, jury and lord high executioner."

The term was first applied to Anastasia by Brooklyn *Daily Eagle* reporter Ed Reid, but became popular when William O'Dwyer used it when speaking before the Senate Crime Investigating Committee.

U.S. Attorney Franklin J. Parker of the Eastern District of New

York issued a press release announcing that he was opening an investigation into Albert Anastasia and his connection with a ship-repair firm called Sancor Corp. that had declared bankruptcy in Brooklyn Federal Court in 1937.

The press release noted that this was the same Albert Anastasia who would no doubt have been convicted of the murder of Morris Diamond had Kid Twist not taken his dive. Another of Sancor's investors, Benedict Macri, another guy who turned himself in at Walter Winchell's suggestion, was on the hook for the May 9, 1949, murder of union organizer William Lurye, of the AFL International Ladies Garment Workers Union.

The press, the government, the public, were all into the numbers game. Everyone knew Albert Anastasia was a killer and had been getting away with murder for three decades, but how many goons had he whacked? What was the *number*?

The answer was hard to come by. If you only counted murders for which he'd been convicted, the answer was one—although the conviction was later overturned. Did you count murders for which he'd been arrested but never convicted? And what if those convictions didn't take place because the witnesses were also murdered? Did you count the guys he'd whacked himself, or the ones he'd ordered, as well? There were years when many gangland-style murders in New York (and elsewhere) were done by Murder Inc. Did you give Anastasia credit for all of them? Then there were the kills they didn't even know about, guys who'd been disappeared, accidented, or suicided. The answer was probably more than a thousand.

Sure, the St. Valentine's Day Massacre and Hollywood movies had put American gangsters a generation earlier on the dreamscape of the nation's collective imagination. And for years, dead hoods *in situ* had made the wood on yellowing tabloids.

But mobsters first truly became super-*duper* stars in 1951 with the Kefauver Committee . . .

Albert Anastasia, a stone-cold killer. Although he did time for gun possession and tax evasion, he was never punished for doing the one thing he did best.
(*Brooklyn Daily Eagle* photograph—Brooklyn Public Library—Brooklyn Collection)

Here's something you didn't frequently see: Albert Anastasia and an NYC cop sharing a laugh. Maybe they were talking about a broad. Anastasia was not known as a cheerful guy. Usually he only smiled when inserting an ice pick under some goon's occipital bump. (*Brooklyn Daily Eagle* photograph—Brooklyn Public Library—Brooklyn Collection)

7 ★★★★★★★ Complete

BROOKLYN EAGLE

5 CENTS EVERYWHERE

ANASTASIA DEFIES QUIZ

Expert Awaits Trial in March
Free in $2,000 Bail, For East

IKE NOMINATES

COULDN'T KEEP RECORDS, ILA OFFICER SAYS

Hoodlum Clams Up At Crime Hearing —Snaps at Probers

Albert Anastasia, triggerman of Murder, Inc., and top boss of the waterfront underworld, defied the State Crime Commission today and refused to discuss his finances or murders he is alleged to have committed. He refused to give his occupation between 1919 and 1942. He refused to list the occupations of four brothers, and grew angry when asked about a fifth brother.

On December 19, 1952, Albert Anastasia was called before the State Crime Commission and refused to discuss the murders he was supposed to have committed, refused to give his occupation between 1919 and 1942, and refused to give any information about his brothers. His defiance earned huge headlines. (*Brooklyn Daily Eagle* photograph —Brooklyn Public Library—Brooklyn Collection)

At 9:15 a.m. on April 28, 1923, Anastasia was driving bootlegger Biago Giordano west on Sackett Street, approaching the corner of Sackett and Henry, when two men, with a rifle and a shotgun, fired a fusillade through open windows of this house on Sackett Street. Albert's left side and stomach were peppered with buckshot, while Giordano took a slug to the chest and died. (Author photo)

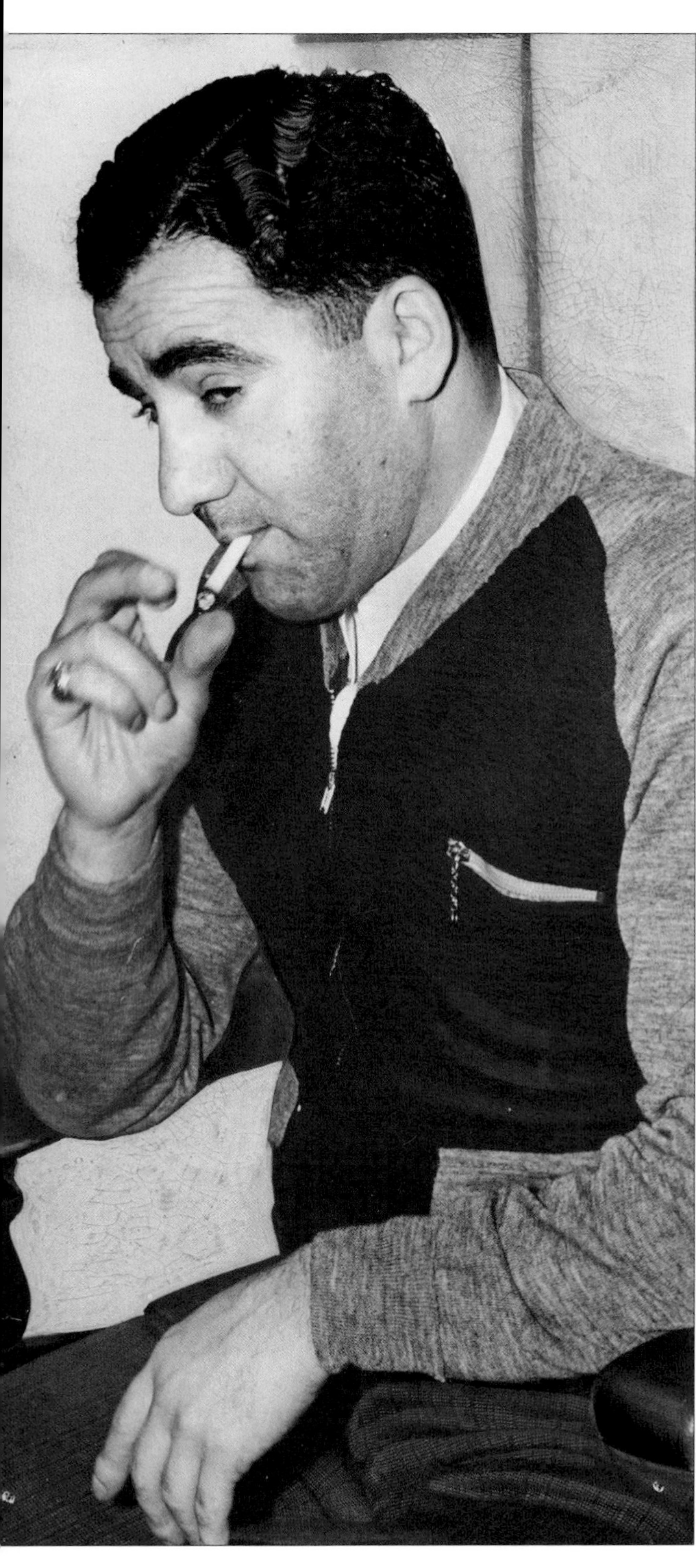

Abe "Kid Twist" Reles liked to twist a guy's neck until he was dead and was one of Albert Anastasia's top pro killers in Murder Inc. He then turned government witness, put a few hoods in the chair, but dramatically died before he had a chance to testify against the Mad Hatter. (*Brooklyn Daily Eagle* photograph—Brooklyn Public Library—Brooklyn Collection)

On November 12, 1941, the eve of his scheduled testimony against Anastasia, Twist was under heavy protection, with six NYPD detectives guarding him, holed up in the Half Moon Hotel. In other words, right up against the boardwalk and the Atlantic Ocean in Coney Island. None of that protection did any good, as Twist "fell" out the hotel window and plummeted sixty feet to his death. (*Brooklyn Daily Eagle* photograph—Brooklyn Public Library—Brooklyn Collection)

Gerardo "Bang Bang" Anastasia leaves court after being granted his citizenship, despite the fact that his sponsors were bookies. "This is one of the happiest days of my life," he told the reporter from the Brooklyn Eagle. "I'm happy to be an American citizen." (*Brooklyn Daily Eagle* photograph—Brooklyn Public Library—Brooklyn Collection)

Louis Capone was part owner of the Oriental Danceland Restaurant on Stillwell Avene in Coney Island. During the summer of 1939, when Lepke was hiding out, he stayed in an apartment here, now called Riviera Catering. It's also where I got married in 1979! (Author photo)

On March 8, 1952, Arnold Schuster left his home on 45th Street in the Borough Park section of Brooklyn and was promptly whacked by Anastasia's gunmen. The reason? He fingered Willie Sutton, a hood who had nothing to do with Anastasia. "I don't like squealers," Anastasia said. The hit pissed off the commission, who disapproved of icing guys for personal reasons. (Author photo)

For syndicate guys, a kiss from former Miss America contestant Janice Drake was like the kiss of death. She made a habit of getting next to hoods just before they were chilled. (*Brooklyn Daily Eagle* photograph—Brooklyn Public Library—Brooklyn Collection)

Louis "Lepke" Buchalter was betrayed by his "pal" Albert Anastasia and ended up sizzling in Ol' Sparky. He and his Murder Inc. brother, Mendy Weiss, died within fifteen minutes of ach another in the Sing Sing electric chair and were buried within hours of each another only a few hundred yards apart in Mount Hebron Cemetery in Flushing, Queens. (Author photos)

Gurney's Inn, out in Montauk, for New Year's, 1980. That's my uncle Joe Schipiani, aka Joe Shep, front and center. He was in a crew with Anastasia and saw some things in perso that the rest of the world only got to imagine. My dad, Rick Dimatteo, is at the top left, my uncle Chubby is top middle, and I'm at the top right with my porno mustache. In the middle row, left to right, are Uncle Joe's wife, Ann, my mom, Dee, and my wife, Emily The lady next to Uncle Joe is Chubby's wife, Teresa. (Author photo)

Tough Tony Anastasio and Louis Capone managed to be buried in consecrated ground, Holy Cross Cemetery in East Flatbush, Brooklyn, but only by being dumped into an already crowded plot with their in-laws. In order to locate their final resting places, you have to read the small print. (Author photos)

Charles "Lucky" Luciano was, more than anyone else, responsible for Albert Anastasia's rise to the top of the mob world. He was Albert's champion and defender. Lucky's final resting place, in St. John's Cemetery, Middle Village, Queens, is no smaller than the average Manhattan apartment. (Author photo)

Grasso's Barber Shop, where Albert Anastasia was brutally murdered, is now a Starbucks. Hipsters and tourists can grab a Venti White Chocolate Mocha with an extra shot and whip just inches away from the once-upon-a-time position of chair number four, where Albert Anastasia was whacked more than sixty years ago. (Author photo)

Catholic cemeteries refused to take Albert's body, so he had to be buried in Green-Wood Cemetery, very close to Fifth Avenue in Brooklyn, in a modest section, far from the huge monuments and statues that the cemetery is known for. (Author photo)

Senator Estes Kefauver of Tennessee saw mob-busting as a way to accrue power. Kefauver spoke up about subjects previously kept hush-hush. What he did was launch a craze, like the Hula Hoop and The Twist to follow—TV's first reality show, and gangsters took top billing day after day.

Authorities were good at never asking questions they couldn't answer. (For example, up until the death of J. Edgar Hoover, it was the official stance of the FBI that the American Mafia didn't exist.) Kefauver not only talked about the mob out loud, he shouted it out.

He told America that organized crime had infiltrated every city in the country, and that they had their hands in every business. He talked about the violence of mobsters, who lent money to degenerate gamblers and broke their arms if they didn't pay back on time. He called the mob a "supergovernment."

Kefauver's committee, the Senate Crime Investigating Committee, made like Sinatra singing to bobbysoxers and went on a fourteen-city tour. More than eight-hundred witnesses were interviewed. Kansas City, America learned, was operated under the "law of the jungle." In Chicago, the cops were bought and paid for.

It was during the Kefauver hearings that Americans first became acquainted with the phrase "Taking the Fifth," an abbreviation that became necessary because "I impose my Fifth Amendment rights and refuse to answer on the grounds that it might tend to incriminate me" was quite a mouthful for some hoods.

Windy City thug Jake Guzik told the committee that he wasn't answering because he "don't want to be discriminated." Frank Erickson said he wasn't answering because his answers might "criminate him." So "I take the Fifth" it was. Just about everyone could say that—and most of them did.

TV cameras followed.

When Frank Costello testified, his lawyer demanded that the TV cameras not show his client's face, so thirty million Americans watched hypnotized for hours at a close up of Costello's nervous hands as he tried with varying success to adequately answer the committee's questions. Ratings were better than those of that year's World Series. Kids were let out of school to watch the hearings, to get an education they couldn't get in a classroom.

Bugsy Siegel's girlfriend Virginia Hill took the stand in a mink coat and chatted about the "fellas" she knew, generous guys who showered her with gifts, guys who knew who was going to win the horse race before the gates opened. On her way out of the room, Miss Hill was inundated by eager-beaver boys from the press—and one woman, Marjorie Farnworth from the *New York Journal-American*. Farnworth asked a question Hill didn't like and Virginia smacked her in the face right there in the elevator. She then spit at the men, wishing aloud that an "atom bomb" would fall on all their heads.

"Nice mouth, lady."

"Fuck you. Go fuck yourself."

A couple of guys wrote down the quote. Outside, Virginia was hurried into a taxi and sped away.

During his testimony, Joe Adonis was asked, "Who killed Philip Mangano?"

"That could not have been a gangland murder," Adonis said, as if stating a simple truth. "The guy was found with no pants. Looks to me like a simple crime of passion."

Adonis turned out to be Kefauver's biggest victim. He ended up being indicted on gambling charges. He skipped bail, hopped a ship, and spent the rest of his life in Italy.

And, of course, the Kefauver tour came to New York. Some guys took a powder in advance of the government invasion. They said they were on Holy Pilgrimages to the Vatican, trips during which they might just drop in and pay their respects to the exiled Lucky Luciano. But two guys stayed: Willie Moretti and Albert Anastasia.

Moretti took a page out of J. Edgar Hoover's book and testified, "You guys should be after communists, not bookmakers. They're the real criminals, not us."

* * *

In 1951 Albert Anastasia was called to the Kefauver stand and swore to tell the truth, the whole truth, and nothing but the truth. His lawyer demanded TV cameras be turned off, and they were.

Republican senator from New Hampshire, Charles W. Tobey asked the questions: "How do you make a living, Mr. Anastasia?"

"I own part of a dress manufacturing business."

"Make dresses?"

"That's right."

"Where abouts?"

"Hazleton, Pennsylvania."

"Do you know a Benedict Macri?" Tobey asked.

"Sure."

"You own a mansion in the Palisades section of Fort Lee, New Jersey, is that correct?"

"It's a nice place."

"How many rooms?"

"Thirty-four."

"Baths?"

"Five."

"Did Benedict Macri ever supply you with workmen or supplies for the construction of that home?"

Of course, the answer was yes. Albert even hired Benedict's brother Vincent as his personal bodyguard. Vincent lived in that expensive house with Albert and his family so he would always be available in case Albert needed something done. But that's not what Albert said. What he said was: "I refuse to answer on the grounds that my answer might tend to incriminate me."

The crime Anastasia was worried about was vague—but hindsight tells us that the government had tax evasion on its mind. But at that moment, Anastasia was not allowed to take government contracts because, ever since he went to Blackwell for gun possession, he was a convicted felon. And yet he was working with Macri to the tune of $100,000 worth of work on his house. Plus, Macri was the treasurer of Sancor Corporation, a ship-repair firm, which was created following a major investment by Anastasia and in turn took contracts from the United States Maritime Commission.

Word was that when Sancor folded, declaring bankruptcy, it owed the government a half million dollars, and the reason for going belly up was that Anastasia bled it to death.

"What was the name of your contractor on the building of your house?"

Anastasia consulted briefly with his counsel, James A. Major of Hackensack, and took the Fifth.

The questioning turned to whether or not Anastasia had committed many murders, and again he refused to answer. Kefauver later said that the questioning on the subject of murder went on for some time, but never once did Anastasia seem indignant. He just repeated his rights again and again, as cool as Jamaica Bay in February, the same chilliness Albert exhibited when inserting the icepick.

Frustrated, Kefauver said he was considering bringing contempt charges against Anastasia. Albert shrugged. James Major told his client not to sweat it. Kefauver couldn't just do it. It was a complicated process. He would have to propose the charges, which would then be voted on by the full committee, and then by the entire Senate.

Anastasia admitted during questioning that he was "friends" with Joe Adonis, Willie Moretti, Vito Genovese, and Augie Pisano—guys the government referred to as "important thugs."

During the questioning, Anastasia's brain was humming. *Benedict Macri is a rat—and a dead man.*

The FBI distributed a memo that said Albert was using the piers of Brooklyn to smuggle heroin into the country. That kind of rumor made no one happy. At the time it was forbidden by the Commission to smuggle the *babonia,* but the practice was allowed with only mild disapproval if the junk was distributed in black neighborhoods.

In the meantime, Anastasia was slated for a return appearance before Kefauver. He spent several days playing solitaire in a committee witness room, waiting for his turn, but when that turn came, Anastasia complained of extreme discomfort from inflamed eyes.

He was sent to St. Mary's Hospital in Passaic, New Jersey, suffering from "running conjunctivitis," the highly contagious pink eye. He was given a raincheck and told to return next week to testify in public.

In Albert's stead, the committee recalled Frank Costello to the stand. Mr. Hands was back. They grilled him about reports that he'd made political statements, supporting Italian-American candidates because they might be sympathetic with the plight of Italian-American people.

He said yeah, so what?

They grilled him about his legitimate businesses. They told him they had evidence that he had a lot of money, a hundred grand in a strong box, six-figure bank account. They wanted to know where his money was and where it came from.

Costello said, "I might have more money, but I couldn't tell you where." He pretended he was a guy who knew nothing about business. Sure, he had a part of four businesses—an infra-red broiler company, an oil field, a realty concern, and the Beverly Club, a gambling joint in suburban New Orleans—but he didn't know how big of a part or how much those companies made.

After intense questioning, Mr. Hands let slip on TV that his realty concern was just a dummy corporation. He admitted that he didn't know what an infra-red broiler was.

"I understand it's very practical for the home, everyone should have one," he said, taking advantage of the fact that he was on TV to get a commercial in.

He didn't know where his oil wells were either. He'd gone in on a deal involving oil fields with a friend's wife. That was all he knew. They asked him if he owned any land. He said no. Asked if his wife owned any land, he said yeah, but nothing exciting, just some empty lots down in Florida.

While Albert was waiting to be re-scheduled, he returned home with his prescription eyedrops, where New Jersey authorities questioned him.

"What do you guys want?"

Assistant District Attorney Louis Andreozzi said he had a few questions regarding the Philip Mangano case.

"He got whacked by a hooker or a pimp or something, that's all I know."

"He was a friend of yours?"

"An acquaintance. I knew him when he lived and operated in Brooklyn," Albert said.

"Know him well?"

"No."

"When was the last time you saw him?"

"Many years ago."

And that was that. If Andreozzi was aware that he was asking about the wrong Mangano brother, he didn't let on.

During the Kefauver hearings, an Associated Press reporter named Saul Pett went to Fort Lee to talk to Albert in person and get his take on what was going on. Pett talked to Albert's teenage son, and was told to take a hike. The reporter did manage to leave his name and number and soon thereafter Albert called him and granted him a phone interview. There were some points, as it turned out, that Albert was eager to get off his chest.

"O'Dwyer never had a perfect case against me," Albert said. "If he had, he would have indicted me in fifteen minutes. He never even brought me in for questioning."

Pett didn't interrupt but later pointed out in print that this was mostly because Albert was in hiding.

"I'm not scared of any new witnesses they might get," Albert continued. "They just picked on me in the first place because I made good reading. They had to wipe their filthy knife on somebody's shoulder and they picked mine."

Pett asked why he'd been arrested so many times.

"It all started in 1921. In those days the cops used to put a letter after a guy's name. P for panhandling. M for murder. I got the M.

From then on, they had me branded, even though I was never really convicted of murder. The one conviction was reversed by the Court of Appeals. You know who was on that court? Benjamin Cardozo." Of Supreme Court fame. "Now, you don't think I had him in my pocket, do you?"

Estes Kefauver described Anastasia as one of the "Big Six" gangsters in the national crime syndicate. He asked aloud why the guy wasn't in prison? Senator Tobey was outraged, as well, and asked why the justice system was so lame and mealy-mouthed regarding anything Anastasia.

Speaking of mealy-mouthed . . . on March 14, 1951, Frank C. Bals was called to the Kefauver stand. Bals was a former police captain, former NYPD deputy police commissioner, a close friend of William O'Dwyer. He was also the guy in charge of the disgraced Kid Twist security detail. And did I mention, his name was Frank Bals?

"Will Frank Bals please come to the stand?" a bailiff called out. There was a stifled giggle in the gallery, which earned from the judge a steely glare.

"Do you promise to tell the truth the whole truth and nothing but the truth, so help you God?"

"I do."

"State your name."

"Frank Bals."

A full-blown laugh came from the back, and the judge pounded his gavel.

"Mr. Bals," Tobey said, "if you had a witness with murder evidence against him, why was there never a prosecution of Albert Anastasia?"

"I don't know," Bals said. "We did everything to apprehend him, but we just didn't apprehend him."

"Have you ever heard that William O'Dwyer, as the District Attorney, said, 'We have a perfect case against Anastasia'?"

"Yes, I've heard that."

"Then why was Anastasia allowed to go unprosecuted?"

"I have no opinion on that. I am not an attorney."

"Did you continue to follow up on the matter?"

Bals didn't answer verbally. He merely shrugged.

"Did you try the draft board, check to see if maybe Anastasia was in the army?"

"The draft board would be the last place I would look for him," Bals testified.

Tobey was now visibly steamed. "The whole thing is a tawdry mess," Tobey snapped. "Did you want to find him or didn't you? Who told you not to find him?"

"Personally, I wanted to find him. Nobody told me not to find him. I just didn't have the opportunity."

"Why wasn't the Anastasia case pursued?"

"I would say, as far as I'm concerned, there wasn't very much done about it."

"Did you know that a 'wanted card' for Anastasia had been removed from the police files?"

"Yes, I heard about that. I don't think the whole story has been told."

"Do you have a theory as to the circumstances surrounding the death of Abe Reles?"

"I think he was just trying to kid around and he fell," Bals opined.

"Kid around?" Senator Tobey spat angrily.

"Yeah, his captors were staying right below him. I think he wanted to pop in on them by surprise."

Tobey set about now to air Bals' own dirty laundry. There were certainly some numbers that didn't add up. Bals had made $1,000 a year as a police captain and had retired with a pension of $2,700 a year. He had come out of retirement at the request of Mayor O'Dwyer to be a deputy commissioner with a salary of $5,800 and had retired a second time with a pension of $6,000.

Asked to explain those numbers, Bals shrugged again and said, "It's the law."

"It looks to me like special privilege to the nth degree," Tobey replied.

During his time as Deputy Commissioner, Bals had headed a twelve-man "Police Confidential" squad, which operated for eleven months before being abolished.

"There is a record of the squad's operations?" Tobey asked.

"Yes. There are plenty of records left behind. They're in department files."

"Special committee counsel James Walsh has disclosed that those records are no longer there and cannot be found."

Again Bals shrugged.

"Well, would you say they were stolen?"

"I wouldn't venture a guess on that, Senator."

Tobey had done a pretty good job of grilling Bals, but there was one matter in which he didn't press the ex-cop. Many thought Bals should've asked why, if a gangster by the name of Allie Tannenbaum was "just as good" of a witness as Abe Reles, why had Tic Toc never been called as a witness?

O'Dwyer himself later testified before the committee. He told it that Albert headed the mob's "secret police" and "liquidation squad." He said he'd had the perfect case against Albert Anastasia—perfect, that is, until Abe Reles dove. Again, Tic Toc's name didn't come up.

The committee was at war with the whole Anastasia clan. All four brothers were being hassled. Tough Tony, boss of the stevedores, said, "To be an Anastasio is like an empty barrel. Everyone wants to put their garbage in it."

In March 1951, Gerardo "Bang Bang" Anastasia, of Woodhull Street in Red Hook, then thirty-eight years old, was applying for U.S. citizenship, and the headlines being created by Kefauver and brother Albert were not helping. Gerardo had taken the oath of citizenship on March 20, but his status didn't become official until he had his application signed by a federal judge.

On Thursday, March 22, Federal Judge Albert Inch postponed signing Gerardo's application. Gerardo wasn't the big-time crook that his brothers were, true—but he wasn't a priest either, like his other brother. He'd been convicted three times for bookmaking.

He was scheduled to testify before the Kefauver committee, and the judge thought it wise to see how that went before granting Gerardo a bunch of rights.

The technical reason for the delay did not include Kefauver. Judge Inch put off the hearing because Gerardo's application itself was being scrutinized. Bang Bang's sponsors—Angelo Lonardo of Sackett Street and Rosario Purpurra of East Flatbush—were under investigation by the feds. Both sponsors listed their occupation as Red Hook longshoremen. Judge Inch's delay came after argument by U.S. Attorney Frank J. Parker, who said he'd recently had a case where an applicant's sponsors claimed to be legit but weren't.

"Your honor, they claimed to be in real estate, but they were actually engaging in illegal activities," Parker said.

"Who was the applicant?" the judge inquired.

"Frank Costello, your honor."

Judge Inch set down his pen. Gerardo Anastasia would have to wait.

Gerardo's sponsors were investigated and it was discovered that both had failed to report that they had arrest records, an unspectacular list of various misdemeanor charges. One was a gambler, and the other had once had a "meretricious relationship" with a woman, which means he got caught with a hooker.

Gerardo's mouthpiece, Ralph L. Negri, with offices conveniently located on Court Street, did a nice job of disassociating Bang Bang from his notorious brothers, stating that Gerardo and his brother Albert, for example, only saw one another a couple of times a year. Thanksgiving and Christmas, maybe. Gerardo saw his brother Tough Tony more frequently, the lawyer admitted, but only in the line of work as they both worked the docks, so there was no avoiding one another.

The court recognized the fact that a deportation order for Gerardo was cancelled on January 11, 1946 because his was determined to be a hardship case. Bang Bang was married to an American woman with three kids at the time. His wife, however, died in 1949, and he now lived with his children and mother-in-law in a modest home in Red Hook.

Gerardo directly addressed Judge Inch at one point, "Your honor, I knew nothing about the record of my witnesses [sponsors]. I work with them and consider them friends. I didn't know they'd gotten into trouble."

On April 24, 1951, Judge Inch ruled that Bang Bang's pros outweighed his cons and made Gerardo a U.S. citizen. The skimpy criminal record of Bang Bang's sponsors was disregarded.

The decision was made despite the fact that Gerardo had entered the U.S. illegally, but largely based on the fact that he'd had a clean legal record for the previous three years. Leaving the courtroom, Bang Bang was all smiles.

"This is one of the happiest days of my life," he told a reporter from the *Brooklyn Eagle*. "I'm happy to be an American citizen."

In April 1951, the ten-year-old Kid Twist cold case heated up, as District Attorney Miles F. McDonald told the *Brooklyn Eagle* that a Kings County Grand Jury was going to hear evidence in the case, and thirty witnesses were scheduled. McDonald pointed out that Twist had been the "sole witness" who could've put Albert Anastasia in jail for good.

All eighteen cops who'd been assigned to guard duty at the Half Moon Hotel were called to testify. Frank Bals' boys. There were nine other police assigned to the case, but they were guarding Mrs. Reles and her kids at the time of Abe's death.

Chief Assistant District Attorney Edward S. Silver disclosed that two bed sheets used by Twist in his escape attempt were being sent to the FBI labs in Washington D.C. for analysis. The sheets were to be checked for evidence of strain such as might be imposed by Kid Twist hanging from them out the window. Silver clearly suspected that the sheets had been tied together and hung out the window in an attempt to make it look like Twist died during an escape attempt and to cover up the fact that he'd been simply tossed out the window to his death by someone sympathetic to the plight of Albert Anastasia.

In April 1951, Tough Tony—who had a sixteen-year-old daughter, and lived in a brownstone six doors away from the 76th precinct house, a building he'd never been inside—was questioned about his finances, which seemed robust for his position in life. They made him deny that he used strong-arm techniques on the piers to maintain control.

"Mr. Anastasio, how did you and your brothers happen to come to America?"

"We come over on the boat."

"Did you go through Ellis Island?"

"No, we jump ship."

"Are you here illegally?"

"No, sir. My wife and I went to Canada, re-entered this country legally, and we became naturalized citizens."

"What about your brothers?"

"They came in same way."

"Jumped ship?"

"That's right."

That bit of truth brought the brothers trouble. Joseph Anastasia, then forty-six years old, who had entered the country illegally in 1929, was arrested. "Your brother ratted you out," they told him. He was held in the immigration jail on Ellis Island for deportation. On April 5, he was released on $2,000 bail. "Bang Bang" was a new citizen but there were non-committal threats to "re-open his case." It struck Tough Tony as ironic. He once told Associated Press reporter Saul Pett that Joe was the most conservative of the Anastasio brothers, if you didn't count Father Sal.

"Joe never drank, never looked at a card, never gambled a dollar in his life. Joe got the most money saved, maybe four grand."

The reporter thought this an exaggeration. Surely, Albert was the richest, right?

Tony said no. "Albert don't have no money. No real money. Maybe a thousand dollars. He likes to play the horses like the rest of us. But Joe, never! All he knows is house and work, house and work."

Tony seemed like a pretty gentle guy until the reporter mentioned the rackets.

Tony said, "Anybody who says Tony Anastasia is the boss of the waterfront is a liar! I'll tell that to any senator or judge or committee in the world. In five minutes, I can get a thousand other longshoremen to testify who are the real gangsters and dictators on the docks. Sure, gangsters are running the waterfront but Adonis, Albert, any of those guys, they got nothing to do with it. I'll swear that on a Bible, as much as I love my mother."

Who were the real gangsters? Tony didn't want to say. He was asked about his brother the priest.

That was Salvatore, "Fadduh Sally," youngest of the brothers, a small-boned man with blue eyes and a sensitive manner. There is no evidence that Sal was in any way tough. He'd been a delicate lad, and no one was shocked when he married Jesus.

He joined the monastery in Italy, came to America in 1949, but never took to the New World. His brothers were Italian *and* they were American. Albert served in the U.S. Army. But Sally was just Italian—and homesick. That was the state of his fragile psyche when the bad news about his brothers began to make it from the newspapers and radio into his cloistered consciousness. Father Sal promptly had a nervous breakdown.

Tough Tony saw Sally only as a victim, a kid who couldn't catch a break and now he was suffering because of his blood family. Tony said, "He does not want to do any more masses. He keeps thinking the people in his parish are pointing at him and saying 'that is Albert's brother, that is Albert's brother.' He is the favorite brother and this has been terrible for him."

Father Salvatore spent three weeks in the hospital for nerves, and upon his release was transferred by the diocese to a small parish where he hoped to remain out of the Anastasia fray. Eventually, the priest's frayed nerves healed to the point where the diocese assigned him to once again say mass at St. Lucy's Church on Bronxwood Avenue in the Bronx.

On April 22, 1951, the *Tampa Tribune* ran a piece on the Anastasias, Albert and Elsa, a domestic piece, better homes and gardens-style. They described the dad as "in the dress business . . . father of three . . . home in Fort Lee." The assumption among his neighbors, and everyone else for that matter, was that dad was a big-time hood, a notion they got when he was called before the Kefauver Committee. Neighbors told the Florida paper that the Anastasias didn't hang out much with their neighbors. They were "quiet and standoffish, definitely not the type to cross the backyard for a cup of sugar or a fourth at bridge." Mom they saw at church, but she wasn't much of a joiner.

The kids were strangers to the neighbors as well. They didn't go to school with the neighbor kids. No one knew what all they did.

During the 1950s it was considered too dangerous to send Albert and Elsa's children to school, so a tutor was brought in. They were home-schooled, to use the modern phrase. The teacher was a guy named Don Modica. He had been teaching the philosophy of education at New York University when he met Albert at a club and became the mob's number-one tutor at a considerable pay raise. Modica also taught the kids of Joe Adonis and Willie Moretti. Albert's hood buddies called Modica "the professor." Modica was called before a subsequent government investigation, the McClellan Committee, and was asked about the goings on inside Anastasia's clifftop home. He took the Fifth.

During the summer of 1951, Walt Disney released his latest animated movie, *Alice in Wonderland*, which became one of the studio's most popular pictures ever. Guys that would never have read the book in a million years now knew all about the whacky characters in the story, including the Mad Hatter, whose main characteristics were madness, impulsiveness, and hat wearing. The madness part came from the notion that the glue used to hold hats together made hatters screwy. Well, you know what happened. Hat, nuts, impulsive—described Albert Anastasia to a tee. The nickname stuck. On President Street no one ever called Anastasia the Lord High Executioner. That was for the *literati*. We called him the Mad Hatter.

In June 1951, Albert traveled north by northwest to Utica, N.Y., to attend the wedding of his nephew to the lovely Concietta Miletto, the sister of a former bootlegger.

Albert knew Utica well. He had worked there for a time and owned a house there. Before there was the Fort Lee mansion, Albert the family man used Utica as a place to get relief from the heat, both from the weather and the Law.

But this time there was drama. Albert was too big of a celebrity now for his movements to go unnoticed. News leaked, death threats were phoned in, Utica police responded and provided Albert protection at the wedding.

(Concietta passed away in early 1957 and Albert again went to Utica, where rumors were that he was to be met by a hit squad. This time Albert traveled with his own five-man security team so the Utica taxpayers didn't have to shell out for his safety.

The Utica wedding in 1951 was still making the news in 1958 when government committees were growing like weeds, and a New York State anti-rackets crew was quizzing Joseph Falcone, the boss in Utica. They asked him if he knew about Concietta Miletto's wedding, if he attended the wedding, if he knew Albert Anastasia, if he attended Concietta's funeral, and when was the last time he saw Anastasia. Falcone pleaded the Fifth to all of those questions.)

TWENTY-THREE

The Savage Death of William Moretti

IN OCTOBER 1951, according to an FBI memo, Albert was asked by Frank Costello to suppress the case against a cage-full of crooked cops. Corrupt cops were a hood's best friends, so it made sense that crooks would come to the cops' rescue if they got in trouble.

The memo said that Anastasia and Willie Moretti were to "act as emissaries for the purpose of paying off convicted bookie Harry Gross to insure silence in connection with the trial . . ."

Without Gross testifying, it was believed, Judge Samuel Leibowicz (done defending mobsters and now putting them away) would be forced to dismiss the indictments. It didn't go smoothly. The payoff was supposed to be $200,000, but by the time the package was delivered it was considerably lighter.

Albert's fellow commissioners called Albert onto the carpet and asked him where the money went. "I wasn't in on the payoff itself," Albert said. "I don't know what Moretti did."

Albert made a gesture like Moretti wasn't all there mentally. Everybody knew he had a bad brain. Syphilis ate away at him. Once known for his stylish clothes and sharp tongue, Moretti was now on the decline, an unpredictable commodity, an embarrassment to leadership that needed to be lanced like a boil on the mob's ass.

Anastasia was in the doghouse, but Moretti was on a hit list.

* * *

According to an FBI informant, Moretti erred in a different way. After Moretti and Anastasia arranged and completed a contract between Gross and the dirty cops, and after Gross had completed his part of the contract, Moretti, apparently with Anastasia's backing, had indicated a "shakedown" of the indicted policemen and their co-conspirator to the tune of a hundred grand. In response, a group of plainclothesmen agreed to discuss the matter with Anastasia and Moretti. But that never happened . . .

Vito Genovese was all in on the agreement to whack Moretti, who was Costello's muscle and without him Costello was weakened. Plus, Moretti had his own rackets in New Jersey. Bumping him off would create a power vacuum that Genovese thought he could exploit.

Also, one of the symptoms of Moretti's STD was he couldn't keep his mouth shut. Lately he'd been saying shit about Genovese and Costello in public. It was like noise pollution with this guy. Moretti never shut his mouth. Silencing him permanent-like would be like a gift to the world.

Early on the morning of October 4, 1951, Albert Anastasia called Moretti on the phone.

"You got to come get me," Albert said. "I threw my back out again. I got to go to the hospital."

"Be right there," Moretti said. He picked up Anastasia in Fort Lee and took him to St. Mary's Hospital.

"You go. I'll be fine now," Anastasia said in the emergency waiting room.

Albert knew that Moretti only had hours to live, and wanted to make sure he was in a place with plenty of witnesses. In the hospital whining about his back he had an airtight alibi.

In the summertime, you stepped out of Joe's Elbow Room on Palisades Avenue in Cliffsdale Park, New Jersey, and you could hear the rote enthusiasm of carney barkers, the bells and whistles of arcade games, and the screams from the plummeting rollercoaster.

But it was quiet at 11:00 A.M., when fifty-seven-year-old William Moretti parked his 1951 cream-colored Packard at the curb outside, entered the long and narrow eatery, and sat down at a small square table near the counter.

It wasn't a fancy place. No tablecloths. Each table had a paper napkin dispenser, salt and pepper, a jar of sugar, and a small glass ashtray. The place wasn't busy, but Moretti wasn't the only customer.

There were two guys having breakfast in the front near the window. They left but came back with another pair in fedoras. They walked directly to Moretti's table and for a moment everyone seemed to be having a friendly conversation. Then they blew Moretti away and left him sprawled across the checkerboard-tiled floor with his ankles crossed.

Hearing four shots, waitress Dorothy Novak returned from the kitchen, and screamed as she saw blood soaking through Moretti's brown suit and maroon tie. His left hand was on his chest, and a pool of blood spread beneath his head.

She called the cops. When they arrived, she said, "I left to get menus and, bang, the second I was out of sight, I heard shots."

"Time?"

"It was 11:28."

Within minutes a cluster of people gathered outside, looking at the corpse on the floor through the plate-glass window.

On October 8, 1951, William Moretti's funeral was categorized by the FBI as a "typical gangster type." The gallery was swollen, and the bigs all sent flowers. Floral arrangements arrived from Albert, Joe Adonis, Frank Costello, and Vito Genovese. They all said boo hoo. Moretti was buried in St. Michael's Cemetery in Lodi, New Jersey.

Moretti was dead, and a lot of people thought Anastasia was next—including apparently Anastasia, as he sealed himself up tight inside his Fort Lee mansion. Word was that both Moretti and Anastasia were mob targets because they'd double-crossed the wrong people.

Rumor had it Anastasia had been offered a deal where his life would be spared as long as he moved to Hot Springs, Arkansas, and discontinued all mob activities. Some might have mistaken Anastasia's holed-up posture as a sign of weakness. That would have been a mistake. He was a very powerful man and his phone worked fine.

During the last months of 1951, the Kefauver Committee was eager to get Albert back on the witness stand, but Albert continued to work medical excuses: "I got a bad back. Had it a long time. From throwing the hook. Most days I can't get out of bed," he said. "I could give you a doctor's note if you want."

In the meantime, the FBI was going door to door in Fort Lee trying to dig up dirt. During one of those interviews, the feds found that Albert and Anthony Strollo, also of Fort Lee, had fixed the union elections for Teamsters Local 560. To keep the job—and probably his life—whoever was elected was "under constant obligation" to Anastasia and Strollo.

At about 8:00 P.M. on January 3, 1952, Gioacchino "Jack" Sparacino, a fifty-one-year-old Coney Island pizza-parlor owner who'd been questioned following the murder of his friend Philip Mangano, was burned down in the middle of 26th Avenue near Harway Avenue in Bath Beach, Brooklyn.

According to family members, Sparacino left his house for the final time saying he had to meet two unnamed business friends. He was shot on the run from behind, once in the back of the head, once in the chest, and twice in the back.

Sparacino had been ordered out of the car and told to run for his life. It was a sadistic game, and said a lot about the guys who juked him. They were having fun. Sparacino managed to move about fifty feet trying to escape the gunmen but was unable to out-race hot lead. Running wasn't his strong point anyway. He was short and pudgy. Two-hundred-pounds-plus of goo. A small-time hood with a minuscule shoe size.

One of the great mysteries of journalism seventy years ago was why they published the names and addresses of witnesses to mob hits, but they did, so on January 4 anyone reading the *Daily News* knew that Angela Basile, a twenty-nine-year-old file clerk, had talked to police, and reported that she'd heard the shots and rushed to the front upstairs window of her house in time to see two men climb back into a car and speed away. Could she recognize the men if she saw them again? That was left to the imagination. Imagine Miss Basile's terror when she realized her situation.

We don't know if no one in the neighborhood bothered to call the police or if the cops thought another dead hood was no big deal, but the body was allowed to lie akimbo in the street for more than an hour. That was when foot patrolman Alfred Frontera on his regular rounds tripped on it. Only then did an ambulance from Israel Zion Hospital show up and a doctor proclaim the man dead. After some crime-scene dicks poked around for a while, the body was transported to the morgue, which was just across the street from Kings County Hospital. Jack's brother-in-law came to the morgue to make the official identification and fill in some details for authorities, including Jack's actual address. The brother-in-law said that Jack was a longshoreman and a dressmaker. This wasn't the first time someone had tried to kill him. Back in 1944, Jack had been shot and seriously wounded by Ernest "The Hawk" Rupolo.

Cops figured Sparacino, like his friend Philip Mangano, was another guy forever silenced.

Eight blocks from where the body ended up was Sparacino's green 1947 two-door sedan. He had apparently driven to a rendezvous under the el near the corner of 86th Street and 23rd Avenue from his home on 80th Street in Dyker Heights (although the I.D. in his wallet listed his address as on Corso Court in Gravesend), and there had transferred to his executioners' car for the final eight blocks to the site of his death.

TWENTY-FOUR
"I Hate Squealers!"

BEFORE I CAN TELL YOU about Albert Anastasia having Arnold Schuster whacked, I got to tell you about the legendary Willie "The Actor" Sutton, greatest of the bank robbers. Sutton was raised in Hell's Kitchen, and he was a Houdini when it came to getting out of prison. He cut his way out of Sing Sing, tunneled out of a Pennsylvania facility, climbed the wall at a third prison. His escapes were legendary. Plus, he was a brazen bank robber. He didn't hurt anybody and was seen as a hero by most of the public.

On March 9, 1950, an on-the-lam Sutton knocked over the Manufacturer's Trust on Queens Boulevard in Sunnyside, Queens, getting away with almost $70,000, which he lived off of in a home on Dean Street in Brooklyn. He grew a moustache and lived practically next door to the precinct house, but no one recognized him.

Almost no one. Enter Arnold Schuster, annoyingly observant twenty-two-year-old Coast Guard vet, solid citizen, and squealer. Schuster was aboard an Uptown BMT train at Fourth Avenue and 45th Street in Brooklyn one day and looked at the guy across from him.

"Hey, that's Willie Sutton," Schuster said to himself.

When Sutton got off at Pacific Street, Schuster got off too, and he followed Sutton to a gas station at Bergen Street and Third Avenue. When he ran into a cop on the beat, he said, "You're probably going to think I'm crazy but . . ."

Cops approached the man Schuster had pointed out.

"You Willie Sutton?"

"Nope, my name's Gordon."

"Oh, okay."

The cop did tell the story to a supervisor, who in turn decided to check out Mr. Gordon for himself, and Sutton was eventually arrested. The papers lauded the cops and didn't mention the civilian who'd first pointed Sutton out.

A smart guy would have felt he'd done a good deed and gone on with his life, but that wasn't Schuster. How dare they not give him credit in the newspapers? He was a hero and he wanted to be treated like a hero. Where was his reward money?

Schuster went to Police Commissioner George Monaghan and next thing you knew, he was all over the papers as the smart guy who fingered Sutton. There was no reward money, but he did get a couple of paying gigs (total of $750) on those newfangled television shows. Police offered him protection after Sutton's arrest, but Schuster said no thanks. After all, Sutton's reputation was as a nonviolent guy.

Then Schuster began getting threatening mail and phone calls, so most of the time he stayed inside. He still refused protection but allowed cops to make a wellness check on him now and again.

One of the guys who read about Schuster in the papers was the Mad Hatter.

"I can't stand squealers!" Anastasia said. "I want him hit."

On Saturday night, March 8, 1952, Schuster was found shot four times with a .38, through both eyes and in the groin, in an alleyway on 45th Street, just down the block from his home in the Borough Park section of Brooklyn. Although there were several witnesses within two-hundred yards of the murder, it was very dark and police had small hope that anyone would be able to identify the shooter.

At the time of the shooting, kids across New York City were listening to the radio show, *Gang Busters,* which that evening was discussing the recent capture of the legendary Willie Sutton.

Police from Borough Park's 66th Precinct station believed that Schuster had been followed to the murder site from his father's store, Mac's Pants, at Fifth Avenue and 55th Street.

Investigators started out with the usual canvassing of the neighborhood but nobody knew nothing, a sure sign that neighbors smelled mob.

An early person of interest was Frederick J. "Angel of Death" Tenuto, who escaped from prison with Sutton and was described by police as a "maddog killer." Tenuto made a great suspect in any murder. Since this one tied in with Sutton, he went to the top of the list.

Trouble was, no one knew where Tenuto was. The only tip came from an anonymous cab driver who said he dropped Tenuto off on East 53rd Street in Manhattan early Monday morning and had received a fifty-five-cent tip.

Years later, super-rat Joseph Valachi filled in the blanks. Tenuto really was the guy who hit Schuster, and the reason no one could find him was because Anastasia had Tenuto whacked soon thereafter, exact date unknown. At the time of his death Tenuto was number fourteen on the FBI's most-wanted list and had been on the list for longer than ten years, which was then a record. Since his body was never found, he stayed on the list for another four years.

Initial reaction was that an insane person must have done the Schuster killing. Experts, however, said not so fast. Dr. Clarence H. Bellinger, director of the Brooklyn State Hospital for the Mentally Ill said, "Based on forty-two years of experience, the murder was perpetrated by an ex-convict, a hardened criminal who has shot and killed before. It was not perpetrated by an insane man or by anyone who had been in a mental institution because mental patients do not commit this type of crime." The murderer of Schuster was bold and brazen, more like a gangster than a psycho. The killing, the doctor said, was meant to set an example, to "close Schuster's eyes forever. The murderer planned to shoot him in the eyes as a lesson not to see too much. He was saying to the world—if you do see more than you should, you'll get your eyes blown out, too."

What about the shot to the groin?

"That," Dr. Bellinger said, "rose out of a vindictive desire on the part of the criminal to mutilate Schuster's person."

The doctor offered some early-days criminal profiling, suggesting that the killer probably had less than a high-school education. Two types of people committed crimes of this sort: those who had no other option, and those who liked it.

Motive? The psychiatrist said—accurately, by the way—he thought the killing was related to the arrest of famed bank robber Willie Sutton, although he didn't think Sutton himself was behind the killing. Sutton had a reputation as a guy who had never hurt anyone, in fact, and it was doubtful that he'd had that dramatic of a shift in personality. Though Schuster was no friend, Sutton was smart enough to know that killing the man who "fingered" him would not help his case, and might hurt it.

When Sutton heard that the witness against him had been offed, he reportedly said, "This sinks me."

The NYPD was saying nothing about nothing. They kept a lid on leaks regarding the investigation. They wanted to be sure that potential witnesses could come forward without their name appearing in a tabloid the next day.

Police Commissioner George P. Monaghan ordered his investigators to "clam-up" regarding the search for Schuster's killer. The news media was playing the murder up big. Next to the death of the Lindbergh baby, they said, this murder had outraged the American public more than any other killing. The victim, after all, was an honest citizen doing his duty, and his death had to make people afraid of cooperating with the police in the future.

On the day after the murder, a truck with a loud speaker mounted on its roof, went up and down the streets in the vicinity of the murder (from Sixth Avenue to 12th Avenue, and 35th Street to 55th Street in Brooklyn), urging people who knew something to come forward. A sign on the side of the truck read, "Help Find the Killer." Those who were fearful of talking to the police were urged to give the relevant information to their priest or rabbi.

On the Monday following the murder, a letter showed up at Schuster's home, which turned out to be the twelfth in a series, urging Schuster to forget everything he ever knew about Willie Sutton. The letters appeared to have been written by different people—although several of the letters were in the same handwriting. The letters began arriving on February 20, soon after police first made public that Schuster was a witness against Sutton. The letters were written on unlined paper and mailed from a postal zone in Upper Manhattan.

Schuster was buried in Montefiore Cemetery, Springfield Gardens, Queens. The Schuster family sued the city of New York for failing to protect Arnold, and the city settled for $41,000.

The question of who ordered the hit on Schuster remained a mystery until mob turncoat Joseph Valachi spilled the beans. Valachi made it clear that Albert Anastasia would have a guy killed solely because his behavior was offensive to him. That character appraisal jives with Lucky Luciano's memories of Albert: "Anastasia was really off his rocker. He was starting to see himself like some guy in the old gangster movies."

Strike One: Abe Reles squeals on Albert. Strike Two: Albert whacks the Manganos. Strike Three: Albert whacks a civilian for a non-business reason. It was the beginning of the end. The commission took a look at the up-and-comers under Albert, came upon capo Carlo Gambino, and they gave him a little, just a little wink.

Gambino was an impatient and ambitious man, about the same age as Albert, unwilling to await an act of God to ascend to what he felt was his rightful spot at the top of one of the Five Families.

TWENTY-FIVE

Bang Bang

THE KEFAUVER SHOW carried on, but was now joined by other committees run by politicians saying, “hey, look at me, I’m tough on crime, too.” In December 1952, with Albert still holed up in his Fort Lee fortress with his “sore back,” it came time for brother Bang Bang to testify before the New York State Crime Commission.

Bang Bang took the stand but remained mute as his mouthpiece, Joseph J. Petito, argued for him that the commission hearings were illegal, so there was no way to force him to comply.

Despite Gerardo’s keeping mum, it wasn’t a good day at the hearings for the Anastasio brothers. A former steamship executive named Willard L. Swain testified that Joseph was kingpin of the East River piers’ “pilferage rackets.” Swain was executive assistant to the chairman of the New York Shipping Association and was the former head of the Agwi shipping line. He said that despite the pervasive extortion of Joseph Anastasia on those piers, he found that contracting stevedores, including the John W. McGrath Co., were “unable to fire” Joseph.

The state commission announced that they’d found evidence buried deep in the files of former D.A. William O’Dwyer linking Albert Anastasia with the Peter Panto murder. The evidence, perhaps a statement made by Anthony Romeo before he was whacked, had seemingly been suppressed by the original investigation. When O’Dwyer was quizzed about the unspecified evidence, the former

D.A. said, "If they're so interested in Anastasia then why in hell don't they prosecute the bastard?" Asked why he never did anything about Albert and the Panto murder, O'Dwyer said, "Because the murder took place in New Jersey, smart guy."

Later that month the commission heard the testimony of Anthony Guistra, financial secretary of an ILA local. He said the fix seemed to be in for several of Albert Anastasia's brothers, that Gerardo Anastasia had run in an election for delegate of his local, lost the election, and was appointed delegate nonetheless.

The state hearings rolled on. On December 5, 1952, Bang Bang was again scheduled to testify. Since his last appearance, he had been arrested for refusing to answer questions. At this hearing, he was again accompanied by his lawyer. Although Gerardo managed to speak this time, it was still Petito who did most of the talking.

Commission counsel Theodore Kiendl asked, "Why did you not speak to the commission the last time you were called to this stand, Mr. Anastasia?"

"I was sick. Very, very sick," Gerardo said. "I had just gotten out of a hospital bed."

"Why didn't you tell us that at the time?"

"I couldn't speak."

That brought a slight tittering from the gallery.

"You spoke your name. Why couldn't you say you were sick?"

Gerardo had a long conference with Petito before answering: "You didn't ask me if I was sick."

Presiding over the hearing was Commissioner Ignatius Wilkinson, who didn't care for the witness/lawyer sidebars.

"Mr. Petito," Wilkinson said. "You may advise your client of his rights, but you may not tell him what to say."

Kiendl took up the questioning and pointed a finger as he asked: "Mr. Anastasia, do you have a criminal record?"

"I got some convictions for bookmaking, but I was never a bookmaker."

"How many convictions?"

"Three."

"You were innocent of all three charges?"

There was another whisper fest between Gerardo and his lawyer. Finally, Gerardo replied, "The record shows I was convicted."

"The record shows you pleaded guilty, correct?"

"Yes."

"Did you ever receive gifts from stevedores who employ the longshoremen for whom you are a delegate?"

"At Christmas, yeah, sometimes."

Kiendl tried and tried but couldn't get Gerardo to specify a single dollar amount for these gifts, or the name of an individual who gave him the Christmas present.

"Can you tell me which ship lines the stevedores who gave you gifts worked for?"

After a sidebar with Petito, Gerardo took the Fifth.

"In general terms, can you tell us how much money you made from stevedore gifts at Christmas?"

"I never counted it. Maybe three-hundred fifty. Something like that."

"What did you spend the money on?"

"Fun. I ate and drank with it. It was Christmas."

The whole "I couldn't speak because I was sick" angle lost its humor when soon thereafter, Gerardo was diagnosed with throat cancer.

Illness didn't stop Bang Bang from continuing to get into trouble. In October 1953, there were three pitched battles between union factions. Even though a judge had ordered an injunction against a work stoppage, Tough Tony was able to blockade the unloading of a freighter. A thousand cops were on hand to help light the fuse.

Opponents screamed for Tony to be arrested for inciting to riot, but nothing was done. A subsequent grand jury indicted Bang Bang and a dozen others as instigators and throwers of bricks and bottles, however Kings County Judge Samuel S. Leibowicz granted Bang Bang severance, being that he was in critical condition in the hospital following his first throat cancer operation.

* * *

Years later, Joseph Valachi testified that he and his partner were in a Bronx bar and got into a fist fight in the restaurant kitchen over divvying up profits. The partners ended up in court, but not a court of law. This court was in the back of a social club and the judge was Albert Anastasia. The partners each brought mouthpieces who did most of the talking, and the proceedings could not have been more orderly if they'd taken place in the Supreme Court. After listening to both sides, Albert scolded both men, but mostly Valachi, for "taking the law into your own hands." Beefs needed to be decided by the bosses, that was what they were there for. Settling a beef without approval was the sort of shit that started gang wars, Albert said. He ordered Valachi to pay his partner "a couple of thousand dollars and call it even."

The partner started to squawk but Judge Anastasia pacified him with the tiniest gesture of his hand. The ruling had been made and that was it.

TWENTY-SIX
The Dire Wolf

GODFATHER JOSEPH BONNANO had his nose in a newspaper in Tucson, Arizona, when he came to a troubling item: Vincent Mangano had vanished. Nobody remembered the last time they saw him. Bonnano knew they'd never find him, and that this meant trouble.

Mangano chaired Commission meetings, rapped the gavel for the distinguished panel, the Five Fathers—plus Chicago and Buffalo. "Chicago" included everything west of Chicago. With Mangano disappeared, Bonnano would preside over Commission meetings, and Albert Anastasia, Lucky Luciano's maniac psychokiller friend, would get a seat at the table.

Everyone felt it in their bones that Anastasia had disappeared Mangano, but Albert rarely spoke on the subject.

Luciano had set up the Five Families to better distribute the power and hopefully cut down on guys whacking their bosses to get ahead. It might have helped, but the way to get ahead in the mob remained the same as it had been since the nineteenth century in Sicily: you kill the guy above you and you take his place. Not a lot of guys had the balls to do it, because payback could be a bitch. That's why you often ended up with a nut in charge. That was part of the excitement.

Frank Costello had to worry about Vito Genovese, who was hugely popular and a rising star in his gang. Costello figured he would need re-enforcements and aligned himself with Anastasia. Genovese could make friends, too, and aligned himself with Tommy "Three-Finger" Lucchese who had his own family ever since the natural death of Gaetano Gagliano.

So it was Costello-Anastasia versus Lucchese-Genovese. Profaci was off to one side worrying about his own civil war with the Gallos. Everyone else shut up and took orders if they knew what was good for them. You couldn't take the matter to the Commission, because the commissioners themselves were the ones lining up their ducks for war.

Guys that enjoyed staying neutral were forced to take sides. Luciano's five-family plan was on the verge of annihilation. Lucchese claimed neutrality at the sit-downs, but privately admitted to gearing up "to defend himself" against Anastasia.

Anyone in their right mind would be scared shitless of Anastasia, and Tommy Three-Finger didn't like having a beef with him. He feared that Anastasia would attack because, keeping it real, that was what he did. Vito Genovese had a private meeting with Lucchese and told him to keep his guard up.

"I know," Genovese said. "Anastasia is trying to eliminate me. If he succeeds, you will be next, my friend."

Lucchese shivered. There was only one way to prevent an attack—and that was to attack first. It was Joseph Bonnano who talked Lucchese out of striking first. Instead, Bonnano suggested, he should place himself at Anastasia's mercy.

"Albert Anastasia does not kill people who beg for his mercy," Albert had once said to Bonanno, and he believed it to be true. Bonnano told Three-Finger that he knew the mercy gambit would work.

"I understood something about Anastasia," Bonanno later said. "In the wild, when wolves fight, one wolf will indicate that he is ready to yield by offering his throat; then the fighting stops."

The unseen hand in all of this was Luciano, who still exerted his formidable will over this bunch of quarreling wiseguys. His liaison was primarily Costello, who it seemed was being overwhelmed by the powerful personalities and fearsome reputation of his fellow fathers.

* * *

By December 1952, the New York State Crime Commission was setting the stage for a solid decade of government investigations into organized crime. A frequent topic of testimony was the iron fist with which waterfront racketeers ruled their Red Hook Empire.

Involved in the investigation was one of Albert Anastasia's arch-enemies during the days of being waterfront czar and boss of Murder Inc. It was that economic crusader in a cassock named Rev. John Corridan, a Harlem-born Irishman and man of the cloth, who made it his business to learn about the mistreatment of the laborers on the piers by the racketeer unions version of waterfront economics.

Corridan knew he was battling a shrewd and powerful enemy. Corridan's crusade went on for many years, taking him from being a young man to a middle-aged man. Corridan gambled that Catholic hoods wouldn't whack a religious man, that it would mean too much bad karma and they feared hell. He used spies and ingenuity to learn the details, complex details, regarding the corrupt political and business relationships that fortified Anastasia's control. Corridan used his knowledge, which constituted a large blackmail file, to put a damper on mob retributions, and he gets credit for keeping the body count of men like Peter Panto from being much higher.

During the 1950s, some of Rev. John Corridan's tempering was visible, as "Tough" Tony Anastasia cut back on dumping bodies into the tide-angry waters of Buttermilk Channel running between Red Hook and Governor's Island, and instead simply called his union enemies Communists, and that usually shut them up one way or another.

"Tough Tony" was never a made guy. He was a union big wig and ran the docks like a dangerous hood, but he usually didn't require back-up from gangsters. Being the brother of the Mad Hatter was enough. Who but the stupidest of men would cross Tough Tony?

Albert's brother was a rich, rich man. He drove expensive cars and had a strong sense of fashion, white tie, white carnation, preferring double-breasted suits with lapels the size of Staten Island.

Corridan went to Albany and gave the New York State Crime Commission an eight-point reform program. Then he took the train to Washington, D.C., and testified for the feds. He said that it was a mismatch on the piers, that the criminal elements were strong and ruthless, the maritime unions and businesses lacked the gumption to stick up for themselves.

Nobody cared about stevedores. The way the public saw it, tough guys were pushing around an overcrowded herd of immigrant laborers. So what?

But there was shock when the commissioners learned from Rev. Corridan that legitimate suit-wearing men with businesses in New York Harbor had to deal with the same organization that played God over desperate longshoremen. The corruption involved the piers of Manhattan, the piers of New Jersey. One legit stevedoring company admitted to officials that they'd paid $15,500 to street thugs to prevent a strike. Another admitted paying nearly $10,000 in order to save a boatload of lemons worth a hundred grand that would have been allowed to rot without the bribe. Goons told the bosses who to hire and who not to hire. The guys that got hired expected to be paid even when they didn't show up. Witnesses were tight-lipped on the stand, but in private *Albert Anastasia* was the name they whispered the most. He was the guy they were most afraid of. For that matter, Corridan said, Albert's brothers Tough Tony and Bang Bang, were right up there on the fear scale, as well.

Albert Anastasia, who thought his worries of being deported went away after he was naturalized in the army, had to start worrying all over again. Deportation proceedings against him were scheduled in 1952 in New York City in connection with the Lepke case.

Albert's strategy remained the same, to malinger and lock himself inside his Fort Lee mansion—which was highly effective. The New Jersey state commission had a subpoena for Albert, but was unable to serve it.

Discussions of why so many people were afraid of Albert were held in his absence, and among federal authorities there was talk of stripping Anastasia of his naturalized status and deporting him to Tropea where he came from.

Albert was pretty much under house arrest. He couldn't even step outside for a breath of fresh air. New Jersey State Troopers surrounded his house. He stayed away from the windows.

One guy who *was* successfully subpoenaed was Jersey City Mayor John Kenny, who said he was an honest man working among pirates and admitted to having a business relationship and friendship with dock boss Charlie Yanowsky, who'd been bumped off a few years prior. One of the witnesses who could put Kenny and Yanowsky together was a guy named Frank "Biffo" DiLorenzo who suddenly passed away. The medical examiner said coronary occlusion, but other witnesses nonetheless asked for protection. Much of the fear was inspired by Jersey City cops, who back then sometimes freelanced as mob muscle.

By this time William O'Dwyer, once a perceived enemy of the mob, was a U.S. Ambassador to Mexico, and his brother Paul O'Dwyer was a defense attorney kept busy by Anastasia's crew.

Before the bullshit RICO laws, law enforcement sought creative ways to incarcerate guys they knew were ordering hits, but who maintained plausible denial. When Capone went down for not paying his taxes, it molded the template.

So in January 1953 the feds went after Albert Anastasia for tax evasion and sought evidence to prove Albert was making tons more moolah than he was reporting. For the tax guys, this was an easy one, as they weren't expected to launch an investigation of their own.

If the waterfront investigation—a combo of the Domestic Intelligence Division and the Investigative Division, already in high gear—came up with evidence the tax department could use, they'd be sure to pass it along.

The foundation for the charges came when the FBI unearthed some dollar figures regarding Anastasia's mansion. The thirty-four-room house had cost Albert more than fifty grand to build and was estimated to be worth $125,000. Many of the witnesses at Albert's trial would be contractors who would describe what they had done and how much they'd been paid to do it.

The idea was to compare these numbers with Albert's reported income and call the obvious discrepancy proof of tax evasion. United States Treasury agents would testify that they had visited 110 banks in New York and New Jersey, pretty much all of them, and had found no, zero, accounts, loans, inheritances, or safety deposit boxes.

The feds assembled Albert's own version of his life. He'd been a longshoreman, he claimed, from 1928 to 1936. From 1936 to 1940, he ran his own cheese business. After that, right up until the time he went into the army, he worked for $100 a month at a sand and gravel company in Utica, New York.

The FBI also compiled a bio of Albert largely culled from a *New York Times* investigation published the previous year. During the Murder Inc. years, the FBI said, Albert ordered sixty-three hits. How they came up with that number I don't know. Sixty-three sounds like an average month of Murder Inc. carnage.

They, of course, discussed how slippery Albert could be in court due to his intimidation of witnesses, and complained that they could've had Albert for the murder of Peter Panto if it weren't for Kid Twist's sailor dive.

An FBI memo summarized Anastasia's situation: Brooklyn District Attorney William O'Dwyer had bragged of having a "perfect case" against the Mad Hatter. Oops. They might've had him for the murder of Morris Diamond, too. But no. That also imploded with the death of Abe Reles. World War II got Albert off the hook, and he shook off his legal woes by enlisting in the army, ridding himself of his illegal alien status. Now the war was over, and Albert was again a pain in the justice system's ass, only now the prospect of deportation had been taken off the table. Or had it? Fed legal beagles were looking into that subject.

On December 9, 1952, the feds instituted proceedings to set aside the naturalization decree that Albert had been given during WWII and cancel the certificate of naturalization on the ground that the letter had been illegally procured and based on a fraudulent Certificate of Registry issued to Anastasia in 1931.

Back then, when Albert was asked if he had a criminal record, he said, "Nah."

The commission finally got Anastasia to sit down for questions on December 19, 1952, but it didn't do them any good. Answers were few. They asked him just about the murders he had been arrested for, about what he did for a living between 1919 and 1942, about the activities of his brothers. He took the Fifth.

Albert maintained his cool until they crossed a line and he flared up. They asked him about his youngest brother Salvatore, the priest. At that Albert snapped, "Why should I drag an innocent man into this?"

According to an FBI memo, in September 1953, Albert attended secret meetings at a hotel near Lake Tahoe, Nevada, a meeting attended by top "criminal syndicate members and top union men" from around the country. The subject: building a gambler's paradise in the desert, one that was strictly legit, one that flipped off the federal government.

TWENTY-SEVEN

Albert's Tax Evasion Case and the Murders of the Macri Brothers

ON MARCH 10, 1954, a federal grand jury indicted Albert on two counts of "knowingly and willfully attempting to defeat and evade income tax filed." He turned himself in immediately, appeared in a Newark courtroom, pleaded not guilty, and was released on $10,000 bail. Specifically, the charges were that Albert had failed to pay $11,742 in taxes for the years 1947 and 1948. He was defended by Anthony A. Calandra, who had offices very close to the courthouse in Newark.

The *Daily News* published details from Anastasia's filed tax returns for 1947. According to Albert's accountant, he made $5,960 that year and paid $789 in taxes. The government said those numbers should be $25,728 and $8,930. The FBI talked to Albert's tax preparer for 1947, who was Alfred Esposito of Cliffside Real Estate and Insurance Broker. He told the feds that, according to Albert, he won $4,500 at the racetrack that year.

The FBI learned that in 1948 Albert's taxes were filed by accountant Nat Bennett of Lynbrook, Long Island. According to that tax return, all of Albert's income derived from the profits of his company, Madison Dress.

On April 14, 1954, the U.S. District Court in Newark upheld the denaturalization petition against Albert. This was a necessary step in the Attorney General's Denaturalization and Deportation Program.

The FBI memo regarding the decision referred to Albert as Umberto (for the first time in years) to make him sound foreign.

A tax lien was filed against his Fort Lee property as a result of his tax evasion indictment. Anastasia appealed the revocation, and his case was argued before the Third Circuit Court of Appeals. On September 20, 1954, the appellate court announced it had made a decision, but there were delays in announcing what the decision was, and obviously Albert was never deported.

That same spring, between court appearances, Albert attended a series of meetings with other "top echelon hoodlums" at the Rivera Hotel in Cliffside Park, New Jersey, to discuss "labor and racket matters along the waterfront in the New York area." Someone at the meeting yakked to the FBI.

The government had rounded up guys inside Anastasia's private world. Among those who would testify on behalf of the government at the trial was Anastasia's old neighbor and plumber, Charles Ferri.

Benedict Macri remained on Albert's hit list. He was the garment center hood who beat the rap in 1951 in the fatal stabbing of union organizer William Lurye. His acquittal was obtained through perjured testimony and a friendly all-male jury. One witness later admitted he was paid off, but Benedict remained free. Albert knew Macri had blabbed to the feds from the questions he was asked by the Kefauver Committee. Now Macri would be joined on Albert's shit list by Ferri.

Albert's tax evasion trial began on October 19, 1954, in Newark. The Honorable Alfred E. Modarelli sat on the bench. In the courtroom, Assistant U.S. Attorney Frederick B. Lacey's opening statement for the government was more like a lecture in Accounting 101. What was the difference between gross and net, what is a deduction, an expenditure, an asset, a liability, partnership profit? Stuff like that. Jurors dozed.

The prosecution's strategy would be to show that Anastasia bought things during 1947 and '48 that he couldn't possibly afford had he made only what he claimed to make. Assets were hidden by putting them in Mrs. Anastasia's name—her maiden name. Their focus would be on the Anastasia mansion. How much did it cost? How much work went into it? How much did that cost? And where the hell did the money come from?

The house, Lacey noted, was in the name of Elsa Bargnesi, a.k.a. Mrs. Anastasia. How could they afford to build a mansion without money? Easy answer: they couldn't. They had money and lied about it. They didn't blame Elsa. She wasn't being prosecuted here. She was just a name on a piece of paper. Albert was the brains behind this scam, and he was the one who would have to be punished.

Elsa sat in the gallery directly behind the defendant's table, looking like a Jersey housewife on her way to a cocktail party, sitting next to a man who had "separate counsel" written all over him. The prosecution was saying evidence would show that Elsa had borne out two mortgages for a total sum of $30,000, and that "Elsa" had sold a different house in her name in 1946 for $25,000. (When the time came Elsa's lawyer stood and objected to the submission of the evidence, but the judge, after making Elsa's lawyer identify himself, overruled.)

Lacey said that Anastasia's net worth had been calculated using "recognized accounting principles," a.k.a. standard deduction against the gross, and the tax Anastasia should have paid was determined using that amount. His gross was determined by what he spent rather than what he claimed to have earned. He told the jurors about the Madison Dress Company in Hazleton, which Anastasia claimed was his sole source of income. He gave the jury a small lesson in logic and criminology also, explaining the scientific basis and value behind "circumstantial evidence."

At one point defense counsel called for a five-minute piss break, which the judge granted and some wondered if they really had to go to the bathroom, or if they were just disrupting Lacey's momentum. Bottom line was that Anastasia claimed an income of $18,769 for the years 1947 and '48 but spent during those years a whopping $51,074. The jury was invited to do the math.

The prosecution closed its opening statement with a heads-up.

Settle in. This was going to take a while. They intended to call Rudolph Halley, former chief counsel for the Senate Crime Investigating Committee, to the stand—along with more than one hundred other witnesses.

But the witness we are going to concentrate on is Charles Ferri, who was questioned by Lacey. Ferri, to his chagrin, had to say and spell his name, and then state his address, which was on Northeast Sixth Avenue in North Miami, Florida. Anastasia no doubt made a mental note.

Ferri testified that he was retired now, but back in 1947 he was a plumbing and heating contractor. Yes, he knew Anastasia, met him when he and his architect came to Ferri's office with blueprints for the Bluff Road house, asking for a plumbing and heating estimate. Over the next few days he gave the estimate and Anastasia asked him to draw up a contract. Ferri had the contract on him and it was entered into evidence.

The defendant, it was noted, signed the contract on Valentine's Day 1947 as "Albert Bargnesi," his real first name and his wife's maiden name. Ferri couldn't testify that it was Anastasia who signed the contract, however, because it wasn't signed in his presence. Ferri testified that he provided best quality service and materials and was paid $8,700 for his work on the house.

"While you were doing the work," Lacey said, "did you observe the other construction activities going on at the same time?"

"Yes."

"And what was the quality of those services and materials."

"Best," Ferri said.

Calandra leaped to his feet with an objection. Ferri's opinion of others' work lacked credibility. He wasn't an expert. His opinion wasn't binding.

The judge asked the witness if he was an expert in construction materials, and Ferri said he knew a top-notch cinder block when he saw one. The judge allowed the answer. Ferri said the plaster, foundation materials, ceramic tiling, etc., all seemed like the best possible quality.

Lacey shifted back to the witness's personal history with the construction project. In what manner was the witness paid? Much of that money was delivered in cash to Ferri's Fort Lee office with the message that it was from "Mr. Bargnesi."

"Mr. Bargnesi and the defendant are one and the same, is that correct, Mr. Ferri?"

"Yes."

Also entered into evidence were pages from Ferri's ledger, where his bookkeeper kept track of "Mr. Bargnesi" incrementally paying his bill.

"Did you also do work for the defendant in 1948?"

"Yes, sir. We cleaned out some stoppages and repaired a few faucets," Ferri said.

"In whose name was the bill paid?"

"Mrs. Elsa Bargnesi."

The witness described the house thoroughly. At one point the judge's eyes went wide.

"You want me to understand that there are four complete bathrooms in that house?"

"Yes," the witness said. Not "just powder rooms," but full baths.

Lacey ended his direct questioning of Ferri, and Calandra immediately launched into cross-examination. Ferri told the defense attorney that he'd had his own business for thirty years and retired to Florida because of doctor's orders.

Calandra asked if it wasn't the contractor's job to determine the owner of the house before beginning work.

"I have to admit I was a little lax in that regard," Ferri said. "I generally have a witness present when a contract is signed."

"You always want to know the true owner before you begin ordering expensive merchandise, right?"

"Right."

"And it was your belief that the home was owned by an Elsa Bargnesi, is that correct?"

"Yes, sir."

"Did you ever meet Mrs. Bargnesi in person?"

"Not at that time, no, sir." He did meet her later, when the house was almost finished. Mrs. Anastasia, that is. He still didn't know she was "Mrs. Bargnesi."

Calandra called attention to the permits the witness had acquired at Borough Hall from the Board of Health. They all listed Elsa Bargnesi as the owner of the house.

"According to your testimony then, Mr. Ferri, you never gave much thought to who actually owned the house."

"I was lax."

"At some point you must've realized that Mrs. Anastasia and Mrs. Bargnesi were one and the same."

"Yes."

"When was that?"

"About a year into the job."

"And how did that meeting take place?"

"She viewed the new house and asked that a sink be relocated."

On re-direct, Lacey asked Ferri if the reason he was lax about the true ownership of the house was that he was being paid in envelopes full of one-hundred-dollar bills.

Ferri denied it.

The entire time Ferri was on the stand, the defendant glared at him, Anastasia's eyes telepathically squeezing the black spot into Ferri's trembling hand.

The trial lasted for five weeks and was turned over to the jury on November 20, 1954. After almost eighteen hours of deliberation, the jury declared itself hopelessly deadlocked. Judge Modarelli discharged the panel, and a mistrial was declared. U.S. Attorney Raymond Del Tupo said a retrial would be held as soon as possible.

Del Tupo said, "I have a hundred witnesses. He'll do ten years and pay a fine—and then we'll kick him out of the country."

Point was, Ferri and Macri were among those who might have to testify at the re-trial. Or not. To do that, they would need to survive.

That re-trial was scheduled to begin on February 11, 1955, before Judge William F. Smith, but there was a series of postponements. Albert's citizenship came up yet again. Smith eventually determined that Albert had achieved his citizenship by fraud and ordered it cancelled.

While plans were being made to deport Albert back to Italy, as they had Luciano, the U.S. Court of Appeals in Philadelphia reversed Judge Smith's decision, on the grounds that a naturalization examiner "might with greater diligence have discovered Anastasia's fraud upon the naturalization court and so the government was not deceived into granting his citizenship in 1943."

Appealing to the Supreme Court, the Justice Department said the Philadelphia court's action was erroneous and undermined the foundation of denaturalization law.

Hey, I don't know what that means either but the bottom line was that Albert didn't have to go back to Italy. Once again, a justice system with the cards stacked against Albert, failed to dish out punishment.

On March 17, 1954, according to the FBI, Albert and his brother Tough Tony held a meeting at an undisclosed location to discuss obtaining a cut of the lucrative jukebox industry. By using their usual subtle and not-so-subtle intimidation techniques, Albert and Tony were able to get some of their own guys into both the Automatic Coin Operators Association of Long Island and Local 1690 of the Retail Clerks International Association, AFL.

In April 1954, Anastasia had his former bodyguard Vincent Macri killed. Macri was not just the brother of Benedict, who had testified for Kefauver against Albert, but had for a time lived in Anastasia's mansion so he would always be on hand when Albert needed him. It was a shame, but the guy now knew way too much. Nobody ever called Albert Anastasia "Mr. Sentimental."

Albert noticed that since Benedict Macri cooperated with the government, Vincent Macri had been moving up in the world. He'd lived in Bath Beach, Brooklyn—Bensonhurst's southern "suburb"—with his wife and three kids, and for the past year many miles away in the northwest Bronx in a swank and expensive apartment on Henry Hudson Parkway in Riverdale.

Vincent was found murdered on April 25 at 3:40 P.M. on Wickham Avenue, a quiet street in the Bronx, all five-nine, two-hundred pounds of him, legs doubled under, stuffed into the trunk of a flashy two-tone 1952 green Pontiac convertible.

The guy who lived across the street—a retired transit worker who'd noticed the car parked there for a couple days—discovered the body. Investigating, the snoopy neighbor found the door unlocked and opened it. He found the ignition and trunk keys on the interior floor. A tan topcoat was on the backseat. He unlocked the trunk, took one look, and slammed the lid shut. Terrified, he fled and called police.

Macri had been shot once in the right temple and once in the back of the head with a small caliber gun. Both wounds were through and through, and no bullets were recovered. The knees of the victim's blue suit were soiled. In his pockets were a handkerchief, tortoise-shell glasses, and a pocket watch. And, bingo!

A little black book.

A team of detectives were assigned the book, which was chock full of potentially pertinent contact information. Detectives visited Macri's friends, and hauled them in for questioning. Who wanted him dead? No one knew. There were so many underworld connections in the little black book that investigators were confounded. Any one of them could have known the motive for Macri's murder. One working theory was that Macri had been shaking down bookmakers to create a defense fund for Albert Anastasia and keep Anastasia in the United States where he belonged.

The body was autopsied by Assistant Medical Examiner Philip Goldstein, and eventually officially identified through fingerprints at eight o'clock that evening.

Time of death could not be determined.

Macri's prints were on file because he'd served ninety days for attempted extortion back in 1933. He and two others were arrested that year trying to extort $10,000 from a Dr. Jacob Wachsman, under the threat of kidnapping him. For that, he got three months on Raymond Street.

First response was to bring in Benedict Macri for questioning. The last they'd heard from the brother he was in Hell's Kitchen trying to unload a hot U.S. bond worth $100,000. Trouble was, Benedict was nowhere to be found. This was starting to feel like the Mangano brothers, with one corpse and one missing.

The car Vincent Macri was found in was registered in the name of Macri's nephew, Carmelo Lazzaro from Bensonhurst, Brooklyn—15th Avenue in the sixties. Lazzaro, too, had a record. Everybody had a record. Lazzaro did one solid for drugs and paid a couple of fines for bookmaking. Cops found Lazzaro's wife Rita, and she said he might've lent the car to his Uncle Vince. That's the sort of thing that could've happened.

On April 28, police located a second crime scene. It was Benedict's car, which was pretty gory, found "on the Harrison, New Jersey, waterfront," near the bank of the Passaic River. The luggage compartment, spare-wheel well, and convertible-top boot-cover were covered in blood.

Vincent Macri was buried on April 29 in Saint Charles Cemetery, East Farmingdale, Long Island. Vincent's widow was given forty-eight hours to grieve, then cops took her downtown and grilled her for four hours. The next day they picked her up again and asked her questions for two more hours.

On May 19, 1954, a barge captain reported to the tender of the bridge at Avondale Avenue in Lyndhurst, N.J., that he'd seen a body submerged beneath the waters of the Passaic River below. Police noted that the body was not floating and theorized that it might be weighted down with concrete underwear or whatever. Police searched along the banks by radio car.

A reporter showed up and asked, "Do you think the body might be that of Benedict Macri?"

One cop muttered a reply, "That's what we're hoping."

But no body. Lyndhurst cops dispatched a teletype, BOLO for a corpse in the river. Because the river in Lyndhurst is tidal water, there was a chance that the body moved upstream from where it was spotted.

Benedict's gory car had been found close enough to the Passaic that it was possible his body was dumped in there and had moved downstream to Lyndhurst. The body, hoped to be that of Benedict Macri, was never found.

TWENTY-EIGHT
The Ferris Get No Mercy

THE MACRIS WERE OFF THE BOARD, but there was one more order of business, a guy scheduled to testify at Anastasia's re-trial, Albert's neighbor Charles Ferri.

During the spring of 1955, Charles Ferri and his wife Marian left their Miami, Florida, home, a $40,000 bungalow on Northeast Sixth Avenue, and were never seen again. The Ferris were still at the same address that Ferri had been forced to say aloud in court with Anastasia listening.

Ferri, according to his public persona, was a retired New Jersey plumbing contractor, a volunteer fireman, a Square & Compass Mason, and a member of the Fort Lee Board of Health. He was sixty-eight years old, his wife sixty-one. They'd last been seen on Friday night, April 29, 1955, by their daughter, Pauline Lopiano, who was grown, married, herself a mother of two. The couple had only recently moved to Florida from Fort Lee, New Jersey, and had been candidly photographed for the *Miami News* as they enjoyed the thoroughbred races at Hialeah Park. Not everyone knew it but Charles Ferri's wife Marian sometimes required a paid companion because of a nervous condition. (This fact pattern of course could be seen as the Ferris fearing for their lives, fleeing to Florida, being outed inadvertently by a photographer, and hiring a bodyguard for the wife.)

The Ferris' son-in-law Mike made the discovery. The Ferris did not answer their telephone on Saturday. On Sunday morning, Mike bopped by to do a quick wellness check. All was not well.

The first thing Mike noticed, the porch light had been left on. Two folded newspapers, Saturday's and Sunday's, lay untouched on the finely manicured front lawn. The mailbox was full to overstuffed. The door was unlocked. Inside was the horror. Mike called police, who at first insisted he must be exaggerating.

The Ferris' caged parakeet chirped anxiously at the intrusion of official personnel. The crime scene was found between twenty-four and thirty-six hours after the couple got juked, this based on the state of the buckets of blood they left behind.

Crime scene investigators went over the Ferri home and found blood in many locations. There were splotches spattered on a bedroom night table, and a large coagulated pool on the floor. Fingerprint expert E.G. Bugler caressed the scene with his dust and brush. Spencer Pierce from the *News* took photos of everything. The entire block was cluttered with Dade County Sheriff's cars, lights flashing, neighbors stepping out with arms crossed to see what was going on.

Another large stain of blood was found on the carpet only a few feet from the front door. Sheriff's Criminal Bureau of Investigation deputies theorized that Mr. Ferri had just answered the door when he was struck down, fell, and bled at that spot on the carpet. The fall had broken a vase that had been atop a bric-a-brac stand.

His wife went down in the bedroom. She had just gotten out of bed, probably to see what the fuss was, and was struck down. There was a lot of blood next to the bed and on the night table, but not on the bed itself.

A pile of bloody green drapes and blankets were found on the floor of the rear bathroom. The drapes had been yanked violently from the wall and had a severely bent traverse. There was a crimson smear on the bedroom curtains. One of the killers, it seemed, had pulled the curtain aside with bloody fingers to peek out the window and make sure the coast was clear.

There was little indication of a struggle. No indication of a search. Neighbors heard nothing. Police figured the couple had efficiently been rendered harmless and were removed. No one wanted to toss and turn the place. Charles and his wife Marian were the targets, not their possessions. Just to be on the safe side, all of the hospitals, police stations, and other emergency locations were contacted with negative results.

Mr. Ferri's slippers were found twenty feet from the house, leading police to speculate that he'd been dragged from his home, his slippers falling off in that spot. There was smeared blood on the floor of the carport where something had been dragged.

Deputy Floyd Alsbury spent many hours at the crime scene and said, "We can't call it murder until we have bodies—but it sure looks bad."

The search for the couple went on for weeks. They searched by airplane, by lines of men walking through heavy woods pushing toward Biscayne Bay, by cops going door to door in north Miami.

The couple's daughter and son-in-law said they had nothing helpful to offer. Charles had been retired for about eighteen months and had come to Florida from New Jersey to be closer to Pauline who herself moved to Florida three years earlier because of failing health. As far as the kids knew, the missing couple didn't have an enemy in the world.

"They had to have had at least one," an investigator said, flipping a page in his spiral notebook.

All very normal stuff, nothing for investigators to latch onto. Moving to Florida was an American pastime for northeasterners of a certain age and temperament. It was an annual migration, like the birds.

It was when investigators checked Charles Ferri's books that the lightbulb went on. The list of customers formed an unusual pattern. Ferri fixed pipes for a disproportionate number of hoods: There was Bergen, N.J., bookmaking emperor Frank Erickson—he had a leaky faucet.

There was Ferri's old Fort Lee, N.J., neighbor Albert Anastasia. Everybody knew who he was. He was the guy who went from death row back to the streets. Ferri testified at Anastasia's tax trial. Albert became suspect number one. On the day of his disappearance, Ferri had been subpoenaed to testify at Anastasia's re-trial.

The way it looked, someone had rung the Ferris' doorbell on Friday night, or perhaps during the wee hours of Saturday morning. Charles opened the door, got his head busted, Marian called out, giving away her location and earning her some quick blunt-force trauma. The bodies were, for a time, wrapped in drapery and blankets, and were dragged from one spot to another while wrapped up.

With all of this Anastasia info under their belt, investigators returned to Mike LoPiano, the son-in-law with nothing helpful to say.

"You guys are nuts," LoPiano said, shivery and nervously adjusting his collar. He was trying to scoff at the notion that a hit had been put on his in-laws by the Mad Hatter. "I can't believe you're dragging all of this Anastasia business into it."

With the disappearance of the Ferris still in the headlines, a meeting was called at the Atlantic Highlands, N.J., home of Vito Genovese. Joe Adonis and Albert Anastasia were there. The topic of discussion was Genovese's discomfort with the optics of their new notoriety, how they had to be extra-careful in the media age to avoid coincidences. He didn't like the newsprint juxtaposition of Anastasia's tax evasion trial and Ferri's tragic disappearance along with his lovely wife.

He thought people's minds would bridge that gap in a way that wouldn't have been possible had Anastasia had more patience and better timing when it came to icing guys he didn't like. With Albert, every day was execution day. It was always no time like the present.

Normally, the whacking of a godfather like Anastasia was prohibited. But Anastasia himself, by knocking off Mangano, had shattered that rule. As far as Genovese was concerned, Anastasia was getting to be a pain in the ass in too many ways.

Vito went to the commission and described the Big Picture with Anastasia out of it. They gave him approval to take out Anastasia and put Carlo Gambino in charge of the family, which would become known forevermore as the Gambino Crime Family.

Soon thereafter, Anastasia's defense attorney Anthony Calandra began a disinformation campaign designed to soften public (and mob) opinion regarding his client. He explained that the notion that Anastasia was better off without Ferri around was nonsense. Calandra said that at Anastasia's tax evasion trial Ferri had been a *good* witness for Anastasia. Ferri testified that Anastasia's home was worth $43,000. The government said $90,000.

At the same time, a counter-rumor spread that Ferri was a degenerate gambler who owed money. Nothing to do with the Hatter, *capisce*?

TWENTY-NINE
One Solid in Milan

THE FERRI INVESTIGATION caused rifts within law enforcement, which happens when some cops are actually trying to solve the crime and others, for reasons we can only speculate upon, ain't. John P. Berdeaux, chief of the sheriff's Homicide Bureau, resigned after attempting to follow up on a clue in the Ferri case only to be ordered to return to his office by the chief of the sheriff's Criminal Bureau of Investigation.

In the meantime, Albert's second tax evasion trial was delayed again and again, as Albert's legal team successfully argued for a change of venue. On May 16, 1955, a judge moved the re-trial to Camden, New Jersey.

Federal Judge Richard Hartsthorne had a long and intense meeting with representatives of the U.S. attorney's office and counsel for Anastasia. The judge postponed the start of the second trial for six days without explanation. There was speculation that the search for the Ferris had something to do with it.

But that wasn't it. Truth was, Albert had been offered a deal, and he'd decided to take it. There was no second tax evasion trial. On May 23, 1955, Anastasia entered a guilty plea to two counts of income tax evasion. On June 3, Albert was sentenced in U.S. District Court, Camden, N.J., to one year in the fed pen in Michigan, and a fine of $20,000, which was paid on June 8 and disbursed on June 27 to the IRS.

According to an FBI memo, there were "rumors" that Albert had pleaded guilty at the instruction of "other hoodlums who feared an investigation into the garment industry," who feared that the trial would cause unfavorable publicity when Albert, as anticipated, would have all of the potential witnesses against him murdered. The Macris and the Ferris were already unavailable to testify.

In the late winter of 1956, while the feds had Albert in captivity, they continued to work his case, continued their goal to pin murder on him and put him away for good. The Macri and Ferri investigations forged on.

On March 14, 1956, Bronx assistant district attorneys Albert Binder and Fred Baroni revealed that they, with the help of law enforcement in Miami, were tying together the Ferri and Macri murders, and trying to pin the whole ball of wax on Anastasia.

"Anastasia is what ties them together," Binder said. "Vincent and Benedict Macri, Mr. and Mrs. Charles Ferri. The only common denominator in all of these cases is Albert Anastasia. They were important in Anastasia's tax case. Without them as potential witnesses, Anastasia was allowed to cop a plea."

On March 13, 1956, the *World-Telegram* reported that, as part of the Anastasia investigation, authorities in Miami were seeking to interview former world featherweight boxing champion Willie Pep, who turned out to be easy to find as he was fighting that night in Tampa.

Pep was a favorite of boxing purists who liked the science of pugilism, but not well-loved by the casual fan. Pep was an expert, indeed a wizard, at defense, and won fights by how often he wasn't hit as opposed to how many times he hit the other guy. Legend had it that he'd once won a round on all judges' cards without throwing a punch. I'm not what you call a boxing purist, even though my biological dad fought at the Garden. I like a slobberknocker myself.

Point is, Pep was a friend of murder victim Vincent Macri, and had already been questioned by feds once in New York. Now there was "new confidential info," and they wanted to talk to him again.

On March 28, 1956, Albert was released from the fed pen in Milan,

Michigan. A month later, the FBI obtained information that a plan to deport Albert wasn't going to work out because he had been "refused entry" into Italy. If Italy didn't want him, there was no place to deport him to. That ended the push to deport.

On Sunday, May 13, 1956, Albert's brother Joseph Anastasio (only Albert and Tony officially changed the spelling) who had spent his life as hiring boss of Pier 14 on the Hudson, died at the age of fifty-one in Long Island College Hospital. He lived in a house Albert bought for him on 73rd Street in Dyker Heights, Brooklyn.

His funeral was held on Thursday, May 17, and it was said to be the "grandest" funeral in the borough of churches since Frankie Yale kicked the bucket in 1928. The sweetest of the Anastasio brothers, Father Sal Anastasio, said the funeral mass at the Regina Pacis Votive Shrine at 65th Street and 12th Avenue in Bensonhurst. The proceedings began at eight o'clock in the morning when mourners gathered at the Andrew Torregrossa & Sons Funeral Home, a handsome white cement building with angels on plaques under the roof eaves, set on a terrace and located in Dyker Heights, Brooklyn. Hundreds of longshoremen were on hand to pay their respects.

A *Daily News* photographer—they were everywhere—managed to photograph Albert and a few other mourners as they left the unreal parlor and got into their limo. Albert, however, managed to spot the shutterbug in the nick of time, and the next day there was a photo of Albert in the newspaper holding a handkerchief over his face.

The procession from the church to the cemetery was no longer than your average Columbus Day Parade. It was five full street blocks long and consisted of thirty-three black flower cars, carrying fifteen grand worth of purple-ribboned wreathes. Following the flower cars came the hearse carrying Joseph's body, which was inside a six-grand bronze casket. Transport of the casket in and out of the church and to the gravesite required eight pallbearers.

Inside the hearse with Joe's stiff was the widow, forty-eight-year-old Stella, all in black with a soggy handkerchief in her gloved hand, perpetually dabbing away under her veil. With her were children Robert, Rosemary, and Joe Jr., who were twenty-one, sixteen, and nine, and brothers Hatter, Tough Tony, and Bang Bang.

The police department got caught with their pants down. It figured Joseph wasn't one of the important brothers and was stunned at the size of the crowds.

Of course, much of that crowd—and it was almost all men—were there to pay tribute to Joseph's more powerful brothers. Cops had to take some last-second steps to re-direct traffic away from the proceedings. A sergeant and a bunch of patrolmen were dispatched from the Bath Beach Station.

Because he was an Anastasio brother, the Associated Press felt it necessary to print Joseph's criminal record as part of his obituary. He had been charged with murder, bookmaking, and illegal entry into the country—but he was a man who always had well-tailored mouthpieces and every charge was eventually dismissed. He was once successfully deported. He laid low in Italy for a time and then came back, jumping ship once again just as he had as a kid.

In some papers, the news of Joseph Anastasio's death ran side by side with a story of labor syndicated columnist Victor Riesel, who had been blinded when someone threw acid in his face as he was strolling near Broadway in the city, in apparent retaliation for things he'd written about racketeers who extorted laborers and exercised dictatorial rule.

It was rare for mobsters to go after a writer, but Riesel apparently crossed a line, and got his eyeballs burned out for his trouble. He called the American Mafia "the Second Government." He said this government had a Secretary of Labor, and labor "experts." Some worked the garment and trucking fields; some worked the waterfront. There were guys who either had close ties with or were themselves imbedded in the Teamster locals. There were guys who extorted sanitation workers, guys who skimmed restaurant employees. Riesel said Albert Anastasia was top of the heap, chief executioner, and when it came his turn to face his maker, there would need to be a major mob conference to divvy up his power and turf. It was like, though blind, he could see the future.

In another column, Riesel told a story about Albert cozying up to a beautiful woman in the bar of a "fashionable Park Avenue Hotel." He introduced himself.

"But you're the president of Murder Inc.," the woman exclaimed.

"Not true," he said. "I am just a businessman." He then complained about how tough it was to make a buck because prices kept going up and up—which struck her as funny.

"You're sore about inflation?" she said.

"Of course," he replied. "Look, lady, when I was a kid of eighteen or nineteen I was in the death house." He didn't pronounce that final H, and at first she thought he said debt house. "I wanted to get out. A relative got five-hundred bucks. He finds me a lawyer. I've got days to live. He gets me out with a *nolly prose*, whatever that is. A couple years ago, I got into tax trouble. I try to find a lawyer. I ask all the blue bloods. All of them say no. One lawyer, he asks me if I got a record. I leave. Finally, I got a lawyer. He costs me $40,000. So years ago, to get out of the death house it cost five-hundred bucks and today it costs forty grand to spend a year in a nice prison like Milan. That's inflation, lady!"

In May 1956, around the time of brother Joseph's death, the FBI acquired information that Albert Anastasia's godson Vincent J. Squillante, working as a front man for Albert, had been shaking down all of Nassau County on Long Island with a "garbage collection racket." Albert, the FBI learned, was Squillante's godfather and the "labor relations counselor" for the Greater New York Cartmen's Association.

Back in 1951, a middle-aged ILA delegate named Frank Russo visited a stevedore firm to inform them that they were to add the name Gerardo Anastasio to their payroll, and that he should receive a check just like the others even though he wasn't going to be showing up.

This no-show shit went on all the time, and it was no big whoop, until 1956 when Russo was called to testify before a federal grand jury and was asked about his arranging the no-show job for the Boss's kid brother. Russo told his questioner that it wasn't true and he'd never done anything like that. That resulted in Russo being charged with lying to a federal investigator. He could have done jail time after Russo pleaded guilty, but Judge Sylvester Ryan took a look at Russo's finances and concluded that this guy was too poor to be on the take and sentenced him to a three-year suspended sentence.

In November 1956, the FBI received information that permission had been granted by "high figures in the New York underworld" to kill Tough Tony. The hit, the FBI believed, was scheduled to take place as soon as the ILA signed a new contract with the New York Shipping Association, but never took place.

Around the same time, the feds learned that hoodlums were not eager to be seen in public with Albert. The Boss had never been one for making friends, but now he couldn't even get anyone to walk on the same side of the street. Hoods, the FBI believed, felt they "might receive some notoriety in the newspapers if they were seen in his company." There was also the possibility of, you know, incoming.

On January 7, 1957, Senator John McClellan, a Democrat from Arkansas, and chairman of the Permanent Investigations Subcommittee, announced he needed a quarter of a million dollars to investigate underworld/labor union racketeering. He got it, and the fed versus mob reality show went back on the air. And this time it had Kennedys.

McClellan said that there were a half-dozen top mobsters that he wanted to grill and Albert Anastasia "of Murder Inc." was on the short list. Also on the list were Johnny Dio, now charged with the 1956 acid blinding of Victor Riesel, and Joseph Profaci, boss of one of the Five Families.

By spring, the McClellan committee was in full swing, holding regular hearings, and then contempt hearings for the wise guys who refused to cooperate during the regular hearings. One of the guys refusing to cooperate was Ninzio J. "Jimmy" Squillante, a Long Island garbage collector whose brother Vincent was godson of Anastasia and by reputation the real boss of the New York Cartmen's Association. He was also an admitted policy racketeer and had done time for tax evasion.

On Monday evening, April 29, 1957, at the Universal Notre Dame Night Celebration in Washington, D.C., one of the speakers was the Senator from Massachusetts and future president John Kennedy—who along with his brother were pains in the mob's ass and look where that got them—but that was down the road, and on April 29, JFK did some namedropping. He explained that he was a member of the McClellan Committee, whose job it was to investigate labor racketeering. He gave a quick lesson in what labor racketeering was, illegal practices on the piers, unions corrupted. He said the guys they were investigating were all so-called businessmen, and he named "Jimmy Hoffa, Johnny Dio, Three-Finger Brown (Tommy Lucchese) and Albert Anastasia . . ."

It was around this time that JFK's kid brother Bobby Kennedy was gaining his first national attention as Chief Counsel for the McClellan Committee. This was the committee that would never get a shot at Anastasia because he was dead.

THIRTY
Wacky Gets Whacked

ACCORDING TO AN FBI MEMO, during the first week of June 1957, Albert sent a message to Italy. He wanted to take out his underboss Frank Scalise for failure to pay proper tribute. A sit down was held between Luciano and Adonis, who approved the hit. That's according to the FBI. Who knows?

Here's what we know: On June 17, 1957, Albert's underboss, Francesco "Wacky" Scalise, breathed his last.

Scalise, no relation to union-racketeer George Scalise, was an original Sicilian, born in Palermo in 1893, came over on the boat, and set up business in the Little Italy section of the Bronx. He and Albert had hit a guy together once, a former boss on the decline named Giuseppe "Peter" Morello, twenty-seven years earlier. His name and number were in Lucky Luciano's little black book.

When police questioned Scalise, he said he was a contractor. He lived on Kirby Street on City Island (which was technically the Bronx but poked up out of Long Island Sound between the mainland and Nassau County), although a police tail once reported that he didn't seem to be there much. He was the subject of several dope trafficking investigations, and in 1955 he testified before a Senate committee investigating narcotics.

Scalise was made by Salvatore D'Aquila as a capo. D'Aquila was replaced by Manfredi Mineo who was on the losing side of the

Castellammarese War, and got whacked. Joe the Boss got whacked, and Scalise was briefly the head of one of the original Five Families (1930–31) and known to his underlings as Don Ciccio (most often pronounced Don Cheech).

He went on to be one of the first hoods to develop Vegas, helping to open the Flamingo Hotel and Casino, working under Bugsy Siegel, and by 1957 he was back in the Bronx.

Through all of it, police couldn't touch him. His record was a short one, a burglary arrest in 1920, and a vagrancy charge a few years later. Other than that, clean as a whistle, despite his reputation as a lifelong mobster, and an upper echelon guy at that.

On that hot day, Scalise had just finished an ordeal. Bronx County Assistant District Attorney Albert Binder had quizzed him for hours about several murders—although the majority of the questions focused on who put the chill on Vincent Macri and disappeared his brother Benedict.

Wacky had a disorderly mind. He had guys who didn't properly respect him for the things he'd done in the past. He was Don Cheech! He also had a reputation as a guy who'd sell a button for fifty grand, very bad form, and when a recent shipment of *babonia* was seized by police, he didn't reimburse his partners. That could mean nothing but trouble.

Although it was technically still springtime in the Belmont section of the Bronx, the direct sun of the approaching solstice baked the teeming tenements and pavement, and rising humidity created an out-of-season dog-day steaminess.

It was just after one-thirty in the afternoon and Wacky had just purchased ninety cents' worth of fruit from Enrico Mazzaro—at Mazzaro's Fruit and Vegetable Store on Arthur Avenue just north of East 186th Street. He was putting his dime change in his pocket.

The proprietor walked in front of Wacky outside to straighten up his sidewalk displays.

Two men brushed by Mazzaro. He heard some shots and looked around. These two men were hurrying by him again. They weren't wearing coats and they had their sleeves rolled up. They got into an old black sedan and headed north on Arthur Avenue.

There was no telling how well Mazzaro saw the killers, one of whom was believed to be Jimmy Squillante. He was smart enough to say that it wasn't very well.

"I couldn't even tell how old they were," Mazzaro said.

Wacky received four wounds: one in the Adam's apple, left cheek, right shoulder, and right side of the neck. He fell onto his left side. A pool of blood grew from under his head.

Within minutes of the shooting, the Bronx grapevine had summoned the victim's brothers, Philip and Thomas. They tried to get to their brother's body, still sprawled on the floor of the store but were restrained at the door by cops.

Seconds later, another brother, Jack, showed up, having run all the way from the candy shop he owned on Crescent Avenue. The three brothers were corralled by detectives from the Ryer Avenue squad and questioned.

Don Cheech's 1956 blue Cadillac coupe was found two blocks away from the shooting, on Crescent Avenue, just down the street a ways from his brother's candy store.

Deputy Inspector Martin Donelon put fifty dicks on the case. Bronx County D.A. Daniel Sullivan promised he would fully support the investigation. To get a bead on the case, Inspector James J. Walsh, a Mafia expert with sixteen citations (one for his work on the Lindbergh kidnapping), was brought up from Brooklyn.

With great ceremony, Assistant District Attorney Albert Blinder sought and received a court order, then opened Frank Scalise's safety deposit box at the Dollar Savings Bank on the Grand Concourse. The box, which technically belonged to Frank's widow Joan, contained $950 in cash, $2,000 in bonds, and a dazzling array of sparkling jewelry—but nothing that might help cops figure out who killed Frank.

A search warrant was granted for Frank's house, and one of the items seized was an address book, every page of which contained a potential lead. We may assume that Scalise's loan book was also discovered as cops began to visit the scores of men who owed Scalise money. Police established that Scalise, despite his seniority, remained an active shylock, but they came no closer to figuring out who killed him.

Wacky's funeral was held at Scocozza Funeral Home in the Bronx, and he was buried in Woodlawn Cemetery, also in the Bronx. His brother Joe began to scream about revenge. Whoever offed Frank had better watch his ass, because Joe was coming for him.

There was a lot of bluster, but it had to stop. On September 7, 1957, Joe Scalise accepted an invitation to a party at Jimmy Squillante's house. In a nightmarish scene, all of the other guests at the party were stone-cold killers with an unquenchable blood lust.

Joe Scalise was no sooner in the door when they fell upon him with knifes, slit his throat, and chopped him into pieces. Because Squillante and his brother were in the waste management biz, they bagged up what was left of Joe and put him in a trash truck.

Following Wacky's death, Carlo Gambino moved up a notch and became underboss, under Albert Anastasia. Today, it is believed that Albert himself ordered Wacky to be shot, the motive being that Wacky was selling buttons, which resulted in made men who were not trustworthy. Wacky had outlived his usefulness. Maybe the FBI memo, that Wacky was hit for failure to pay tribute, wasn't that far off.

In July 1957, Albert demonstrated that he'd learned a lesson from his tax evasion conviction and his year in the fed pen. If he was going to continue to live as a rich man, he was going to need a more substantial cover as a legitimate businessman. He purchased a second company, the Nuremberg Dress Company, in Nuremberg, Pennsylvania.

On September 12, 1957, FBI agents interviewed Albert Anastasia for about a half hour. The interview was conducted in connection with an anti-racketeering investigation requested by Assistant U.S. Attorney Charles H. Miller.

The questions dealt with his connection to and association with the Hazleton dress manufacturing company. He said that he'd owned half the company since 1948 but had never participated in the operation of the company.

The FBI's Newark Division completed the investigation on September 20. An internal FBI memo took note of a comment made by Victor Riesel on the "Three-Star Extra" news show on NBC that Anastasia had been grilled for three weeks by the FBI, and confirmed that this report was inaccurate. The half-hour interview was all there was.

Coming out of the interview, Albert Anastasia boasted, "Nobody's got nothing on me. I'll die in bed."

THIRTY-ONE

Costello Gets Creased

IT WAS MAY 2, 1957, spring was in the air, and sixty-five-year-old Frank Costello, just out of stir, was still taking those deep-nostril inhales of freedom. He'd been in bad trouble for six straight years and over that span had done stretches for contempt of court and tax evasion.

Costello had just enjoyed a steam and a rubdown at a Turkish bath at the Hotel Biltmore and hopped in a cab with theatrical agent Philip Kennedy, head of the Huntington Hartford model agency. It was just shy of 11:00 P.M. The cab pulled to the curb and Costello got out, home sweet home.

Costello lived in the fancy posh apartment building—the Majestic Apartments on Central Park West and 71st Street. Costello entered the building, tiptoed down the steps, crossed the foyer, and was about to pass into the lobby proper.

Just then the world's largest hit man, a three-hundred pounder, stepped from the sidewalk through the open front door and from the top step fired one shot, downward at Costello's head. The bullet danced and plowed and skipped and ricocheted, tearing up Costello's scalp but never penetrating the bone to enter the brain.

The bullet came to a near stop next to Costello's right ear, then fell—all pooped out—to the lobby floor.

* * *

Costello didn't even go down. He was stunned for an instant, and when he began to walk his gait was punch-drunk, a boxer ready to call it a night. He made it into the lobby, found a chair, and plopped into it. What a headache he had.

The tall, heavyset gunman didn't track Costello's movements. He waved his gun menacingly at the terrified doorman and dashed toward the street, on feet pretty fleet for a big guy. The shooter climbed into the shotgun seat of a black Cadillac sedan, driven by an accomplice.

Witnesses couldn't see in the rear window of the getaway car because "the shades were drawn." The little light that was supposed to illuminate the license plate was apparently out. The car laid a patch of rubber and rocketed southward on Central Park West.

It all happened so fast that Philip Kennedy's cab was still parked at the curb. He and the hack heard the shots and then the getaway. Kennedy hopped out and ran into the building, and became the first person to Costello's side. Costello looked like he should be dead meat but instead was only dazed.

"Are you all right, Uncle Frank?" Kennedy asked.

"Somebody tried to get me," Costello said, teeth clenched with pain. "Get a doctor. Call an ambulance. My head . . ."

The apartment building's night service manager arrived at that moment and quickly called the house physician—but the doctor was out. So they helped Costello into a cab, and he was taken to Roosevelt Hospital.

The injury was quickly treated, cleaned out and stitched, and at about 1:00 A.M., with a turban of bandages around his head and two aspirins in his belly, Costello was joined by Kennedy and Mrs. Costello, the lovely Loretta. Police arrived and Costello was taken directly from the hospital to the West 54th Street station for questioning.

Because of the gunplay's organized crime connotations, the interview was conducted on the second floor of the precinct house, which had been declared for the occasion by Chief of Detectives

James B. Leggett off limits to the press, and any other visitors for that matter. Costello's wife was just shy of crisp when she arrived, dressed after a long night in a black cocktail dress and a mink stole. She and concerned friends were also kept on the second floor where they were questioned separately.

"Ever see the guy that shot you, Frank?"

"No."

"Hear the shot?"

"Yes, and then a sting in the right side of my head. When I felt the blood oozing down the side of my head, I knew I was hit. That's all I know."

"Who do you think shot you?"

"No clue. I'm sorry boys. I know you got a job to do and I'd love to help you out, but I can't. I didn't see nothing."

Cops found a slip of paper in his pocket that they found interesting, and Costello had a hell of a time convincing them he didn't know what those numbers meant. Santa Anita? What is that?

As Costello was receiving medical care, police at the Majestic Apartments found the bullet on the lobby floor badly flattened. Clearly a bullet versus Costello's skull was a mismatch.

They learned from the doorman that the shooter had been a behemoth. So they went in search of shooters who resembled mountains, who looked like they could work the pro wrestling circuit grappling with Killer Kowalski. It was a short list—and before long cops nabbed Vincent "The Chin" Gigante. They brought him in for Costello to look at.

"This the guy?"

It was obviously the guy.

"Never seen him before," Costello said.

"Look careful."

"Nope," he said, and then added, "I seriously don't know why anyone would want to ice me. Things ain't that great for me as it is. I'm old, my health is heading south, and tax evasion prosecutions are sucking at my will to live."

Costello hinted that he might've—once upon a time back in the bad old days when it was like the wild wild west in the five boroughs—dabbled in the rackets, but that shit was behind him now.

In reality, Costello was thinking it might be a good time to retire in peace to his Sands Point, Long Island, mansion. But one thing first. What Costello was thinking was, *"Anastasia should say his prayers because Anastasia is a dead man."*

Talk about punishing the victim: Costello was shot, had about a hundred stitches in his scalp, a major migraine, and he was jailed for contempt when he refused to testify regarding the meaning of the betting slip found in his pocket. Seriously?

Anastasia knew the instant he heard the hit on Costello had failed that his own life expectancy was not good. He only hoped that they'd hit him, and not members of his family. He prayed the target wouldn't be his son, who was only twenty-two. They did that sometimes, Albert had done it himself, to bust up dynasties and prevent vendetta. Albert Jr. had just graduated from Fordham and was in graduate school.

Albert Sr. pumped up security after Costello was shot. Three men now guarded him, and his wife and son now had full-time guards, as well. The pressure was getting to him. One Saturday he was spotted at Jamaica Racetrack tearing up a handful of $100 losing tickets.

He looked old. Asked what was up, he said he was worried about his family.

Cops talked to people at the Biltmore Hotel. Anything unusual happen with Frank Costello? The manager said, yeah, there was something. Didn't seem like a big deal at the time. Minutes after Costello left, there was a phone call from someone looking for him, a voice the manager didn't recognize.

"What did you say to the guy?"

"Said sorry, you just missed him."

In the papers there were photos of Costello, blood on his double-breasted brown suit, blood on his white shirt, his bandages visible under his now ill-fitting fedora. The victim was referred to as "gambler Frank Costello." The joke was that the shooter put a new part in

Costello's hair. Costello was the world's luckiest guy and scared shitless.

Every time a hood took a bullet, Albert Anastasia's name came up, but at police headquarters, he was not a heavy suspect in the Costello shooting. As one police official put it. "Couldn't have been Anastasia. If it had been Anastasia, Costello would be dead. Albert's boys don't bungle a job."

A couple of days after Costello was shot, crime reporter Fred J. Cook of the New York *World-Telegram and Sun* received a phone call from a guy who didn't want to identify himself. The mystery caller had a simple message. "If Albert or Freddie steps in, they get it, too," the caller said, and hung up. It was easy enough to figure out who Albert was. Who was Freddie? Perhaps Frederick J. "Angel of Death" Tenuto, one of Albert's favorite enforcers.

During the summer of 1957, the feds came after Albert for what seemed like the umpteenth time. Again, it was taxes, Albert's Achilles heel. In August, tax agents filed a civil suit against the Hatter to recover more than a quarter million dollars in back taxes and penalties.

Albert answered back by charging the government with harassment, saying their figures were based on "exaggerated estimates." The suit covered 1946–52 when Anastasia was boss of the waterfront. The suit stemmed back to the 1954 tax case. Albert endured his year in Milan, but still owed the tax.

In September 1957, there were further indications that the authorities had put a target on Anastasia. For one thing they surprise-arrested forty-five-year-old Anthony "Tony Cappy" Coppola, Anastasia's chauffeur and head bodyguard.

Coppola was rolled up as he left the San Carlos Hotel on East 50th Street for his daily duties: picking up his shiny 1957 Oldsmobile at the lot and driving to Fort Lee to see the Boss. He was charged with six ignored traffic tickets dating back to 1953, and released on $3,000 bail—$500 for each ticket.

While they had him, all they wanted to talk about was Albert, Albert, Albert. This was apparently a new ploy as several scofflaw gangsters with access to bosses had been brought in and grilled.

Cops kept an eye on Coppola and learned that he had two massive subordinates who helped him with Anastasia's security, and all three were with Anastasia whenever he went out. This was Coppola's second arrest of the year, as he'd also been held for questioning following the Frank Costello shooting.

According to U.S. Attorney Paul Williams, during the early autumn of 1957, the FBI was going after Albert with renewed vigor, and the fear was that Albert was in such big trouble that he was a candidate to flip. Even if he didn't flip, the fact that law enforcement seemed on the verge of nabbing him for good was wearisome to the hoods who were trying to earn money without it showing up in the next day's headlines.

The constant attention Albert was receiving had the mob feeling weary. The commission was urging Anastasia to make like Costello and retire. The commissioners were wealthy men, and it seemed that with each scandal Anastasia caused with his impulsiveness Treasury agents were menacing their accountants, scrutinizing their books, and pretty soon "everybody knows their business."

They were fed up with unwanted headlines and with a man whose name had become in America synonymous with brutal gangland violence.

Albert's last date with a woman before his date with death came on Saturday night, October 19, 1957. It was with a married beauty queen named Janice Drake. She'd been Miss New Jersey in 1944, a pinup girl for the boys overseas during World War II. She'd been a pro dancer, had spectacular gams with silken thighs, and arched her back nicely while wearing the bullet bra.

If she caught the whiff of mob on a guy, she was about as hard to get as a haircut but just as dangerous. She was married to comedian Alan Drake. The Drakes were swingers. One was just as apt to step out as the other. There was no jealous-husband angle.

For syndicate guys, a kiss from Janice Drake was like the kiss of death. She made a habit of getting next to hoods just before they were chilled, and going down on guys on a hit list turned out to be her fatal flaw, as well.

Janice bar-hopped with garment-district-powerbroker Nathan "Nat the Bookie" Nelson on the night he was killed, taking bullets to the belly and the mouth inside his West 55th Street bachelor pad in 1952.

Her last meal came on September 25, 1959, in Kew Gardens, Queens, with mob killer Little Augie Pisano. A dapper dresser, Augie was known for his white felt fedora with black silk band, his finely tailored suits and his shiny shoes. He was a caporegime for Genovese, ran nightclubs, and was a man with a history and many real enemies. He would kill for Genovese, of course, but for a price he sometimes shot people for Lucky Luciano and Frank Costello, as well. Before he was through, Augie would be arrested for murder six times, but each time they had to cut him loose. Augie was in charge of collecting the Genovese cut from New York's garment district. Because of his status, Augie also controlled labor unions there, and may have used his muscle to rig a few city elections. On that last night, after dinner Augie and Janice drove around in Augie's Cadillac. Their killer was in the backseat. Augie and the thirty-two-year-old Janice were each shot in the head as they drove down a dark street near Junction Boulevard in Queens. The crime scene was not far from the airport at the time known as LaGuardia Field. The car had continued on after the shooting, went up onto the sidewalk, and crashed into a small apartment building. The killer climbed out and scurried into the Queens night. The hit became famous because a *New York Daily News* photographer, of course, was on the scene immediately. The photo that ran in the paper, big, showed Drake, slumped to one side but eyes open, staring at the glove compartment, with a bullet hole in the center of her forehead. Augie had fallen over to his right, so that his head was now in Janice's lap—a clear reversal of the way her dates usually went.

* * *

You don't often hear Albert Anastasia and John F. Kennedy in the same breath, but most would agree they have something in common. They both went out so spectacularly, in public, like Fourth of July fireworks, that it colored and, in some cases, obscured what they had done in life.

If one was an assassinator of men, and wanted to execute the most spectacular assassination, there were two requirements: one, hit someone big, someone worthy of splash headlines; and two, do it in a spot where many people could see it. Do it in public, where people gather, where witnesses have cameras.

There had to be *visuals*. (Six years later these requirements were taken to the extreme, with the leader of the free world whacked in public with multiple cameras clicking and several movie cameras purring away from all directions.)

As Anastasia's days grew few, his killers knew that his name would earn the front page of the tabloids, so they picked a spot where the crime could get maximum exposure. They chose a barbershop with a big storefront window, on an over-crowded Manhattan avenue, cattycorner from Carnegie Hall, right in the middle of everything.

It had long been the policy of reputable newspapers to never show dead bodies. It was considered too sad, gross, disturbing, and invasive of the victim's privacy. That is, unless you were the *Daily News* and the dead body belonged to a gangster, in which case the gory details would be shown vividly on the front page. Apparently, there was nothing sad about a dead hood; nobody cared about a gory goon's privacy.

Anastasia's demise involved a barbershop quartet of ambitious men, out to make their bones, and I knew all four of them.

THIRTY-TWO
Albert's Last Shave

AT 10:15 A.M., FRIDAY, October 25, 1957, fifty-three-year-old Albert Anastasia entered Grasso's Barbershop off the lobby of the Park Sheraton Hotel at Seventh Avenue and 55th Street in the city. With him was his godson Vince Squillante, Long Island trash czar.

Albert's bodyguard Cappy was parking the car. Cappy's two massive subordinates weren't around. There was no security in the barber shop.

"Albert, your usual?" the proprietor said.

"Thank you, Arthur."

"Your favorite chair is free."

"Lucky number four."

"Have a seat and I'll get you ready," he said. Arthur heated up the towel.

"Joe available to shave me? I like the way he does it," Albert said.

"Sure, Albert, sure. You going to the fights tonight?"

"Yeah, I just talked to a kid fighting tonight. Managed by a friend of mine."

"Close your eyes, towel's hot."

At 10:18 A.M., four men in business suits, each wearing a black glove on their right hand, a scarf, a fedora, and aviator shades arrived at the Park Sheraton. One stood near the front entrance, one stood in the lobby just outside the barbershop, and two entered the shop with guns in their gloved hands.

As the hitmen entered, they didn't start firing right away. They were too cool for that. Anastasia's face was wrapped in a hot towel. He wasn't going anywhere.

One of the gunmen used the muzzle of his gun to push Joe the barber out of the way. The shooters positioned themselves so that one was on either side of Anastasia's chair.

Anastasia now sensed the interruption, pulled the towel off his face and had time to look around. He started to get up. He raised his left hand to protect himself, and two slugs tore through it, one gun so close that it left powder burns on his hand.

And as Albert Anastasia's brain was ripped to shreds, there was a brief explosion of electricity. Synapses sought to bridge the gaps and snapped. But just before the end, perhaps, Albert got a quick but vivid glimpse of the lamentations, horrors painted from his earthquake nightmares, that naked pack of scavengers that scuttled about like spiders in the chalky Italian dust worming their boney hands into the pockets of the dead. He knew in that instant that he was still and had always been on the dusty road to hell, scalding wind on his face, marching down, down, down through the ruins of the dancing land and into the boiling river of blood.

The gunmen fired ten shots. The victim was shot three times in the head, once in the hip, twice in the hands. Four shots caught nothing but barbershop. The victim managed to get up even as he was being shot. He lurched in an aggressive manner, but toward the reflection of his killers in the mirror. It was his last move as he fell to the floor on his back between chairs two and three.

The gunmen paid no attention to Squillante, who shivered violently only a few feet away in chair number three, paralyzed by fear. There was a moment of silence as Anastasia lay still, until the manicurist screamed and slumped over in a faint.

The killing squad retreated into the lobby, and then to the street, so that once again there were four of them. Three climbed into an American-made car that squealed as it burned rubber down West 55th Street. The fourth walked briskly north two blocks and ducked into a nearby subway, downtown BMT to Brooklyn.

Virginia Nelson—the red-headed owner of The Red-Headed Woman, a hotel dress shop—was first to call police. Next to Grasso's was a flower shop owned by Constantine Alexis, who heard about six shots in three flurries: one shot, pause, two shots, pause, three more shots. There were more, of course, but sometimes the gunmen fired simultaneously.

Alexis saw "five or six" men run out of the hotel. Some went out the Seventh Avenue exit, and others ran out the 55th Street exit. Not all of the running men were with the kill team. Terrified barbershop customers also ran. One of those customers was probably Squillante who had vanished into the Manhattan tumult by the time police arrived. Alexis told police he ran into the barbershop and recognized the body on the floor as that of Albert Anastasia. He knew him because he used to come into his shop for flowers.

Arthur Grasso told cops it was his shop. He rented the space from the hotel and was head barber. When Anastasia came in for his regular trim, Grasso himself made sure to greet him.

"I set him up, but he was going to be shaved by Joseph Bocchino."

"How come?"

"He liked Joe's touch."

"Describe the shooters?"

"Nah, faces covered."

"Anything unusual about them?"

"Yeah, they were both wearing one black glove—on their shooting hand. One five-five, one five-seven."

Along the same corridor that led to the barbershop was a luggage shop owned by Joseph March. He said he was entering the hotel and ran into several men running out. One still had a little shaving cream on his face. One running man stumbled and fell to the floor on his back.

While he was down, he screamed, "They're going crazy in there! They're shooting!"

There were many newspapers in New York back then. Morning papers, afternoon, and evening. And competition between them was intense. So, when word of the barbershop assassination hit the telephone wires, there was a rush on the location. Within minutes of the shooting, a herd of reporters and photographers, crumpled and jabbering, barged into the shop to observe and photograph the body. The photographers' flashbulbs back then were literally explosive and strobe-lit the scene, memorializing the carnage. For an instant, with excitement heavy on congested hearts, the lightning of eager 1957 photography, and the tight circle of interest around one fellow down for the count, the scene resembled the end of a big fight at the Garden.

One detective just arriving said, "Witnesses?"

"Yes, sir," a uniformed cop replied, "Two customers, five barbers, a manicurist, and a couple of bootblacks."

"What did they see?"

"Might as well be blind, sir."

One witness said the shooters might have been Italian men and everyone laughed.

Someone had covered Anastasia's ghastly head with a towel, but it was still a vivid sight. Even after police managed to keep members of the press outside the shop, spectators could still look in the window and see the body on the floor.

It was the biggest mob hit in New York in thirty years, and you could watch from one of Manhattan's busiest sidewalks. Every few minutes, another official vehicle would scream to a halt outside. Detectives, assistant D.A.s, and press converged. The first doctor on the scene was Dr. Robert Cestari of St. Clair's Hospital who pronounced Anastasia dead, and then got on the horn with Chief Medical Examiner Milton Helpern.

An officer was assigned to contact next of kin, who was Albert's brother Tony, the leader of Brooklyn's longshoremen. The cop headed out to the docks to do the notification, but a reporter from the omniscient *Daily News* got there first and broke the news to Tough Tony.

Mr. Sensitive with a police press card said, "Tony, your brother Albert just got blown the hell away."

Tony went straight to the hotel.

At Anastasia's Fort Lee fortress, a *Daily News* reporter parked outside the front gate and called out to a handyman who was puttering in the yard.

"I need to talk to Mrs. Anastasia," the reporter said.

"What for?"

"Anastasia has been killed."

"Which one?"

"Albert."

"Father or son."

"I think it's the father."

"Sorry, she's not here. She's out shopping," the handyman lied.

Elsa was sedated at the news her husband was dead.

On the other side of the Hudson, additional barber sheets were used so Albert's body was covered completely.

Police asked folks from the hotel if they had folding screens, and someone ran over to the dress shop and returned with temporary walls that were placed around Anastasia's body. That helped to disperse the crowd outside the barbershop window.

Tough Tony arrived at 11:17 A.M. weeping like a child. He threw himself on the floor of the barbershop. He threw his arms around the body, pulled away the sheet so he could kiss his brother's face. He had to be pulled away so Dr. Helpern could have the body transported to Bellevue Hospital morgue for autopsy. Later in the day, Tony was seen stoically entering the West 54th Street police station.

Tony Cappy, done "parking the car," strolled back to the murder scene. Seeing a fuss, he scrammed. Later he voluntarily went to the police station to give a statement, saying that he missed the whole thing, that he had no idea who might have wanted to bump off his boss, and that he himself was retired because of his arthritis.

At Bellevue, Dr. Helpern determined that either one of two bullets, one in the back, one in the back of the head, could have been responsible for death. Albert Jr. arrived with his cousin Robert and officially identified the body. In the paperwork, the son listed dad's occupation as "dress maker."

Law enforcement knew that the *who* of this murder mystery was going to hinge on the *why*—which was troublesome because there were so many motives to choose from. Maybe Anastasia put a hit out on Costello, didn't get the job done, and blowback was fatal. Maybe Anastasia and Costello were friends, in which case both hits could have come from the same source. Maybe someone thought Anastasia was one government questioning away from bringing down the whole show.

While patrol cars searched for the gunmen's vehicle, beat cops near the hotel interviewed those who hadn't run away, including lightweight boxer Johnny Busso who was staying with his manager Andrew Alberti in a room at the hotel because Busso had a fight at the Garden that night. Minutes before the shooting, Busso said he ran into Anastasia "by coincidence" and had a conversation in the hotel lobby during which the upcoming fight was discussed. The happenstance of the meeting was thrown into doubt by Alberti's long association with Anastasia, which earned the boxer Busso a grilling. (Busso won his fight that night, by the way. Apparently unaffected by his interrogation, he won a unanimous decision over Gale Kerwin.)

Sketchy information later gathered by the FBI indicated that the guns used in the Anastasia hit were stored for pick-up in the hotel room occupied by Busso and Alberti. The information wasn't good enough to cause Busso legal troubles, but Alberti lost his boxing manager license and in 1962 blew his brains out with a shotgun rather than give grand jury testimony against a friend.

Cops wondered about the black gloves. Prevent fingerprints?

Sure. Keep off gunpowder residue? Absolutely. Or . . . some speculated that the killers were paying homage to assassins of old, their black gloves being symbolic of the Black Hand murders a generation earlier, in which the killers left the impression of a black hand somewhere on the victim's person.

Reporters hung out at the police station and watched the parade of underworld characters that came in for questioning. Little Augie Pisano was questioned—what you might call one of the usual suspects. Augie was never a real suspect, though. The hit on Anastasia served him poorly. His position as a Genovese lieutenant would grow shaky. Augie's allegiance was questioned. (In 1959, Vito would call for a meeting of his lieutenants because he was worried about family solidarity. Everybody showed up except Augie. He was discussed in his absence. Then he went out with Janice Drake and you know how that turned out.)

Harry Stasser, Anastasia's garment partner, came in for questioning, as did Anniello Ercole, who brought his lawyer with him.

Others questioned included Mike Miranti, one of Albert's hoodlum pals, and Pete DeFeo, who'd been indicted for murder but released when five of the witnesses disappeared.

Two guns were discovered in the hours after the shooting. One, a .38 Colt, was found immediately as it had been dropped in the hallway outside the barbershop. The other, found later in the day, was a .32 Smith & Wesson. It was in a garbage disposal unit in the 57th Street subway system. At least one of the gunmen, it appeared, had escaped the scene by train. The guns turned out to be antiques. The .32 was traced back to 1920, the .38 to 1934, both purchased from "out-of-town dealers."

Anastasia's body was still warm when the phone rang at the news desk of the *New York World-Telegram and Sun*. It was a guy who asked to speak with crime reporter Fred J. Cook.

Cook took the call and heard a familiar but unidentified voice on the other end. "You remember I called you last spring after Costello was shot and printed a warning we issued to Anastasia not to butt in?"

"I remember," Cook said.

"Well, we're giving another warning now," the caller said.

"Warning who?"

"This time we're telling Frankie—and I don't mean Costello. Frankie is not to interfere and we're not fooling."

"Frankie who?"

"Frankie C.—but it's not Costello. That's all."

With that the mystery caller hung up.

The FBI wondered how the killers knew where Anastasia was going to be. Although Arthur Grasso tried to cleanse the taint from his shop by saying Albert was a bouncer who bounced from shop to shop, it turned out that finding Albert wasn't that hard. He had been a creature of habit. You could time his haircuts like clockwork, same shop, same chair, every two weeks.

His back to the door.

THIRTY-THREE

Funeral of Albert Anastasia

WHEN ALBERT ANASTASIA DIED, there were few mourners. His funeral, on Monday, October 28, 1957, was austere, especially when compared to brother Joe's funeral with his five-block-long parade of flower cars and $6,000 mahogany and bronze casket.

Albert had only six cars, which included the hearse, one flower car, and four limos full of mourners. Maybe Albert paid for his brother's funeral but not for his own.

Because of his reputation as a killer, the Catholic Church did not want Albert buried in consecrated ground. So, despite brother Salvatore's oddly delicate lobbying—"my brother is not accused of killing for personal satisfaction, but strictly in the line of business"—Albert's body was not allowed in a Catholic cemetery. Holy Cross and St. John were out of the question.

He would have to be laid to rest under a simple flat headstone, in Brooklyn's Green-Wood Cemetery, which was nondenominational. The procession entered the cemetery at the 25th Street and Fifth Avenue gate. Albert's services were simple and brief—maybe even hurried. There was a sense that bullets were in the air, and it was best to not spend too much time out in the open.

Mourners were scarce, but their numbers were matched and bettered by police, with men stationed along a hill to the east and sitting in parked cars on Fifth Avenue near the corner of 32nd Street to the west. The only thing resembling a crowd consisted of a group of nervous spectators bellying up against the high iron picket fence on Fifth Avenue. Outsiders, hopeful of seeing a "real gangster," were amazed that the burial was taking place so close to a major thoroughfare, and in a such a downscale section of the cemetery, far from the huge monuments and statues that the cemetery was known for.

Witnesses said that, with the exception of Albert's immediate family, there wasn't a wet eye in the house.

Visitation was held earlier in the day at the Andrew Torregrossa & Sons funeral parlor, the Dyker Heights facility where brother Joseph had been laid out. There, Albert's body was displayed in an open steel casket, which reportedly cost $900. Curiosity seekers and gawkers gathered across the street, some to pay tribute to the great gangster, some to make sure he was really dead.

The press covered the event *en force*. The *Daily News* reporter, Joseph Kiernan, tried giving Albert a new moniker posthumously and referred to him as "Al the Enforcer," which never had a chance to catch on with The Mad Hatter and Lord High Executioner already in place.

Reporter Al Turk noted that the ghosts of the men Anastasia had killed outnumbered his mourners. Reporters tried to get into the cemetery to get a better view but were stopped at the gate by police, who also remained outside.

The Catholic presence at the burial was limited to Father Sal, then pastor at St. Lucy's in the Bronx, who said prayers at the gravesite for widow Elsa, son Albert Jr., brother Tony and his daughter and her husband Mr. and Mrs. Anthony Scotto Jr., brothers Bang Bang and Frank, two elderly relatives, Mr. and Mrs. John Melito from Utica, and two unidentified women. Albert's daughters, who were eight years old, were not there.

Elsa was the only one demonstrating real emotion, and she appeared close to collapse. Albert Jr. had her firmly by the elbow the whole time and several times seemed to be supporting her weight as her knees buckled. The cops who were there in force with cameras and binoculars were disappointed as the guys they were looking for were no-shows.

"Private visitations" had been arranged at Torregrossa's on Sunday evening for the two-dozen friends and loved ones who were on the down low. This group included Little Augie, and a pair of union bigwigs, ILA president Capt. William Bradley, and ILA chief organizer Thomas "Teddy" Gleason.

For the spectators who did show up at Green-Wood Cemetery, there was not much to see. Because of the exposed nature of the gravesite, some mourners refused to get out of their cars, so a barrier of floral pieces was hastily constructed.

The funeral director Andrew Torregrossa was at the cemetery, mourning himself perhaps because Albert's existence had been so good for business—and gave each mourner a single carnation to place atop the now-closed casket. He, himself, placed a wooden crucifix on Albert's steel box.

As Father Sal cleared his throat and steadied himself to speak loud enough for all to hear, a quick blast of cold wind whipped across the cemetery and toppled the flower display that had been blocking the view from the street. The display was picked up quickly and the frail priest had to clear his throat and gird his loins a second time.

Fadduh Sally spoke for about two and a half minutes. He talked about how devoted Albert had been to his wife and children. He talked about how much Albert enjoyed playing Parcheesi in his Fort Lee home.

He said some other stuff, religious stuff, but nobody was much listening and later nobody remembered the words. The steel casket was placed inside a copper outer coffin as the family returned to their cars. Once everyone was safely inside their limos, the coffin was lowered into the hole, and everyone got the hell out of there. The black cars were in and out of the cemetery in under twenty minutes. Veterans of the mob funeral beat said it was the quickest and quietest funeral for a big-time gangster that they'd ever seen.

In the next day's paper, there was a stunning close-up of the widow in her black dress and fashionable sunglasses.

In other news, Grasso's barbershop was closed, and would remain closed until the police investigation was through. Arthur Grasso wondered what it would be like when his shop re-opened. Would people ever be able to relax and have a shave—or would it forever be stigmatized as the place where *it* happened.

Albert's disgraced forty-nine-year-old bodyguard Anthony "Cappy" Coppola was being held as a material witness, police openly stating that he was safer in jail as there was a bullet with his name on it. Assistant District Attorney in Charge of the Homicide Bureau, Alexander Herman, said, "If this man walks out, it may very well be the beginning of open warfare by the hoodlums of the city."

All of this, Coppola said, was nonsense. At first, he claimed that he was never Anastasia's bodyguard. They were just friends. Maybe they rode in the same car sometimes. Yeah, he drove, but that didn't make him his chauffeur or anything. They started to chum around when Albert bought some fish at a Jersey market that Cappy's parents ran in 1952. That's all.

"I haven't an enemy in the world that I know of," Cappy said. "And I thought Mr. Anastasia hadn't any either. I was just a friend of his. May God have mercy on his soul wherever he is."

The pudgy Coppola not only gave conflicting stories of where he was when his boss was whacked—going to park the car, buying a pack of cigarettes, etc.—but he was a witness to many meetings between Albert and other gangsters that cops were dying to learn about.

A big deal was made of the fact that Cappy was multi-lingual, leading a reporter to quip, "Yeah, he can say 'I don't know nothin' in nineteen languages."

The grieving widow never publicly admitted that any of her husband's notoriety was earned. In public she said, "He worked hard to support our family to maintain our home. He never drank, smoked only cigarettes, and was always home by 9:00 P.M. He never spoke roughly and he used to go to church with me every Sunday."

That said, Elsa was a practical woman and living the remainder of her life as Albert Anastasia's widow figured to be a stressful proposition. She sold the Fort Lee mansion, changed her last name, and moved back to Canada.

On October 30, 1957, NYPD Chief of Detectives James B. Leggett told a reporter from the *Herald-Tribune* that the murder of Albert Anastasia had "150 angles." Investigators, he said, had to be patient. The mystery was a big jigsaw puzzle, and to see the big picture many tiny pieces had to be put together. It was the sort of thing detectives said when they didn't know what happened.

He said that the two guns picked up in association with Albert's murder had been tested by ballistics experts and could not be tied in to any other mob killings. Neither gun had any fingerprints on it.

Murder investigations tend to be simple when the victims are simple, Leggett said, but Anastasia was a complicated guy and had uncountable enemies. The murder could have been committed by a major power in the underworld, or it could've been over a beef, many years old. Could've been the son of any guy bumped off by Murder Inc.

One angle, Chief Leggett said, sang out *"cherchez la femme."* The chief added that Anastasia did not have a reputation as a ladies' man, but he was a man, so there was a chance that there was a woman involved in his murder, "somewhere in the background."

Chief Leggett was asked about Coppola.

"He was Anastasia's coffee sergeant," the chief said. "He was a messenger, driver, whatever. He's complaining that he doesn't have money for the bail. He says our investigation is all a farce. Hard to figure what he means by that."

"Did Anastasia know someone was gunning for him?" a reporter asked.

"As far as we can tell, no," Leggett replied. "Apparently he felt no one was big enough to take him. He felt his fearsome reputation was all the protection he needed."

The NYPD investigation into Anastasia's murder was under the direct command of Commissioner Stephen P. Kennedy, whose team consisted of fifty detectives. Reporters asked Commissioner Kennedy for the motive. He said it was all about "the policy and dice game rackets" that Anastasia held under his thumb. He noted that NYPD involvement began within seconds of the hit. Within moments of the murder, a *fifteen-state alarm* went out for the two gunmen. Too bad no one checked the BMT.

The bragging made reporters antsy.

"You think it was the same guys that creased Costello?"

"No, there was a drastic difference in competence."

The Costello shooting was shaky, tentative even. Hit man stuck out like a sore thumb. The Anastasia hit was deliberately paced, efficient, and thorough. Killers wore shades, black gloves, eyewitnesses were all over the place. No one could give a description.

There was speculation among reporters that Anastasia's murder may have represented the ultimate karma, indicating that perhaps another Murder Inc. was on the rise, to do the job that Albert's crew had done so well during the 1930s.

Some said the killers shouldn't be hunted down at all but instead congratulated and rewarded. Leggett made it clear that his men were looking for Albert's killers just as hard as they would if the victim had been a goody two-shoes. Why? Anastasia's killers were ruthless men, every bit as ruthless as the man they killed and could not be allowed to continue operating as they pleased.

The working theory was that whoever ordered the hit probably used out-of-town talent. First thought was that some guns were brought in from Philadelphia, but that didn't pan out.

The FBI had a report the killers were holed up in Cleveland. Nope. G-men started to think they were getting a sophisticated runaround. They were told that the killers were holed up in the General Sherman Hotel in Atlanta, Georgia, only to find out that there was no such hotel.

They were told that the killers were holed up in the back room of a barbershop near the Sahara Motel in Miami. Turned out that there was a shopping plaza across the street from the motel that did have a barbershop, but the shop didn't have a back room—or an upstairs, or anywhere else where a person could hide out. Desperate, they searched an apartment house on the other side of a wooden picket fence behind the barbershop, performed background checks on all of the tenants and found nothing exciting.

They looked into connections between Albert and Las Vegas. They checked on connections between Albert's death and the organized-crime takeover of the casinos in Havana, Cuba. They spent *considerable* time looking for connections between Albert and the Cuban government, and between Albert and the criminal element in Cuba, two overlapping groups. Nothing.

The *World-Telegram* printed as fact that it was Albert's ploy to grab a chunk of the Cuban operation that got him killed, with Meyer Lansky being the master cylinder behind the assassination. The paper reported that a few days before Anastasia's murder, Lansky (through messengers Santos Trafficante and Joseph "Joe Rivers" Silesi) warned Anastasia to "stay out of Cuba." The meeting, it was said, took place in a suite in a hotel on West 49th Street in the city. Cappy Coppola rented the suite. Albert told Lansky no and that was that.

Trafficante was an early suspect in the Anastasia hit. Not long after Albert's final shave, police learned that Trafficante—who maintained headquarters in Tampa, Florida, and Havana, but rarely came north—was in New York City on the day of the barbershop shooting, registered in a Manhattan hotel under an assumed name and scheduled to have a sit down with Albert to talk about the Havana casinos. That meeting never happened.

Who benefitted most from the victim's death? Number one on that list was Carlo Gambino, who moved up a notch with the death of Scalise, and then another notch all the way to the top with the death of Anastasia. But Trafficante was served well by Anastasia's death, as well. Whatever chunk of Havana that Anastasia planned to take was now going to stay firmly in Trafficante's pocket.

The Cuban investigation by the U.S. government didn't do anything to solve Anastasia's murder but it did result in Meyer Lansky getting the boot off the island by Cuban Minister of Interior Santiago Rey because of pressure brought to bear on Cuba's president Fulgencio Batista by U.S. Ambassador to Cuba Earl E. T. Smith. Lansky's exclusion from Cuba, the FBI hoped, might influence him to tell what he knew about Anastasia's murder.

Barber Arthur Grasso was already having business problems when things went from bad to worse. The hotel wanted Grasso out. Too many sightseers making the guests nervous.

They tried to break his lease but Grasso fought, and a court told the hotel it was out of line. The hotel, with its own financial issues brought about by the murder, then sued Grasso for half a million dollars, charging that Grasso violated a "good conduct" clause in his lease by "soliciting the business of known underworld figures."

The FBI investigation into Albert Anastasia's murder radiated outward from the barbershop floor, and spread as far as Italy, where a tip led investigators to search for a guy named Sonny Pinto, believed to be identical to Carmine DiBiase. According to the *New York Post*, the feds asked the Italian police in Naples to help locate Pinto. Asked for comment, however, the FBI denied that it was looking for Pinto/DiBiase, or anyone else in Italy for that matter.

It was all wasted time. The actual killers were hiding out only a few miles away from Arthur Grasso's barbershop—in Red Hook, on the west end of President Street by the piers.

THIRTY-FOUR
The Men Who Killed Anastasia

THIS BOOK IS A SORT OF PREQUEL to my last book, *Carmine the Snake,* about the long and wild life of the late Carmine Persico. Anastasia's last chapter and Carmine Persico's making of his bones were simultaneous. Albert was in on the whacking of Joe the Boss and Vince Mangano, so that was how it went.

(If you haven't read *Carmine the Snake,* you should do that right now. It's at a bookstore near you. If they don't have it ask them why not.)

Carmine was born into the Great Depression on a hot August night in 1933. Most men who took up The Life had two choices: work on the piers or in the rackets. But that wasn't true of Carmine. He could've done anything. His dad had a white-collar job, legal stenographer, so the Persicos were better off than most, living in the middle-class Park Slope section of Brooklyn. Carmine found trouble anyway.

He belonged to one of the prototypes for Brooklyn street gangs, the Garfield Boys. Like their competitors such as the Degraw Boys, and the Midgets, they wore Brylcream and smoked Chesterfields. They were sharp and violent. They hung out in the late 1940s at Fifth Avenue and Garfield Place in the Park Slope section of Brooklyn, where they had rumbles over turf.

On Memorial Day 1950, Carmine was among those held for questioning following the death of James Fortunato during a rumble in Prospect Park. Six months later Carmine was arrested and charged with the murder of Steve Bove, a twenty-six-year-old dockworker, found in a Carroll Street gutter near the Gowanus Canal, shot three times in the base of the skull. The murder charge was dropped in March, but Carmine continued to be held as a material witness. Carmine's brother eventually went down for the Bove kill.

As far as incarceration went, maybe Carmine was better in than out. Later that year, while out, Carmine was shot in both of his legs while returning from the movies to his Park Slope home on Carroll Street, ambushed by three young gunmen in a stolen car.

Carmine was a kid with ambition and made a smooth transition from the youth street gang into the crew of Frankie "Shots" Abbatemarco, along with the Gallo boys who were considered Carmine's good friends. Though a competent thief and organizer of money rackets, a *good earner,* he was most intense as a killer. Men who saw it never forgot it: the icy look Carmine had on his face as he killed. Anastasia-esque, you might say.

Two years after making his bones by blowing away Albert Anastasia, Carmine was one of two shooters in the hit on Frankie "Shots" Abbatemarco, his old boss. They shot him as Shots exited his cousin's saloon, Cardiello's Tavern. Carmine and another man, in topcoats and fedoras, coolly followed Frankie as he retreated back into the bar, and filled him with holes on the saloon floor.

Like Carmine, the Gallos were fearless. When Larry Gallo got an invitation to the Sahara Lounge on August 20, 1961, a bar in East Flatbush, he went alone. In the dim tavern Larry found Carmine and two others there to meet with him. No one else around. Not even a bartender. Just Carmine, Sally D'Ambrosio, and John Scimone.

While Larry was sitting at the bar talking to Carmine and Scimone, Sally came from behind and wrapped a rope around Larry's neck. Larry looked to be a goner, until a cop walking his beat poked his head in and broke up the attack. Sally shot a cop while making his escape. Larry lived, but he had a mark around his neck for the rest of his life.

In the twenty-four hours after, someone took a shot at Joey

Gallo's car (Joey wasn't in it at the time), and Joe Jelly's finger was delivered to Jackie's Charcolette. The Profaci Family declared war on the Gallos—and Carmine was on the other side. The President Street Boys had balls of titanium, but Profaci badly outgunned them.

Truth was, Carmine betrayed the Gallos well before he was in on the attack on Larry, hanging around President Street while tactics and strategy were discussed, and taking what he learned directly to Profaci. It was the betrayal of Larry that got him called Snake.

The Gallos didn't take Carmine's turn lightly. In May 1963, a hit team—Rick Dimatteo (my dad), Frank "Punchy" Illiano, and Gennaro "Chitoz" Basciano—attempted to take out Carmine. Rick, Punchy and Pete "The Greek" Diapoulis knew an old army vet who knew how to make a bomb and gave them instructions. And it worked. The bomb exploded on cue under Carmine's Cadillac, and under Carmine.

Fortunately for the intended victim, there was a steel plate under Carmine's seat, and he walked away with nothing much worse than a concussion, tinnitus, some cuts and bruises, and a sore ass.

Years later, Dimatteo and Illiano did try to kill Carmine with bullets. Carmine took a bullet to the cheek and spit it out onto the sidewalk.

Bombs couldn't stop Carmine. Bullets couldn't stop him. He rose in the ranks until by the age of thirty-nine he was the Boss of the Colombo (formerly Profaci) Family. Loved dearly by his crime Family, he now had a new nickname: "The Immortal."

Carmine's decades as Boss were eventful, but most noteworthy because Carmine spent most of his time in prison. His arrests and legal history culminated with his 1986 conviction for racketeering, extortion, etc. He was never free again, and died in prison in 2019.

Two of Anastasia's barbershop quartet were Gallo brothers, Joey and Larry. Their mom Mary had a joint called Jackie's Charcolette on Church Avenue in Kensington.

Their dad was Umberto, and he was of Albert Anastasia's generation. He came over from Naples in 1920 and made big-time money during Prohibition. I knew Umberto Gallo as a very old man. I would pick him up and take him to a place on Henry Street where he liked to play cards.

For me, these guys aren't out of some history book. They were real-life guys I knew as a kid. They grew up in the mean streets of Red Hook, and Joey was the leader.

They called him Crazy Joey because you couldn't tell if his head was screwed on straight. He liked to pretend he was crazy, liked to scare people with the nutzo look in his eyes, but then he'd do crazy things, things that demonstrated balls of steel, but crazy nonetheless, until you were wondering if it was an act at all.

He wasn't around much when I was a kid. I knew him when I was very little, remember the way his eyes gleamed when he smiled. I know now that there was a touch of paternal sadism in that gleam because he'd pinch my cheek so hard that tears would come to my eyes, and he enjoyed causing me pain, but he also enjoyed making me tougher, which is what I was going to need to be if I planned on staying on President Street when I grew up.

I was seven when he went away, and I was sixteen when he got out. After that, he didn't hang out on President Street all the time. He wasn't a big guy, a hundred fifty pounds tops, and he was blond and blue-eyed, which made him stand out on the block.

Joey's crazy act was based on a 1947 movie that he saw when he was a kid, called *Kiss of Death*. In it the actor Richard Widmark played a psychopath named Tommy Udo, who dug jazz and laughed in a bizarre way. Joey could do that laugh, and did—striking fear into the hearts of men. It's the same everywhere, from the backroom of a social club to an elementary school playground: crazy beats tough every time.

Joey was like Udo also in that he loved jazz music and seemed to be living to a syncopated beat, snapping his fingers with a black urban vibe running through his veins. Joey even took his fashion sense from *Kiss of Death*. He wore a black suit, black shirt, and white tie. Very striking.

He'd do the Udo laugh anywhere, and I mean anywhere. He'd do it in a courtroom as a judge was sentencing him. When he was a teenager, a judge sent Joey to a shrink to see if he was fit to stand trial and the doctor proclaimed him schizo.

He wore insanity like a badge of honor. We'd seen him do crazy shit. He backed down from no one, went after big guys and worked them over with his fists. He'd go out on a job with a Louisville Slugger in his hand and do the Udo laugh as he was busting some guy's head open.

He only pulled a gun when he was outnumbered. One on one, he liked to be up close and personal when he was dishing out the punishment. He never figured to live to be old and didn't. On April 7, 1972, "Crazy" Joey Gallo was killed at Umberto's Clam House.

Larry Gallo was the Gallo brother I knew best. That's because my dad Ricky was brought into the Gallo crew to be Larry's bodyguard. Larry was the smartest of the bunch.

Joey made everyone afraid of the Gallos, and Larry made the decisions. Larry was considered smart and sane. He was the guy you went to for advice. He was a fantastic earner, a guy who would think outside the box, thought up new ways to tap into the economic flow.

When Larry and Joey put their heads together, they had unquenchable ambition, which is why they kept acting like David taking on Goliath. They were by decree under the regime of the Profaci family, but they didn't like paying tribute, and a lot of guys got shot because they wanted to be their own thing.

At first Persico was one of the crew, and they all worked for Abby. But Persico killed Abby, tried to kill Larry, and war erupted with the Gallo brothers and Persico on opposite sides.

No surprise that all four of the men who were in on the Anastasia hit were themselves the victim of mob violence. Two were killed, two survived attacks. Twice one member of the barbershop quartet tried to kill another.

In 1968, Larry Gallo—my dad's good friend, the guy who bore the Mark of the Snake on his neck—died of natural causes.

* * *

Joe Jelly, real name Joseph Gioelli, was the fourth guy on the scene at Grasso's Barber Shop, and the only one of the four who didn't get his button out of the deal. Mr. Profaci apparently didn't feel Joe Jelly had done enough to warrant a button. Carmine Persico had a new crew, and one of his boys was Freddie No Nose, an ex-boxer who'd taken one too many to the kisser, and had no remaining cartilage in what used to be his nose.

According to Sal Polisi: No Nose, Sally D'Ambrosio, and Carmine Persico were in on the Joe Jelly hit. Sally had a boat he kept at the man-made bulkhead harbor at Sheepshead Bay. He asked Joe Jelly if he wanted to go fishing in the ocean for blues.

Jelly said sure, and left his girlfriend's house that morning in a relaxed mood. Jelly liked to fish, he'd gone fishing with Sally before, so he had no reason to think something was up. He didn't even get it when he learned Carmine Persico, and No Nose were going out on the boat also.

Joe Jelly, as they say, sleeps with the fishes.

They came back with fish but without Joe Jelly—well, all but his ring finger. They turned it into a messy business, removed Joe's clothes, dismembered him, put the pieces in a fifty-gallon drum and dropped the drum overboard into the Atlantic. The hit took place sometime before the attempt on Larry Gallo's life, but the delivery of his finger to Larry's mom was timed so that they occurred the same day.

THIRTY-FIVE
Aftermath

TWENTY DAYS AFTER Anastasia's assassination, on November 14, 1957, a big-league sit-down was attended by many top mobsters and/or their delegates in a small-league western New York State community called Apalachin, population 277. The attendees wore silk suits and most smoked cigars. It turned into a famous meeting for all the wrong reasons.

The cover story was that there was going to be a barbeque in the landscaped backyard behind the rich-and-famous home of bottling czar Joseph Barbara, whose estate was within shooting distance of the Pennsylvania border. Barbara was Mr. Canada Dry, made his millions selling ginger ale.

The real reason for the sit down was to evaluate the state of the five-family system as set up by the great Luciano. With Anastasia's elimination, fear was that chaos would reign. There was also the matter of Anastasia's power and turf, which would need to be divvied.

The Barber estate was known as a busy place, with a lot of comings and goings, but the parade of luxury cars containing Italian gangsters caught the attention of a local yokel cop named Sgt. Edgar Croswell.

When a town has less than three-hundred people in it, cops know every car. They might even know every car just by listening to the engine. The cars they saw for the barbeque would've stood out anyway. Black Cadillacs and Lincolns were the favorites. A few limos chartered from the city. Those hoods looked about as out of place as a bowtie at a biker rally.

Croswell, no dummy, immediately thought mob powwow, and called for backup. In minutes, cops had the place surrounded. They watched through binoculars and jotted down license-plate numbers.

Then they raided the joint. It'd be great to have surveillance footage of that raid. It must've been a comic masterpiece. All of these tough guys suddenly dropping their drinks on the lawn, chucking their ID and hightailing it into the nearby woods. They ran like escaped prisoners popping out of a tunnel, like degenerates fleeing the busted crap game. The moment has been called the American Mafia's single greatest humiliation.

When you're a kid and you flee from the scene of whatever because of a siren, you can run forever, from Red Hook to Canarsie if you have to. But these guys were middle-aged and older a lot of them, and they chain-smoked Chesterfields. They couldn't run very far at all, and the police had no trouble netting them and hauling them into their suddenly overcrowded police station. Fifty arrests were made. Among those arrested were Joseph Bonanno, Joseph Profaci, Jerry Catena, Vincent Rao, Carlo Gambino, Paul Castellano, and Vito Genovese. What a haul.

Of course, the stories the hoods told the cops were all over the place, but most of them agreed on one thing. Their decision to drop in on Joseph Barbera was spontaneous, and they were surprised and delighted to see that there were other guests on hand, as well. A few admitted that there was a planned event, a cookout, some drinks, but denied that it had anything to do with business, legitimate or otherwise.

Meeting for a barbeque was not illegal, so cops didn't hold any of the mobsters for very long. What was accomplished, however, was that a roster of the mob's upper echelon was now written down, a list of names that future U.S. Attorney General Bobby Kennedy would use as a guideline to fight the mob.

Genovese was hurt most. In his mind, the presumed purpose of the meeting was to abolish the five-family system and to proclaim himself king of the underworld. And the whole thing had been horribly botched. His stock plummeted. Luciano took care of it. He didn't whack Genovese—as Anastasia would have. Instead he set Genovese up, got him busted on a bullshit dope charge. While he was at it, he set up the Chin as well, and both Genovese and Gigante did long stretches.

The damage done to the mob in Apalachin couldn't be measured in jail time. One of the things the mob had going for it was that it really was organized, yet law enforcement didn't know how it worked. Now they had a roster, and that would go a long way toward figuring out the infrastructure.

All of the invitees to the party were Sicilian. Eleven of those picked up in the raid ended up appearing before grand juries. I don't know who did the counting, but it is said they took the fifth 870 times.

During the first week of 1958, District Attorney Hogan hastily called a press conference in the Criminal Courts Building where he announced his latest moves against the mob. The scene was being played out on a day when the mob was a hot topic. The New York *Daily News* was running a series of articles about how gangsters had a firm grip on the gambling casinos of pre-Castro Havana, Cuba. A federal grand jury in New York City was investigating racketeering in the garment manufacturing and trucking industries. All of the men rounded up at Apalachin were being questioned, at a pace of four a day. The four on this particular day included an orchestra leader, a drapery and curtain salesman from Pennsylvania, and a garage owner and a former labor union official from New Jersey.

The D.A. said that Chief Assistant D.A. Alfred Scotti, head of the rackets bureau, and Assistant D.A. Alexander Herman, boss of the homicide bureau, were presenting evidence to the grand jury regarding the murder of Albert Anastasia.

Hogan announced that a "nationwide alarm" had been sent out for two hoods for questioning with respect to a Havana gambling concession. He referenced Santos Trafficante, alias Louis Santos, a resident of Tampa, Florida, who was in town when Anastasia bit the dust.

Trafficante earned himself a lot of press later in life with his connections to the assassination of President Kennedy, i.e., his relationship with Jack Ruby. He'd been among those scooped up at Apalachin, and cops learned he was a shadowy guy.

Trafficante operated the Sans Souci in Havana, a great place to gamble, drink, and get a broad. In Tampa, he operated a $500,000 per year policy bank, with a war chest of a million bucks at all times for bail money and payoffs.

The subject of Havana power, in particular control of the Sans Souci casino, Hogan said, had come up in a meeting with Anastasia days before his death, and because of that Hogan felt safe to assume, it was probably a major topic of discussion at the November 1957 Apalachin meeting, as well.

Hogan said, "It has become extremely important to examine Rivers and Trafficante before the grand jury in the recent rubout of Albert Anastasia. We believe their testimony may shed light on the motivation for the assassination of the old Murder Inc. boss."

Trouble was Trafficante was missing, probably in Florida or Cuba, both excellent places to hide, and hadn't been seen in some time. In addition, Hogan was looking for "certain residents of Havana who it is known were interested in the gambling casino concession which was the subject of negotiations. Three persons were in New York and conferred with Anastasia a few days before the killing."

On a snowy morning, December 4, 1957, NYPD bulls nabbed the big-time bookmaker Frank Erickson as he was strolling down Manhattan's Park Avenue. Erickson was dragged to the nearest precinct house and grilled regarding the Anastasia murder.

The pudgy sixty-two-year-old man's cheeks turned pink, and he blustered a bit, but he went. With him was ex-con George D. Uffner, who was brought along for good measure. Both detainees were dressed in finely tailored suits.

They were searched upon their arrival at the station, and found to have no wallets, cards, or identification papers of any kind. They both, however, carried a roll of cash.

Inspector Frederick Lussen later estimated they asked Erickson about a hundred questions. He answered three of them: name, address, and occupation. He said his occupation was "real estate." He took the fifth for the other ninety-seven. In 1950, Erickson told a Senate Committee that he made a hundred grand a year making book. He didn't want to talk about that either.

On the other hand Uffner—who turned out to be more interesting than detectives figured because he was a friend of Costello and Luciano, once did a six-year stretch for forgery, and had a connection with the rackets that dated back to the days of Arnold Rothstein—answered every question he was asked, which was easy for him because he apparently really knew nothing about the Anastasia hit. He didn't know who did it, who ordered it, or why anyone would want Anastasia dead. He did say that he was the president of the Federal Oil Company of Manhattan, which bought and sold oil fields in the Fort Worth, Texas, area. Almost bizarrely, Uffner said he didn't know Frank Erickson either, and it was just a pure coincidence that the two men had been walking near one another when police pounced.

After about three hours, the men were released. Questioning Erickson made oddsmakers think the gambling angle was being investigated. Maybe it was simple. Maybe Albert got in trouble at the track. Nah, it didn't make sense. Albert's access to cash was pretty much limitless. If he were in debt, he'd just steal what he needed to pay it back—or kill the guy he owed it to.

As for Uffner, he didn't have long to live. On September 30, 1959, he was among thirty-four persons killed when a Braniff Airlines turboprop Electra went down near Waco, Texas, on a Houston-to-New York flight.

On February 25, 1958, the Anastasia investigation took a sexy turn. A slinky blonde actress named Liz Renay wore her black sweater exceptionally well as she was questioned for two and a half hours in the District Attorney's office. She'd go on to be in movies like *Date with Death*, *The Thrill Killers*, and *Hot Rods from Hell,* but in 1958, was best known on the Sunset Strip for her spectacular tits—and as Mickey Cohen's girlfriend.

She told the D.A. with a purr that she never met Anastasia and had no idea who clipped him. The bulk of the interview had to do with her role as courier, taking a package of cash from Anthony "Cappy" Coppola, for Anastasia, to Mickey Cohen.

"Did you know Anthony Coppola?" the D.A. asked.

"Oh yeah. Very well! Cappy wanted me to marry him two years ago, but I said no. The only one I go out with now is Mickey Cohen, a very dear friend of mine."

As for the package, she didn't know what was in it or why it was being sent.

Without his godfather, waste-management czar Vince Squillante was left vulnerable, and quickly vanished. Word was he was killed with a bullet through the brain, put into a car that was taken to the dump, crushed into a cube that would fit on your kitchen table, placed in a blast furnace and left somewhere. The Garbage King was now just another piece of trash.

About a month after the Apalachin bust, NYPD Deputy Police Commissioner Walter Arm, reacting to a tip from Lieutenant James Burke and Detective Thomas Fusco of the Manhattan West Detective Headquarters, arrested three of the men who'd been busted in Apalachin.

While the FBI was chasing down leads in Georgia, Florida, and California, every place but Brooklyn, the local police were starting to get a bead on what might've actually happened. Officials denied that the detentions had anything to do with Anastasia, that they were investigating garment-district racketeering, but you had to figure the subject came up.

The three guys they picked up—Joseph Profaci, the olive oil king and the man under whom the actual shooters toiled; Paul Castellano who worked for the man who benefitted most (i.e., Carlo Gambino); and Natale Evola, who told police he was a "garment distributor." They were taken to the Brooklyn police precinct at Sixth Avenue and Bergen Street and questioned for three hours before being released.

Evola and Profaci snuck out the side door when they were through. Big Paul went straight out the front door into the teeth of news photographers and climbed into a waiting car.

Police later divulged that they had been looking for and were unable to find five other men, including Gambino and Joseph Bonanno. Gambino had just finished a round of questioning from New York State Police and was away for the NYPD investigation. According to state records, Gambino said he worked as a "labor relations consultant." Bonanno said he was retired.

On February 23, 1958, Don Ameche and Eli Wallach starred in "Albert Anastasia: His Life and Death," a TV episode of *Climax!*, on CBS, one of the first programs ever to be broadcast in color.

A synopsis of the episode dispatched to newspapers described it as, "A television commentator-analyst (Ameche) attempts to convince his producer that the life story of Albert Anastasia (Wallach) is not the glorification of a waterfront assassin and, in order to prove his point, he recounts some of the grim aspects of Anastasia's life."

The forty-two-minute play, as was the norm back then, was performed live from a studio in Hollywood. Adapted for TV by Malvin Wald and Harold Greenberg from a story by Bernard Girard, it ran opposite the episode of *Dragnet* in which Joe Friday pretends to be a truck driver to bust oil pirates.

About his performance as Albert, Wallach said, "I grew up in Brooklyn, in a neighborhood which produced quite a few of these people. Some of the kids I knew went into bootlegging, and into the mobs, and came to a violent end. Why didn't I follow them into the rackets? Who knows? Who can say what it is that sends one boy one way or the other?"

To prep for the role, Wallach interviewed many persons who

knew Anastasia, including lawyers who defended him. He scouted Grasso's Barber Shop.

The show got mixed reviews. TV columnist Jack O'Brian said that Wallach, though a very good actor, "didn't come close to the real, ugly intensity of Anastasia." Don Ameche "had too much overstuffed moralizing to mouth." Despite all of that, O'Brian wrote, the show was a "fairly fascinating TV drama . . . The wallop of the play was its modern-day lower-depths drama."

By July 1958, mob fever was once again sweeping the nation. Apalachin revved things up. The Kennedys and the Senate Rackets Committee in Washington were conducting a new investigation into the bust, and the bustees.

Hard to believe today now that the word Mafia has become synonymous with Mob, but in 1958, many people associated the word, if they were familiar with it at all, with something distinctly foreign. On July 1, 1958, for example, a story went over the newswire entitled, "Anastasia Killing Tagged to Mafia."

Today, a headline like that would get a snarky response like, "Ya think?"

But then it meant that the killing came from without rather than from within. The lead to the story read, "A federal narcotics agent today testified before Senate rackets probers that the Narcotics Bureau believes Albert Anastasia was murdered by the *Mafia*, the super-secret Italian underworld society."

Times have changed. Sure, the Apalachin bust had netted a herd of hoodlums, but the notion that they might be associated with the *Mafia* was startling. The story went on to say that the agent testified that Anastasia himself had been Mafia, an organization out of Sicily that was, the agent testified, also known as "Black Hand" and *Unione Siciliana*.

The rackets committee released a chart that showed fifty-eight men who'd been busted at the meeting, and designated which ones had been arrested (50), convicted (35), in prison (23), and found guilty of murder (18), guilty of narcotics (15), guilty of gambling

(30), guilty of illegal possession of firearms (23), guilty of liquor infractions (34), and guilty of blackmail (5).

Despite the successes, getting the goons to talk to U.S. senators in public was tough sledding. Most refused outright to say whether they belonged to a crime organization and/or attended a meeting of that organization at the time of the bust. Some admitted that, yeah, they might've been at the house where the meeting took place but it was kind of an accident, and they had no idea what the topics of discussion were.

One guy was John Charles Montana of Buffalo, New York, who was a former member of the Buffalo City Council and "Man of the Year" in Buffalo in 1956. A lot of the guys were ostensibly union officials, hotel and restaurant employees.

"I was just there to get the brakes fixed on my Cadillac," Montana told the gathered senators

"Oh Heavens!" replied Senator Irving M. Ives. "Of all the places along that stretch to get your brakes fixed, you picked this farm?"

"I've known Mr. Barbara for years," Montana said.

"Did you know that he had been arrested two or three times in connection with murder?"

"No, I did not."

Later, an undercover Federal Narcotics Bureau agent testified that it was his belief that Lucky Luciano still ran things from Italy, and the meeting at Apalachin was arranged by Luciano to discuss filling the void left by Anastasia. The committee discovered that it was easy to tell who was a delegate for which mob leader because they were often related by blood or marriage.

Not everyone believed the Mafia was active in the U.S. J. Edgar Hoover didn't buy it, and with good reason. He won every time he went to the track, in particular Santa Anita, and he wanted to keep it that way.

In 1958, there were still newspaper headlines like, "The Mafia: Is It Real or a Fairy Tale?" Part of the lead read, "Is the Mafia ominously real? Or is it a storybook word to catch the headlines?"

The Apalachin meeting was indeed about divvying up the pie, a pie that included Havana casinos, where hoods were treated as lords and no one ever paid any tax ever. But Fidel Castro ruined the deal in Cuba. John Kennedy ruined the plan to rid Cuba of Castro. Goats and pigs were allowed to run wild in the casinos, shitting in the roulette wheels. JFK got whacked. Somehow Castro survived. You could look it up.

On November 30, 1958, Bang Bang died of throat cancer after a four-year battle at the Long Island College Hospital, the closest hospital to Red Hook. The family wanted to keep Jerry's death quiet, and there was no mention of the passing in the paper until a week later when he was buried in St. John Cemetery in the Middle Village section of Queens following a requiem mass at St. Stephen's Roman Catholic Church.

By all accounts, the funeral was a low-key affair, with only five passenger cars and one hearse at the cemetery. Strictly family. The ceremony was in sharp contrast to the traffic-jam-inducing hubbub at brother Joseph's funeral two years earlier.

When Bang Bang's obituary was finally published in early December, much space was reserved for his more famous brothers, Albert and Tough Tony. Jerry, it said, had been a "business agent" for Local 1814. He had only recently been in trouble. He testified that he had not gone to a stevedore's office in 1951 to demand a $100 per week shakedown and later confessed to lying about that. He was sentenced to thirteen months behind bars in 1957 but was released after sixty days because he was in failing health. Bang Bang was a widower and survived by his three kids.

Now there were only two Anastasio brothers left: Tough Tony and Father Sal.

On January 2, 1963, Tough Tony Anastasio suffered a heart attack that left him weak, bedridden. His wife passed away and he continued living with his daughter and son-in-law Anthony Scotto.

Scotto was the organizational director of ILA Local 1814. Tough Tony had three grandkids. He died in a Brooklyn hospital on March

1 at the age of fifty-seven. His obit recounted how he jumped ship, had a criminal record dating back to 1925, assault, murder, but nothing ever stuck.

After Albert died, Carlo Gambino had allowed Tough Tony to retain his position of power on the waterfront, which had to be bittersweet for Tony, who now worked under the auspices of the man who took control of his brother's crime family.

During the summer of 1962 vice cops had raided Local 1814's hall and were shocked, *shocked,* to discover a $500,000 a year gambling racket. Tony was in Houston, Texas, at the time of the raid, and when he returned, he was subpoenaed to testify before a grand jury. Word later leaked out that he'd been asked if he ever made a bet in his own union hall.

Tony said, "Don't get me wrong, I have placed many bets in my life, but in the union hall? Never. No."

In August 1963, Tony had been ousted as co-chairman of the ILA's Wage Scale Negotiating Committee because he reportedly: 1) made troubling pro-management statements; 2) poked fun at the Wage Scale Committee's demands; and 3) interfered with the committee's internal affairs.

But in death all was forgiven, and the union went all out to create a unifying ceremony. On Tuesday, March 5, on a wintry day in the cold wind, as longshoremen crowded along the sides of the street, there slowly passed a procession of sixty-six limos, a hearse containing Tough Tony's bronze casket, and fifty more cars full of mourners.

The route took the vehicles along seven miles of piers, giving the workers a chance to say good-bye to Tough Tony. Some waved, some jerked off their caps and bowed their heads. Some stood tall and looked straight ahead like good soldiers. Tough Tony's hearse was escorted by fifteen coaches banked with elaborate flower arrangements, including one shaped like a steamship. The parade ended at Sacred Heart-St. Stephen's Church where a crowd had gathered. Father Sal, last remaining brother—showing surprising strength and stamina—sang the High Mass at Tony's funeral.

Outside the church there was speculation about who would take over the union. Popular money was on Tony's son-in-law, "Young Tony" Scotto. (Two weeks after Tough Tony's death, Young Tony was elected International V.P.)

From the church the parade hit the streets again, headlights on, next stop Holy Cross Cemetery, where Tough Tony was buried in a sardine plot that he shared with eight of his in-laws. Such a humble resting spot at the end of such an impressive procession. His name was chiseled in small print at the base of the existing gravestone.

In 1963, Joseph Valachi sang from an undisclosed location, and became the government's first well-informed rat. Valachi filled in many blanks for the Law. In the fall of that year, near the tail end of the Kennedy Administration, Valachi sang for the Senate permanent subcommittee of Senator John McClellan of Arkansas. In Red Hook, you could walk down the street and never miss a word for all the radios and TVs that had Valachi on live.

They asked him about the hit on Anastasia. On President Street, everyone was very interested in his answer to that question. As of 1963, the NYPD said that their top suspects for Anastasia's barbershop quartet were Ralph Mafrici, who had been questioned and released, and Joe Jelly who'd been missing since August 1961. That was close to home but still no cigar. Valachi could spill the beans, though. Worse, he was in a place where he couldn't be whacked.

"Mr. Valachi, who ordered the hit on Anastasia?"

"Vito Genovese," Valachi said.

On President Street, everyone relaxed. There would be no questions about the barbershop quartet. The government was interested in the master cylinder.

Valachi said that Genovese iced Anastasia, as well as disappeared Anastasia's Fort Lee neighbor Anthony "Tony Bender" Strollo. Genovese was a guy who ran his crime family from behind bars after getting fifteen years in Atlanta for narcotics. Vito told his boys that it might be better if the family laid off the drug trade for a while. Anastasia's neighbor Strollo disobeyed the command and continued dealing dope. Strollo kissed his wife good-bye on April 8, 1962, said he had to go out for a few minutes and would be right back, but was never seen again. Imagine the ice water in Genovese's veins: Strollo had been the best man at Genovese's wedding.

Valachi said the beef began in May 1957 with the Costello creasing. Costello was a risk to rat, Genovese thought, and the crease was a request from Genovese that Costello relinquish his turf and his power, dead or alive. Costello complied. Anastasia got pissed off at the attempt to kill his friend Frank Costello and asked Genovese for a sit down to discuss things. Genovese told Anastasia to mind his own business. Anastasia was the one making the threats, but it was Genovese that made the move.

Valachi testified that Genovese had the fix in before he hit Anastasia. He cut a deal with Anastasia's top lieutenant, Carlo Gambino.

Valachi said it was Strollo's disappearance that led Valachi to believe he was next on the hit list and to put himself in federal hands. He would live out his days with a $100,000 price on his head.

A reporter asked a government official, "How long would Valachi last if you released him?"

"About a half hour," the official replied.

In 1964, Father Sal wrote a book, which said that all of the libelous things folks read about his brothers was just fake news, and he relentlessly attempted to restore his family's good name. The book could not have been written more sincerely or with a more focused sense of purpose, and it couldn't have been more unintentionally funny. It struck sophisticated Italian readers as campy, over the top—and became a surprise bestseller.

On March 27, 1969, the *Daily News* reported that major new developments into the Anastasia investigation had brought about the questioning of several witnesses. An unnamed "prime suspect" in Albert Anastasia's murder had applied to the New York State Parole Board for permission to leave the U.S. The suspect had been paroled in 1968 after serving seven years in Green Haven Correctional Facility in Beekman, New York, for assault and robbery. The suspect told the parole board that his family was now living in Italy, and he wanted to join them. The board took several months to rule on the request. The newspaper reported that police did "not yet" have enough evidence to arrest the suspect for the Anastasia hit. Police sources said the suspect had been under "loose observation" since he'd been paroled.

Digging into the situation, *News* reporter William Federici reported that the new interest was based on "solid eyewitnesses"—a barber, bootblack, valet, and manicurist—recently re-interviewed, who said they could I.D. the two triggermen. Police were hopeful that people who were too frightened to talk to cops back then might feel more comfortable now.

The story seemed implausible and had no legs. It read like a plant to see who got nervous.

On October 3, 1973, Salvatore Anastasio passed onto his heavenly reward, the last of the brothers to go. He had long served as a priest in the Bronx, but was always homesick for Italy. Sometime during the 1960s he got his wish and was transferred by the Church to Rome. He died at the age of fifty-four of cancer at Rome's Gemelli Polyclinic. His funeral services were held in the Chapel of Sacred Heart University. (For all you math students out there, yeah, Sally was born seven years after his dad died. Maybe mom met a new man. Maybe one of Sally's "big sisters" was actually his mom. That shit used to happen all the time.)

Sal knew they'd made a movie about him, a condescending comedy called *Anastasia, Mio Fratello,* starring comedian Albert Sordi as Father Sal and veteran tough-guy actor Richard Conte (Detective Butler on *77 Sunset Strip*, Barzini in *The Godfather*) as Albert. Based on Sal's 1964 book, which he wrote with a friend named Vincenzo Benassi.

Sal died without ever seeing the movie based on his book. He said he wanted to, but was afraid that resulting publicity might further injure his brother's reputation, which he maintained till the very end was as pure as driven snow.

Benassi saw the movie, though, and didn't like it one bit. Father Sal would have hated it. The movie distorted the truth as Benassi knew it to be. It made fun of Sal's gullibility, portraying a world in which only a comic bungler (and man of the cloth) could truly believe that his brother Albert was a simple family man who sold pretty dresses for a living.

On November 22, 1982, eighty-year-old Burton B. Turkus passed away. Turkus was the prosecutor who, in 1940, took the wind out of Murder Inc.'s sails with the successful prosecutions of killers for hire. Albert Anastasia called Turkus "Mr. Arsenic" because he was death to mobsters, sending them directly from the Kings County Courthouse to the chair. Turkus was co-author with Sid Feder of one of the first full-length books about the American mob, called *Murder Inc.* and published in 1951.

On December 27, the last known member of Murder Inc., Jack "The Dandy" Parisi also passed away, at age eighty-three in his home in Hazleton, Pennsylvania, ending an era. Still dressing to the nines whenever he went out, some said he was still a major player in Jersey rackets. He'd tell you he's just a tailor, with a tailor's face and hands, but Parisi was a triggerman on the Morris Diamond and Joseph Rosen murders—and a suspect in many, many more. He was dynamite with a needle and thread—but better with a gun.

Turkus's and Parisi's paths had crossed forty years earlier, in 1942, during the early days of America's involvement in World War II, when Turkus was investigating Parisi in connection with the murders of Morris Diamond and Irving Penn.

And the beat goes on. Albert Anastasia had a couple of *paisans* in his crime family, Carmine and Daniel Fatico. By the 1970s, almost twenty years after Anastasia bought it, these guys remembered what gave Anastasia star power, and they saw it again in the Gambino family, where a kid named John Gotti radiated star power—plus he had a skill-set rare in the underworld: he could be tough, and he could compromise. He'd scare the shit out of you. If you had balls he might negotiate. It made him a tremendous earner. Gotti was sixteen when Anastasia bought it. Not long thereafter, the name of the family was changed to Gambino—and it's been that way ever since. The Fatico brothers were excellent birddogs, and recruited into the family many of the guys who'd still be around when Gotti lost his Teflon.

In 1997, chair number four from Grasso's Barber Shop was curated! It was a primary display, surrounded by classic photographs of mob hits in New York's Gershwin Gallery. The chair had for years belonged to an "aging lounge singer." The guy claimed that way-back-when a nightclub owner said he didn't have the cash to pay him for that night's show.

"What are we going to do?" the singer asked.

"Tell you what I'll do," the nightclub owner replied. "I've got a beautiful Koken barber's chair recently reupholstered in dark green."

"Sounds nice, but it really wasn't what I had in mind."

"Take it."

"Okay."

The nightclub owner had a reputation as a connected guy, so you didn't want to piss him off.

The chair lived in the singer's basement and then in a storage space. At some point, the chair made the singer antsy and he became hot to unload it.

Among the people he tried to sell it to was Jules Feiler, who gave the story to *News* columnist Mark Kriegel. Feiler was a guy with a reputation for making things happen, and an antique barber chair maybe was in his wheelhouse.

Feiler was publicist for a hotel that had an Andy Warhol Campbell Soup can in the lobby. He'd also tended bar for the greats and written a couple of plays.

Feiler said, "Won't be easy to move a barber chair. Who would want one?"

"This one they'll want."

"How come?"

"It's the Anastasia chair," the singer said.

That got Feiler's attention, and a few months later the chair was on exhibit at the funky midtown hotel where Feiler worked as publicist. The exhibit paid tribute to sudden mob death. Along with Anastasia down for the count, there was a blown-up death photo of Carmine Galante with a cigar still clenched between his teeth.

The exhibit had a Grand Opening. And the message to all visitors was clear: the chair was for sale. Ten grand. The owner did not attend and remained anonymous.

Feiler was tight-lipped on the identity of the aging singer. He verified that the guy was a senior citizen, but added that it was not Frank Sinatra, Jimmy Roselli, or Tony Bennett.

Not long after the opening, there was a claim that another chair was the Anastasia chair, someone paid $7,000 for that one, but the singer verified that his was *the one*.

"The serial number matches the one in the police reports," the singer boasted.

On March 9, 2011, the Mob Museum in downtown Las Vegas acquired the chair. Mayor Oscar Goodman and former FBI agent Ellen Knowlton attended the gala unveiling, along with museum curators Dennis and Kathy Barrie.

Last I heard a collector had the chair in storage someplace in Florida.

Today Grasso's Barber Shop is a Starbucks. You can still look inside from the Seventh Avenue sidewalk, and folks sip their white chocolate mocha venti with whip and a shot right there on the spot where Anastasia got whacked. And nobody thinks a thing of it.

Albert Anastasia's house atop the Palisades Cliffs has exchanged hands a few times since Albert's 1957 assassination. It was purchased from Elsa by Del Webb, who was then part-owner of the New York Yankees.

During the 1960s it belonged to the late comic Buddy Hackett, then to billionaire trucking tycoon Arthur Imperatore, Sr., who lived there until his death. In 2017, the next-door neighbor, Janet Denlinger, purchased the house—along with three other contiguous properties on the street—and was seeking permits to sub-divide the properties into multiple-home structures.

Perspective buyers who toured the house in 2017 said that much of the house has been renovated since the Anastasias moved out, but there were still decorations in one of the children's rooms and in the basement that dated back to the 1940s.

Those in opposition to Denlinger's plan sought help from the Fort Lee Historical Society, which laughed.

"Belonging to the boss of Murder Inc. is hardly a reason to save the house," said Borough Historian Tom Meyers.

BIBLIOGRAPHY

BOOKS

Barbas, Samantha. *Confidential Confidential: The Inside Story of Hollywood's Notorious Scandal Magazine*. Chicago: Chicago Review Press, 2018.

Benson, Michael. *Criminal Investigations: Organized Crime*. New York: Chelsea House, 2008.

Bonnano, Joseph, *A Man of Honor: The Autobiography of Joseph Bonnano*. New York: St. Martin's Press, 1983

Cudahy, Brian J. *The Malbone Street Wreck*. New York: The Fordham University Press, 1999.

Davis, John H. *Mafia Dynasty*. New York: Harper Torch, 1993.

Dimatteo, Frank, and Michael Benson. *Carmine the Snake*. New York: Kensington, 2018.

Feder, Sid, and Burton B. Turkus. *Murder Inc.*, Garden City, N.Y.: Farrar and Strauss, 1951.

Maas, Peter. *The Valachi Papers*. New York: William Morrow Paperbacks, 2003.

Newark, Tim. *Lucky Luciano: The Real and the Fake Gangster*. New York: Thomas Dunne Books, 2010.

Raab, Selwyn. *Five Families: The Rise, Decline, and Resurgence of America's Most Powerful Mafia Empires*. New York: Thomas Dunne Books, 2016.

Varese, Federico. *Mafias on the Move: How Organized Crime Conquers New Territories*. Princeton, New Jersey: Princeton University Press, 2013.

PERIODICALS AND WIRE SERVICES

Akron Beacon-Journal
Albany Times-Union
Anaconda Standard
Associated Press
Baltimore Sun
Binghamton Press and Leader
Brooklyn Daily Eagle
Buffalo Commercial
Chicago Tribune
Confidential Detective Cases
Daily World (Opelousas, Louisiana)
Dayton Daily News
Great Falls Tribune
Hackensack Record
Hagerstown Morning Herald (Maryland)
Laredo Weekly Times
Los Angeles Times
New York Daily News
New York Magazine
New York Post
The New York Times
New York World-Telegram and Sun
Racine Journal-Times
Reuters
Rome Daily Sentinel (Rome, New York)
St. Louis Post-Dispatch
Tampa Tribune
United Press International
Washington Star
Washington Times
Wilkes-Barre News
Windsor Star (Windsor, Ontario)

WEBSITES

Beatsboxingmayhem.com
Correctionhistory.org
Findagrave.com
Mafiahistory.us
Newspapers.com
Northjersey.com
Vault.fbi.gov

ACKNOWLEDGMENTS

The authors would like to acknowledge the following persons and organizations without whose help this book could not have been written: Lisa and Matthew Benson; Gia at the Brooklyn Farmacy & Soda Fountain at Henry and Sackett for the best Egg Cream in town; author Anthony DeStefano, Tekla Dobson, editor extraordinaire Gary Goldstein, our literary agent Doug Grad; Christine Green, Green-Wood Cemetery; Holy Cross Cemetery; Director of Transportation Joan Lenhard; Arthur Maisel; Ashley Miller at The Mob Museum in Las Vegas; Carey Strumm, Archivist, National Archives at New York City; Trina, Tim, and David Treu; private investigator Donald A. Tubman.

And Emily, Chris, Krissy, Matthew, and Frankie Boy.

And to the others, who wish to remain anonymous, our heartfelt thanks.

INDEX

Turn the page for an explosive preview

MAFIA HIT MAN:
Carmine "Sonny Pinto" DiBiase,
the Wiseguy Who Really Killed Joey Gallo

From Frank Dimatteo and Michael Benson, co-authors of mob classics *Lord High Executioner: The Legendary Mafia Boss Albert Anastasia* and *Carmine the Snake: Carmine Persico and His Murderous Mafia Family.*

Frank "The Irishman" Sheeran, in the book *I Heard You Paint Houses*, claims he whacked Joey Gallo on that fateful night of April 7, 1972, a claim that also made it into Martin Scorsese's 2019 movie *The Irishman.*

Total BS, according to Frank *The President Street Boys* Dimatteo and Michael Benson. The real shooter was mobster Carmine DiBiase, alias Sonny Pinto—Sheeran was nowhere near Little Italy's Humberto's Clam House that night.

***Look for* Mafia Hit Man: Carmine "Sonny Pinto" DiBlase,**
the Wiseguy Who Really Killed Joey Gallo
Coming in October 2021 wherever Citadel Books are sold.

Everybody's a gangster . . . until
a real gangster walks into the room.

—John Gotti

ONE
Joey's Back

FOR MOST OF THE TIME WHEN I WAS A KID on the President Street block, Joey Gallo was away. I was there because my dad, Ricky Dimatteo, was Larry Gallo's bodyguard, Larry being the oldest of the three Gallo brothers. Larry found my dad, an ex-boxer, in the late 1950s when he saw Ricky deck a guy with one punch, even more impressive for the fact that the guy he decked was Emile Griffith, the boxer who went on to be welter- and middleweight champion. My dad flattened him, however, and Larry Gallo offered him a job. So he hung out on President Street, where the Gallo crew had their headquarters. Even after Larry died of natural causes, my dad Ricky stuck around as a valued member of the Gallo crew.

As I grew up, things for the President Street Boys seemed to be going well. Scores were made. There was money. Swag. The boys seemed to be thriving and having fun. I got to see the fun part up close as my dad threw parties at our house in Freeport and the guys were all there. But all of that started to crumble the second that Joey Gallo was released from prison.

The block on President Street (technically two blocks) was geographically isolated, perfectly positioned for a fortress, with the piers at one end and the Brooklyn-Queens Expressway at the other. It wasn't always that way.

Here's a mini-history lesson: When Robert Moses, as head of the

Triborough Bridge and Tunnel Authority, took up the difficult and cold-blooded duty of running veins—that is, expressways—through old New York City neighborhoods so that cars could get more efficiently to and from the suburbs, a lot of neighborhoods were destroyed. (No borough suffered as much as the Bronx. To provide easy access for gas guzzlers to make the commute into the city from Westchester County and Connecticut, the borough was vivisected. The whole southern section of the Bronx went to shit.) Brooklyn, where I was born, is larger and survived its adaptation. Much of the Belt Parkway traced a perimeter of swamp that wasn't being used for much anyway. Canarsie lost its little escape spot by the bay, but it was run down and arson bait by that time. Sunset Park lost its main drag, the sunshine gone forever as the highway was built like a roof above the Third Avenue strip, held aloft by fantastic girders. The sealed-in feel erected a psychological barrier and held the legitimate world out. At night it was a juvenile delinquent playground. It was so dark that you could dump anything there without worrying about the heat. You could find bodies, sometimes a rusty refrigerator, both riddled with bullet holes. Mom-and-pop restaurants closed. Theaters closed or went porn. Shops under the road, on Third Avenue, were cursed to perpetual night, and adult storefronts floated stuck out of time. I'll bet today you can still see raggedy signs in storefront windows offering fetish VHS tapes for cheap. In 2021.

The Brooklyn-Queens Expressway cruised through Brooklyn Heights beneath a flimsily cantilevered promenade, and turned into the Gowanus Parkway that cut through South Brooklyn, separating one part of Red Hook from the rest.

But on President Street, Robert Moses's heartless destruction did a wonderful thing. It created an enclave that was easy to defend. The western end of President was now geographically isolated, and that was where the Gallo crew hung out, shot the shit, and planned tactics and strategy.

The Gallo brothers grew up in the Kensington section of Brooklyn but did business out of President Street block because their maternal grandmother, known as Big Mama or Grandma Nunziato, owned a building there (no. 51), and Papa Gallo, Umberto, had a business there (no. 47) before opening Jackie's Charcolette in Kensington. The Gallo boys were always at home on the President Street block.

Larry passed while Joey was away, spending the last months of his stretch at Sing Sing. When the day of Joey's release finally came, everybody on the block was excited. It was March 11, 1971. I was fifteen, but already at my full height.

I was hanging out on the block with my best friend Anthony "Goombabiel" Russo. Goombabiel and I, being kids, were on a "need-to-know" basis a lot of the time, which meant we didn't need to know. That said, usually no cars came on the block that we didn't recognize. Maybe every once in a while a new worker from the docks wandered onto the block on foot to get lunch at one of the clubs, but that was about it as far as strangers were concerned. If we did see strangers we'd say, "You lost? Where yiz headed?" But, you know, not in a welcoming way.

So we were on alert when a black Cadillac limo we didn't recognize pulled up to the curb in front of Mondo's club.

"What the fuck is this?" Goombabiel said.

We found out quick enough.

The day Joey was released, his younger brother Kid Blast rented a limo and went up there to pick him up. On the pick-up committee with Blast was Joey's longtime best friend, Peter "Pete the Greek" Diapoulos, and Tony "The Beard" Bernardo. They were loaded for bear, just in case someone tried to hit Joey the second he emerged into the fresh air.

When Joey came out of the prison gates and got in the car, the boys were shocked by what they saw. It looked like Joey had been on a decade-long hunger strike. His clothes were hanging on him. His face seemed to be wrapped tightly around his skull. Joey had been off his feed, and eventually he got around to telling his inner circle why. In prison everything is color-coded—white guys and black guys, with no mingling—and Joey had sided with the wrong color. To express their displeasure, Aryan Nation assholes were putting shit in Joey's food—that is, actual feces.

The concern over Joey's starvation eased up some the second Joey opened his mouth and began to pinch cheeks. Same old Joey. He might have been pencil-thin, but he still had his spirit.

The first stop was to see Mama and Papa Gallo at the Gallo house in Kensington. In the car, Joey was trying to catch up on the street situation. Profaci was gone and Joe Colombo was in, but the situation was still the same. There were still guys out there who thought they could tell Joey what to do, and Joey still didn't like that.

God himself could have talked to Joey and he'd've said, "Fuck you, Lord. I'm my own boss."

When Joey got out of prison he felt like he'd lost too much time, and he was going to make up for it. He wanted to eat every food and live every life. Since he went upstate the whole world had changed over twice.

Imagine trying to deal with the 1970s when you'd missed the '60s. The future shock must have been insane. Everyone was hairier and wore bell-bottoms. But Joey mostly focused on the women. He'd picked up a lot of starch in prison, and the women on the streets were driving him nuts. It was a time when broads went around bra-less and Joey's every other comment was about the bouncing boobs. He wanted to fuck them all. He wanted to fuck them all *now*.

Despite Joey's perpetual hard-on, the subject always returned to business and that motherfucker Joe Colombo. Profaci had just been greedy, but by Joey's way of thinking Colombo was worse. He was greedy as fuck, too, plus he was a hypocrite. He wanted the world to believe he was a legit businessman and worked to get more respect for Italians.

The limo pulled up in front of the Gallo house. The Gallo brothers' mom and dad were Umberto and Mary. They came from Torre del Greco, Naples. Papa Gallo came over on the boat in 1920, the SS *Canapich*, made a living carving religious figures out of stone and lived at 47 President Street.

Papa told the story to anyone who would listen that he could've been as rich as the Rockefellers during prohibition, but his shipment of booze sank somewhere in the Buttermilk Channel.

Unlike his sons, he knew what it was to put in a back-breaking day of hard labor. Oh sure, the boys would help their mother flip burgers at Jackie's Charcolette now and again, but real hand-blistering work they didn't know—and they didn't want to know. (Jackie's was where the Colombo crew later delivered Joe Jelly's finger after Jelly was whacked by Joe Yak, Carmine the Snake, and John Scimone.)

Papa Gallo didn't become as rich as Rockefeller, but he did end up making a bundle selling homemade booze during Prohibition. With that nest egg, he'd backed a major loansharking operation and eventually bought the greasy spoon in Kensington and cleaned it up. He called it Jackie's Charcolette, which specialized in what were then called "Hamburger Sandwiches," fifteen cents a pop, and chicken plates. Papa these days took it easy.

(When Papa Gallo was very old it was my job to pick him up at the Charcolette and drive him to a spot on Henry Street in Red Hook where he liked to play cards. Once, I was late, and the roar that came out of that little old man's mouth was terrifying. He roared like the lion in Mondo's basement from the old days on President Street.)

After the family reunion in Kensington, the boys got back in the limo and headed for President Street. Next stop: Mondo's club, called the Longshore Rest Room. Armando "Mondo" Illiano was Punchy Illiano's brother, but the first thing you noticed about him was he was a midget. His club was a joint where a guy working the docks could get lunch and shoot pool. It was a dingy place, with an oversized picture of a pack of Kents in the front window. "The finer the filter, the better the taste. *Kent Satisfies Best*," it said.

The Caddy's back door opened and Joey Gallo himself got out.

Goombabiel and I went wide eyed and stopped breathing. I was six years old the last time I saw Joey. Now I was six feet tall. But Joey took one look at me and smiled with recognition.

"You're Ricky's kid," Joey said.

I beamed. "Yeah," I said.

He said, "You know, if anything happens to your dad, you'll always have a home on the block."

I blinked twice and said, "Thanks, Joey."

He pinched both of my cheeks, hard, and nodded at Goombabiel.

"Do me a favor, kid, wash the car," he said.

We washed the car.

Now a lot of people have told the Joey Gallo story, folks that didn't know and weren't there. My dad was with Joey's brother, so they saw each other a lot, and I was the little kid. My primary memory of Joey from when I was small was him pinching my cheek so hard that tears came to my eyes. He told Ricky he was teaching me to be tough, and they laughed.

The Gallo brothers grew up on the block, from the days when they were juvenile delinquents. Right there, just inland from the international piers, in the most mob-dominated community in the country.

Joey went to P.S. 179, on Avenue C in the Kensington section of Brooklyn, then the Brooklyn High School of Automotive Trades in Williamsburg, but he dropped out as soon as he turned sixteen.

He was in a car crash, got a bump on his head, and developed a nervous tic. Joey and his best pal, Peter "The Greek" Diapoulos, hung out at the candy store on 36th Street and 14th Avenue. Pretty soon they were joined by a third, Frankie "Punchy" Illiano. Mostly they shot eight ball in the Ace Pool Room on Church Avenue, upstairs from Joey's mom's lunch joint, and talked about places they should bump off.

Lots of kids talked like that, but this was different. These guys had the balls to carry out their plans. They planned and executed scores, then came home and shared the swag.

Even then Joey had an "explosive personality." Once, when the Greek and Joey were kids, they went horseback riding in Prospect

Park. Joey couldn't get his horse to turn the way he wanted him to, so he got off the horse, circled around in front, and punched it in the face.

In a world filled with swarthy Italian guys, Joey was different. He was blond like his mother. He couldn't have looked less Sicilian, but he was movie-star handsome and he carried himself like he was infused with Hollywood, jamming a wide-brimmed gingerella hat on his head and laughing like Richard Widmark in *Kiss of Death*, rhythmically flipping a silver dollar like George Raft in *Some Like it Hot*, until you had to wonder if he was really nuts or if it was an act to scare people—because, believe me, he scared the living shit out of people.

He became a national figure in 1959, about sixteen months after making his bones as part of the hit squad that whacked Albert "The Mad Hatter" Anastasia in Grasso's Barber Shop. His fame came the day he testified before the Senate Select Committee on Improper Activities in the Labor or Management Field, taking questions from the investigation's chief counsel, Robert F. Kennedy—you've heard of him—by taking the Fifth while wearing Ray-Ban *sunglasses*.

"Er, uh, do you, Joseph Gallo, solemnly swear the evidence you shall give before this Senate Select Committee shall be the truth, the whole truth, and nothing but the truth."

"Sure."

"Pardon me, Mr. Gallo?"

"I do."

Joey lit a cigarette.

"Mr. Gallo, could you tell us where you were born, just a little bit about your background?" Kennedy said.

Joey looked around until he found the TV camera. It said "Channel 5" on it.

"I respectfully decline to answer because I honestly believe my answer might tend to incriminate me."

"Where did you go to school? Can you tell us that?"

Joey took his right arm and swept it outward, knocking a glass of water and an ashtray off the table onto the floor.

"I respectfully decline to answer because I honestly believe my answer might tend to incriminate me."

Kennedy persisted. He asked Joey how and why he got into the union business. He asked Joey if he was married. If his mother and father were living. The answer was always the same.

"I respectfully decline to answer because I honestly believe my answer might tend to incriminate me." It couldn't have sounded more like Joey was saying "Fuck you, Bobby Kennedy."

Now it was the senators who were nervously lighting up cigarettes. By the time Joey was dismissed as a witness, he was a star.

That part America saw on television. What they only heard about was Joey's behavior off-camera, jollying RFK's secretary in his office and commenting that Kennedy's rug would be "nice for a dice game."

Joey later laughed at press reports remarking on the fashion statement he'd made during his television debut. It was just the way he dressed. That expensive designer shirt they wrote about was actually purchased at an Army-Navy store. He'd paid a dollar for it.

As you probably know, Joey's nickname, never ever uttered in his presence, was "Crazy Joe." Ever since he was a kid there were suspicions that he had bats in his belfry. Some thought it was real, some thought it was an act. Most came to the conclusion that it was a unique combo of the two.

Joey and his President Street crew were still just barely grownups when they began to carve out a piece of the rackets pie, taking over coin-operated machines and portions of the policy bank. By 1958, Joey Gallo had already been a star of the underworld for six or seven years.

Papa Gallo married Mary Nunziata, and they had five kids. Joey Gallo was the middle brother of three, with Larry two years older and Albert Jr., a.k.a. Kid Blast, one year younger. (A lot of people think that Blast got his name from shooting people, but that's not the case. The real story, we knew, was that "blast" was Albert's favorite synonym for "fuck"—as in "I gave her a good blast.")

Joey also had two sisters, Carmella and the baby, Jackie.

Joey had first showed up on the public radar way back in 1950 when, at age twenty, he got popped for burglary, showed up for his court hearing in a black zoot suit, and laughed like Widmark at the judge. His performance was so bizarre that the judge had Joey taken to Kings County Hospital to be checked out by a shrink, the first of many such tests. They gave him the Rorschach test.

"What does this look like to you, Mr. Gallo?"

"Looks like you spilled ink on the paper and folded it over," he replied.

Joey got to the point where he ate psychiatric examinations for breakfast. They told him he was a paranoid schizophrenic, a phrase Joey liked and often used when trying to convince some schlub that he should not fall behind on his payments.

"I'm a paranoid schizophrenic. No telling what I'll do," Joey would say.

The guy would always pay up. It was a technique almost as effective as having a lion in the basement.

My conclusion is that there was *always* something calculated about Joey's madness—it had its own intelligence but lacked a sense of nuance. It sharpened his focus and gave him a joyful sense of purpose. But you couldn't be completely sane and act the way he did, either. Over the years he became a master at the "insanity test" given by government shrinks, always being diagnosed with this or that but immediately being released back onto the streets.

The doctors who didn't tell him he was a paranoid schizophrenic told him he had *pseudo-psychopathic schizophrenia*. He told those shrinks fuck you and let loose with his craziest insane gangster laugh. (If you don't remember Richard Widmark playing Tommy Udo, that laugh was also used by Frank Gorshin when he played the Riddler on the old *Batman* TV show.)

So Joey was *complicated*. A lot of the guys lived in America but considered themselves Italian. The music they listened to, the food they ate, all Italian. Joey embraced things that were pure American, including behavior and style associated with African-Americans.

He dug jazz, cool clothes, and jive talk. He knew all the beatnik jargon.

As teens, the Gallo brothers formed a crew called the Cockroach Gang, and they ruled the turf around Sackett Street and Fourth Avenue, at the bottom of Park Slope in the Gowanus Canal section of Brooklyn. The Cockroaches hung out at the same time as the Persico brothers' Garfield Boys, who ran the turf along Garfield Place in Park Slope, just up the hill from the Cockroaches, and the two clubs were rivals and then allies.

Joey talked a lot of shit, and he loved to tell people he "ran with bums" from the time he was a little boy, operated his first crap game at eleven, and by puberty was an established street kid, running numbers for a Profaci guy.

In 1948, he joined the U.S. Navy to see the world and got the boot after six months for emotional immaturity. Some guys—and I know this to be true from personal experience—aren't good at taking orders or being called a maggot or whatever other abuse Joey had to endure during basic training.

He got out of the service, returned to the streets, and he and his brothers ran their own crew out of President Street. Joey's brother Larry hired my dad, who was working as a bouncer at a joint called the Wagon Wheel, to be his bodyguard.

Like most hoods, Joey was nocturnal. He'd be getting to bed about the time others were waking up to the clanging and banging of metal trash and ash cans being tossed around by the sanitation department.

Joey was slippery regarding the law. As a young man his only pop was for burglary in 1950, and he skated. The Garfields and the Cockroaches grew into young adulthood, sort of blended, and worked the rackets under the auspices of Frankie "Shots" Abbatemarco, a bigtime Bensonhurst bookie and policy banker who ran Profaci operations in South Brooklyn. Thus, whenever a President Street boy got in a jam, Profaci sent the best lawyers and he was back in Mondo's having a drink before dark.

But Joey didn't like being under anyone's auspices and, from very early on, ran his own operations, from which he paid tribute to no one. The movie gangster inside his brain thought in very simplistic terms sometimes and had delusions of grandeur. He wasn't going to be happy until he was the don of his own crime family—or he was dead, whichever came first.

Joey's crew reflected his modern thinking. He didn't believe in the exclusivity preached by the men who came over from the old country. He didn't give a shit if a man was Sicilian or Italian, or whatever. He based his judgments on other qualities. His crew had a Greek, a Jew, a Puerto Rican, two Syrians, an Egyptian, an Irishman, and a bunch of Italians, one of which was a midget. And yeah, for a while there was a mountain lion named Cleo in Mondo's basement.

Joey and Larry were in on the Albert Anastasia hit in 1957 and as a result were made by Profaci. Joey's sponsor at his initiation ceremony was Frankie the Bug. The move to give the elder Gallo brothers buttons was controversial, but the whacking of Anastasia in his barber chair in the middle of hustling and bustling of Manhattan was so spectacular that Profaci had to let them in. Besides, they were good earners. Independent thinkers, yes—but they were young. Profaci thought maybe they'd grow out of it. No one stayed an independent thinker long in the mob. You either learned to obey or you were found disassembled and floating in Jamaica Bay.

Profaci was warned against it. Don't make the Gallos. They didn't want Joey for the same reason the Navy didn't want him. He couldn't take orders. He was always going to do his own thing no matter what.

And so, after a decade of hell locked in prison, Joey came back out into the sunshine. He had only been out for a couple of days, briefed by the boys about the situation, when he started to yell that he was going to kill all of those Colombo motherfuckers. Joey was not afraid of change. He needed change. He needed for things to be happening, to be in a state of flux.

"You don't understand," he once said. "I need to *get off.*"

He restructured his life, and then he did it again. He would never stop.

* * *

Joey's first wife, the former feathered Vegas showgirl Jeffie Lee Boyd was best known for her exceptional tits and ass. She lived in Bohemian Central—that is, Greenwich Village—on Eighth Street, a tenement building with a garden in the backyard.

Joey and Jeffie met in a beatnik pad, and he started hanging out there, the first indication to the President Street boys that this bohemian shit had an appeal to Joey, that he didn't just think about juke boxes and scores. Jeffie had lots of contacts in the jazz world.

Her first husband had been sax legend Gerry Mulligan. Joey could rap about poetry and life's great mysteries. Joey wanted to be in show business. Not to perform, but to get his cut, just like he got a cut of so many bars and restaurants. He dug jazz and wanted to manage bass player Charles Mingus.

Joey could mix with that crowd in a way other hoods couldn't even comprehend. He'd sit on the floor of a Lower East Side flat, one with the tub in the kitchen, and talk beatnik shit, how he'd seen the great balls of his generation blown out by hot lead.

Jeffie was a piece of work in her own right. She told Joey again and again he was too soft and he should be tougher on people. Sometimes when he had to hurt a guy he felt sympathy.

"Joey, snap out of it!" Jeffie would say. "Do your job. Don't be such a fucking head case."

But Joey couldn't not be complicated. He created a character in his mind, a movie gangster, and that was the guy he became whenever the job called for it.

Jeffie and Joey were an item for a long time before they got married. They didn't get married until a few months before he went away. In fact, she was pregnant when Joey headed upstate. Joey's daughter, Joie, never really knew her dad. He was in prison for the first decade of her life and preoccupied once he got out.

Jeffie had been busy while Joey was upstate. She had divorced Joey, married a rich Englishman, and lived the high life. But there was something about Joey that was still in her blood, and when she heard Joey was getting out, she divorced her limey beau and came knocking on Joey's door, purring like a kitten.

Joey and Jeffie were remarried after he got out and moved in together in a twenty-one-story apartment building on 14th Street near Fifth Avenue, on the northern border of Greenwich Village. The choice of apartment buildings was kismet for Joey. He had a problem with a tooth and went to a dentist on the ground floor of the building. The dentist wasn't memorable, but his assistant, a divorcee named Sina Essary, made little red hearts fly out of Joey's blue eyes. Sina had long dark hair, green eyes, and the kind of prettiness that Joey associated with beauty pageant contestants.

He asked her where she lived, and she said with a laugh, "Right upstairs. I can commute to work without going outside!"

Joey told her he lived in the building, too, and she reacted like that was good news.

For a while Joey had Jeffie downstairs and Sina upstairs. Jeffie referred to Sina, who had been a country girl in her youth, as Joey's "hillbilly whore." Jeffie wondered out loud why the hillbilly whore lived in the building's penthouse, an apartment larger and more expensive than theirs. Well, she didn't really wonder. She knew the answer. Sina cleaned tubes as well as teeth. Jeffie correctly guessed that Sina's apartment was being paid for by her employer, the dentist—who was not her ex-husband. When Jeffie pointed this out to Joey he cuffed her around pretty good. That only made Jeffie mouthier, and the violence escalated.

It peaked during a New Year's Eve party on President Street. Both Jeffie and Joey had been into the cocktails pretty good, and she wouldn't shut up. Joey's threshold for frustration was never great—like when he punched the horse, for example. When Joey had had it with his wife, he grabbed her by the arm and dragged her into the other room so the other partiers could hear but not see him beating her.

Before long Jeffie was out and Sina was in. Jeffie found out her marriage was over when she got home one day and a moving van was out in front of her building and her stuff was being loaded into it. The driver said he had instructions to take the stuff to California.

After moving Jeffie's stuff out, Joey had all of his stuff taken up the elevator to Sina's penthouse. The dentist was out of luck—except lucky to be alive. The dentist no longer paid the rent. Joey divorced Jeffie for the second time and moved into the penthouse with Sina and Sina's young daughter, Lisa.

When Joey went to parties, and he went to many parties, everyone remembered him—not big, but tough, and so, so cool. Joey Gallo was the only mobster in New York who showed up on the society pages.

He was a trendsetter. His fashion sense was both daring and impeccable. Plus, he was an intellectual, a guy who could sip a cocktail and discuss the commonalities between *film noir* and German expressionism. His new penthouse apartment had a section set aside for his easel. He'd taken up painting, colorful images of raw emotion, and the normally snobby art-world aristocracy was smitten. He wrote jazzy poetry and the kids with Van Dyke beards snapped their fingers instead of clapping their hands in appreciation. The beats came to call on him, smoke dope, and discuss how the cold war was a hoax.

He could talk politics with anyone. He said fascism propped up the paternal hierarchy and thus the repression of the masses. He said he understood communism's appeal but didn't think it was practical in a world of ambition—and ambition was something Joey knew about.

He could talk philosophy, how the ability to distinguish right from wrong was automatically blurred by modern society, that now there was no such thing as right and wrong, just smart and stupid, so you did what you could get away with.

He clearly had dreams of being king of the underworld, and yet his cover was as a bohemian—very charming. And he pulled it off.

New York elite uptown and downtown embraced Joey Gallo, who had spent so much time away and had so much creativity in his soul. Student and professors of the so-called "New Journalism," a freewheeling stream-of-consciousness form of reportage, wrote about Joey like he was Sal Paradise speeding on the sacred urban road.

Here was a guy, a violent maniac, who went to prison for a

decade, learned the speed-reading technique of Evelyn Wood, and read, and read, and read, and in essence gave himself a graduate-degree level of knowledge in just about anything that fell under the liberal arts umbrella.

During the last weeks of his life he was scheduled to appear on TV to discuss the new ways the boys from the press were telling stories. The show was to be called *How They Cover Me*, and he was scheduled to appear alongside Gore Vidal, Abbie Hoffman, Otto Preminger, and Bella Abzug. Joey was on the A list. As it turned out, the show had to go on without him.

He became friends with David Steinberg, a stand-up comic who would go on to have his own TV show. One of Steinberg's funniest characters was a shrink who was nuts himself, who'd shout "booga booga!" at his patients—and you've got to wonder if maybe he didn't, at least a little bit, consider Joey research.

Joey wasn't just making showbiz friends, he was befriending people you've heard of, like actors Ben Gazzara, Peter Falk, and Joan Hackett. Writers, too—perhaps most noteworthy among Joey's bookish pals was playwright Neil Simon, who wrote *The Odd Couple*.

Joey once told a hovering circle of literati that he plowed through ten books at a time in prison because a prospective writer—himself—had to read like a *predator*.

Joey was aware of the effect he had on people—he scared 'em—and how ironic it was that he wanted to write like Gregory Corso, to be the Walt Whitman of the streets, maybe write a book of verse called *Cracked Bricks*. He loved walking into Sardi's, the Time Square restaurant known for its celebrity clientele, because he transcended. Even the celebrities stopped and stared when he came in with the beautiful Sina on his arm.

How crazy was he really, everyone wondered? Would he know when to stop? Would his history be a comedy or a tragedy? Women thought about other things, how tender could a vicious man be? How charming could a psycho killer be? Would he be writing a book? How could his high-beam eyes look both at you and a thousand yards beyond you at the same time?

Years later, when Bob Dylan wrote a song about him and columnist Jimmy Breslin wrote a book about him, and Peter Boyle starred in a movie about him (sort of), it didn't seem strange at all. He was Crazy Joey Gallo, Superstar. And Joey bought into the hype, saw himself as a superhero, invulnerable. It was his fatal flaw.